PRAISE FOR $UPERHUBS

"In $uperHubs, Ms. Navidi skillfully applies network science to the global financial system and the human networks that underpin it. $uperHubs is a topical and relevant book that should be read by anyone seeking a fresh perspective on the human endeavor that is our financial system."

—PROFESSOR LAWRENCE H. SUMMERS, Harvard; former US Secretary of the Treasury, former Director of the US National Economic Council, former president of Harvard University, and author

"Sandra Navidi's book $uperHubs is beautifully and effectively done. Not only is it a fascinating description of the power wielded by elite networks over the financial sector, it is also a meditation on the consequences of this system for the economy and the society. In recent times, we have seen extraordinary ruptures—notably Britain's vote to break away from the European Union and the intensified sense of exclusion felt by much of America's working class. The last chapter of $uperHubs proposes that this ruling system›s "monoculture," its isolation from the rest of society, and its seeming unawareness of the fragility of what it has built are largely responsible for these ruptures, and that the system may lead to a major crisis in the future."

—PROFESSOR EDMUND S. PHELPS, Columbia University, 2006 Nobel Prize in Economics; Director, Center on Capitalism and Society, and author

"$uperHubs" is a book written with great style but also containing a lot of important substance. The style is so engaging, a real page turner, that I finished it in one non-stop session. But the substance of Navidi's text is no less compelling. Unlike many, she does not see the global economy as a predictable machine in the competent hands of policymakers, but rather as a complex, adaptive system prone to catastrophic breakdowns and rising inequality. Further, she situates the financial system at the very core of this economy where a concentrated number of real human beings—the "superhubs"—exercise an unrecognized degree of economic and political power. The values of these people, the networks they maintain, and their resistance to constructive change are crucial components threatening the future stability of the economy and even our democratic political systems. By identifying these systemic problems, Navidi brings us one step closer to appropriate solutions. A "must read," and a pleasure to do so."

—WILLIAM R. WHITE, Chairman of the Economic and Development Review Committee (EDRC) at th...
Member, Head of the Mo...
Economic Adviser at the B...
former Deputy Gove...

"In $uperHubs, Sandra Navidi provides exceedingly illuminating professional and personal insights into the global financial system. She illustrates its structures, interconnections, and inner workings with great expertise and consistent logic. Her analysis is balanced. She critically examines the implications of the increasing interconnections of decision-makers in the financial system and their concentration of power. Of particular benefit is that the book is easy to understand, making it also enjoyable to readers without any prior knowledge. Numerous references allow for further immersion. The thought-provoking impulses make $uperHubs highly recommended reading."

—PROFESSOR JÜRGEN STARK, former Chief Economist and former Executive Board Member of the European Central Bank and former Vice President of the Bundesbank

"Superhubs—what a clever concept! In $uperHubs, Sandra Navidi impresses with a masterful piece of both reporting and analysis."

—PROFESSOR KLAUS SCHWAB, Founder and Chairman of the World Economic Forum, and author

"How are we governed? By whom and how? These are the classic questions to which globalization and the financial markets have given a new urgency. $uperHubs provides a front row seat in the theater of fundamental change."

—OLAFUR RAGNAR GRIMSSON, President of Iceland 1996–2016

"Today's complex and challenging environment requires a fresh approach towards addressing key issues. In her book $uperHubs, Sandra has pointed out the interplay between economic, geopolitical, financial, and human development challenges. She highlights the linkages between key elements of change, which—if well managed and coordinated—can be powerful drivers for growth, and profitability. $uperHubs is an analytical, engaging, and insightful guide for business leaders in markets which are global, dynamic, and complex. It is a must-read for all who are striving for growth and excellence!"

—HIS EXCELLENCY, MR. SHAUKAT AZIZ, former Prime Minister and Finance Minister of Pakistan, former CEO of Citibank Global Wealth Management, and author

"In $uperHubs, Sandra Navidi provides an entertaining and absorbing portrayal of the networks used by many of the top executives in finance. She has a unique set of perceptions of how certain elements of that world work. She describes examples taken from meetings in Switzerland at the World Economic Forum and traces relationships and their network effects on a broader basis. She draws many useful conclusions and provides terrific portraits of some of the major players in finance today."

—STEPHEN A. SCHWARZMAN, Chairman, CEO,
and Cofounder of Blackstone; former Chairman of
U.S. President Donald J. Trump's Strategic and Policy Forum

"An expert tour guide, Ms. Navidi helps us understand the mechanisms that drive our global financial system by ultimately telling a human story of how a select few wield incredible financial and political power. $uperHubs is a substantive book with just the right balance of research and stories to make it an entertaining and satisfying read."

—THE HONORABLE GEORGETTE MOSBACHER,
Entrepreneur, and author

"$uperHubs is an engaging and provocative analysis of how super-empowered individuals and their powerful networks shape the financial system in ways that are potentially perilous. It is as rich in its narrative as it is in its corroborating research. Based on the premise that the financial world is a complex, self-organizing system, Navidi makes the case that these individuals' actions collectively cause complexity and – if unchecked – could lead to the system's breakdown. $uperHubs is a must-read for anyone seeking to fathom global finance and untangle the role of its leading players."

—FREDERICK KEMPE,
President and CEO, Atlantic Council, and author

"In $uperHubs, Sandra Navidi raises a fascinating question: Who are the captains of global society, and how did they earn this privilege? In particular, Navidi details the links between influence within today's global financial system and power. She applies social science to behind-the-scenes interactions at some of the financial world's most exclusive events to paint a compelling portrait of the industry and offer readers new insight into those with the power to quickly change the world."

—IAN BREMMER, President and Founder of Eurasia Group, and author

"$uperHubs shines a light on our financial world and the tremendously powerful titans who are in charge of it. With vivid narratives and systems thinking, Sandra Navidi effortlessly connects the dots between people, institutions and events. Her conclusions demonstrate the systemic pitfalls and potential improvements. I highly recommend this fun and very useful book!"

—ANTHONY SCARAMUCCI, founder and co-managing partner of
SkyBridge Capital, former White House Communications Director,
former Adviser to President Donald J. Trump, and author

"Since finance plays an unprecedented role in today's world order, the crucial question is how its leaders connect and interact while they assume the responsibility for an entire system. By exploring the financial world as a highly complex and powerful human system, Sandra Navidi's book shares a fascinating look behind the scenes of these influential networks, providing expert insight into their mechanisms. In an increasingly digitalized world, human" interaction remains at the core of the global finance system. *$uperHubs* offers a balanced analysis of the system's driving forces and raises controversial issues regarding the far-reaching impact of a few all-powerful individuals, addressing the fundamental aspects of the complex human dynamics ruling finance and the world. A spirited and riveting book that makes for an intriguing read."

—BORIS COLLARDI, CEO of Bank Julius Bär, and author

"As a colleague, confidante, and sometimes critic of prominent financial personalities from Nouriel Roubini to George Soros, Sandra Navidi is in a unique position to observe the factors that give these titans their power. Though brainpower and personalities are important, Navidi shows how the networks they have developed are crucial. Her writing blends personal anecdote and wry observation with a sound grasp of the science of complex self-organizing systems, making *$uperHubs* a uniquely intelligent and engaging insight into financial power."

—PROFESSOR STEVE KEEN, Head of the School of Economics, Politics and History at Kingston University London, and author

"*$uperHubs* is dedicated to a vitally important topic: the state of our financial system and its implications for society. To the non-expert reader, Sandra Navidi's profound analysis of financial systems is made easily comprehensible by illustrating network science-theory with real-life examples. It makes for a tremendously informative and entertaining read. If you want to understand how our world works, this book is for you."

—PROFESSOR DIMITAR D. SASSELOV, Phillips Professor of Astronomy at Harvard University, Director of the Harvard Origins of Life Initiative, and author

"The 1 percent isn't an abstraction; it's people. And here they are, described with clarity, pity, horror, and sympathy by a woman who gained their confidence, traveled the globe as part of their inner circles, offered them counsel, and—after this book—will be remembered as the woman who revealed how they maintain their plutocracy."

—PROFESSOR DOUGLAS RUSHKOFF, Professor of Media Theory and Digital Economics at CUNY Queens, author, and documentarian

"Power rests in the network—but the network itself is a complex and moving target. In this personal account of rising from outsider to insider among today's levers of global power, Sandra Navidi explains how the many high-profile names, readers will recognize in these pages, are themselves hubs and connectors, and how their relations to each other are the bonds of influence that shape the world."

—PARAG KHANNA, Senior Research Fellow in the Centre on Asia and Globalisation at the Lee Kuan Yew School of Public Policy at the National University of Singapore, global strategist, author, Managing Partner of Hybrid Reality, and Cofounder & CEO of Factotum

"This book is unique in describing and analyzing the human behavior in the upper circles of the global financial system. I agree with the author that unethical behavior has aggravated the increasing wealth gap and social stratification, and thus has fundamentally shaken society's trust in our financial system. The need for political action to save banks in the crisis of 2008, made clear that the financial system is not just a private sector but also a common good. It is this focus on the common good and the wellbeing of ordinary people that has to be considered in capitalism in general and in the financial sector in particular. This book will empower readers to advocate for change."

—AART DE GEUS, Chairman and CEO, Bertelsmann Foundation, and author

"Whether a ski weekend in a luxury chalet in Davos or billion-dollar deals on Wall Street—the financial world's exclusive networks make it possible. *$uperHubs* is a must-read for those who want to understand how these discrete circles tick, who the most important players, the "superhubs," are who pull the strings behind the scenes, and how their networks should be reformed to avoid future global crises. Navidi describes vividly and without taboos how the financial elite have created their own cosmos and why it is about time we scrutinize the rules upon which this system is based."

—ANNETTE HEUSER, CEO, Professor Otto Beisheim Foundation

"Taking an original—and innovative—approach, Sandra Navidi applies network science as a conceptual lens to explain the financial system's structure. Using personal anecdotes, she illustrates how network dynamics play out in practice and substantiates the far-reaching economic and social implications with further research. *$uperHubs* is a timely and stimulating reflection on the ramifications of globalization driven by exclusive networks, and an important contribution to the public discourse."

—STEVEN E. SOKOL, President American Council on Germany

"Sandra Navidi has been a keen observer of the world's financial power elite for many years. Her book $uperHubs deftly takes the reader through the global and societal consequences of those people's relationships, power, and money."

—BILL BROWDER, Cofounder and CEO of Hermitage
Capital Management, human rights activist, and author

"$uperHubs is indispensable for readers who want to understand the financial world's dynamics. As a financial markets expert, Sandra Navidi is predestined to explain complex economic and financial issues as she has successfully demonstrated for years as an expert on n-tv. Her fascinating insider's perspective reveals complex linkages among the financial elite and the resulting far-reaching consequences. $uperHubs is a blockbuster!"

—HANS DEMMEL, CEO of n-tv (RTL Group)

"Sandra Navidi is intimately familiar with the financial power brokers and describes them straightforwardly in her book $uperHubs. Superhubs are the people who by virtue of their many superb connections have become gravitational centers in the international financial universe. Sandra Navidi grants us insights into the characters who currently rule our world. She correctly points out that those who influence financial markets influence the entire world. We will see how financial oligarchs—who may be at their zenith, or are perhaps facing their coming demise—tick and how they have instrumentalized most governments to realize their interests. We will see how it has been possible for financial power and wealth to accrue in ever fewer hands. Towards the end, Sandra Navidi suggests solutions. Ultimately, reform can only successfully be achieved through the primacy of politics, but we are very far away from that. $uperHubs demonstrates how far off."

—PROFESSOR MAX OTTE, University of Applied Sciences,
Worms; head of the Cologne-based IFVE; and author

"Money + information + social capital = infinite opportunities. That's the magic formula of the financial elite according to Sandra Navidi. She vividly describes how homogeneous alpha males maximize their opportunities at glamorous parties and exclusive conferences. Readers will wish that this type of financial elite will disappear, or at the very least, include more women."

—PROFESSOR THOMAS MAYER, former Chief Economist of
Deutsche Bank Group, Head of Deutsche Bank Research, and author

"Sandra Navidi has written an absorbing portrayal of the financial elite's power structures. The internationally renowned financial expert takes readers to the world's power epicenters, where an exclusive circle of the most influential people, the "superhubs," rules the world. She demonstrates conclusively how the financial elite's power self-perpetuates. While her analysis is sometimes benevolent and sometimes critical, it is always differentiated. $uperHubs is a definite "buy"!"

—DIRK MÜLLER, financial markets expert, and author

$UPERHUBS

How the Financial Elite and Their Networks Rule Our World

SANDRA NAVIDI

NICHOLAS BREALEY
PUBLISHING

BOSTON • LONDON

This paperback edition first published in 2018 by Nicholas Brealey Publishing
An imprint of John Murray Press
An Hachette company

First published in the English language in 2017 by Nicholas Brealey Publishing

First published in German in 2016 as Super-hubs: Wie die Finanzelite und ihre
Netzwerke die Welt regieren by FinanzBuch Verlag

2

British Library Cataloguing-in-Publication Data
A catalogue record for this book is available from the British Library.

ISBN 978-1-47366-994-9
eBook ISBN (US) 978-1-85788-979-6
eBook ISBN (UK) 978-1-47364-511-0

Printed and bound in Great Britain by Clays Ltd, St Ives plc

John Murray Press policy is to use papers that are natural, renewable
and recyclable products and made from wood grown in sustainable forests.
The logging and manufacturing processes are expected to conform
to the environmental regulations of the country of origin.

Nicholas Brealey Publishing
John Murray Press
Carmelite House
50 Victoria Embankment
London, EC4Y 0DZ, UK
Tel: 020 3122 6000

Nicholas Brealey Publishing
Hachette Book Group
Market Place Center, 53 State Street
Boston, MA 02109, USA
Tel: (617) 263 1834

www.nicholasbrealey.com
www.beyond-global.com

Dedicated to
My Parents and Grandparents
in Gratitude

Contents

Foreword   xix

Introduction   xxiii
   Genesis   xxiii
   About This Book   xxiv
   The Financial Industry and the Power of Networks   xxv
   Applying the Lens of Network Science: Systems Thinking   xxvi
   Crisis Alert   xxvii
   Author's Note   xxviii

CHAPTER 1
THE FINANCIAL UNIVERSE: AN INNATELY HUMAN SYSTEM   1
   The Stratosphere of Power: Davos   1
   The Orbit of the Financial Elite: The Gravitational Force of
   Networks   4
     *The Financial System: Applying the Lens of Network
     Science*   6
     The Human Factor: The Power of Personal Connections   7
     Introduction: Meet the "Superhubs"   8
     Fault Lines: The Fragility of Our Financial System   12

CHAPTER 2
SUPERHUBS: THE FINANCIAL ELITE AND THEIR
NETWORKS   15
   The Superhub Prototype: Hedge Fund Titan George Soros   15

A Blueprint for Networks: Nodes, Hubs, and Superhubs—Bankers,
Executives, and CEOs   18

   Financial Superhubs: Network Equals Networth   21

   Network Geography: Location Matters   21

   Location: Reputation Matters   22

   Reputation: Access Matters   23

   Access: Social Capital Matters   25

CHAPTER 3
THE LINKS THAT CONNECT SUPERHUBS: MONEY,
INFORMATION, AND OPPORTUNITIES   29

Network Nucleus: Larry Fink   29

Network Power: Money   31

   The Printing Presses: Central Banks   32

   *Federal Reserve Chairman: In Charge of the World's
Reserve Currency*   34

   *Central Bank of Central Banks: The Bank for
International Settlements*   37

   A Primer on Banks: Regular and Shadow Banks   37

   *The Perpetual Crisis Manager: The International
Monetary Fund*   38

Network Currency: Information   39

   The Influence of Personal Connections   41

   Information Access and Proximity   42

   The Benefit of Connections in Tumultuous Times   45

   Thought Leaders—Superhubs of Valuable Information   47

Network Investments: Social Capital   51

Money + Information + Social Capital = Infinite Opportunities   52

CHAPTER 4

THE MATRIX: DECODING THE SUPERHUB DNA 55

The Alpha Personality: Jamie Dimon 55

EQ: Connecting Emotionally 58

Master Closers: Steve Schwarzman 59

Inquiring Minds 62

Inventing Ideologies 63

The Cult of Failure 64

CEOs—Chief Ego Officers: Bill Gross 65

On a Monomaniacal Mission: Ray Dalio 69

CHAPTER 5

HOMOPHILY: SIMILARITY BREEDS CONNECTION 75

The Charitable Superhub Network: The Robin Hood Gala 75

A Law of Nature: Why the Rich Get Richer 77

Global Conquest: The Transnational Financial Elite 77

Meeting of the Minds: Circle of Trust 78

The Hegemony of Homogeneity 79

The IQ Elite: A Master's Degree in Networking 81

Network Plutocracy: "The Old Boys' Club" 82

That's Rich: Superhubs and Super-Riches 85

The "Flocking Effect": The Superhub Habitat 89

CHAPTER 6

EXECUTIVE NETWORKING: RELATIONAL CAPITAL 93

The Superhub of Superhubs: Klaus Schwab 93

Friends with Benefits: Capital Networks = Network Capital 97

More an Art than a Science: Attraction + Interaction =
Transaction 98

Digital Bits versus Human Touch   99

Beyond Networking: How to Win Friends and Influence People 100

The Alchemy of Chemistry: Charm Offensive   102

The Lords of Networks and Their Creations   103

Negative Notions on Networking   104

Think Tanks: Network Motherboards   105

INET: Connecting the Connected at Bretton Woods   106

CHAPTER 7
MEMBERS ONLY: THE EXCLUSIVE NETWORKING
PLATFORMS OF THE GLOBAL SUPER-ELITE   109

A Dinner of Consequence: Attack on the Euro   109

Conspiracy Theories:
An Explanation for Attempted Explanations   111

Why Networks Need Platforms: Connectivity   112

The Annual Power Circuit: Dispatch from Davos   112

The Global Financial Power Center: The International
Monetary Fund   117

Washington, D.C.: The Financial Shadow Capital   117

IMF Meetings in Istanbul: Dancing on the Titanic   118

Power Summit: The Bilderberg Conference   120

Stealth Power: Family Office Gatherings   122

Feeding Off Power: Power Lunches   124

Power Workout: Networking, Working, and Working Out   125

"Superhub-Nobbing": Private Parties   126

The Higher Purpose of Networking: The Charity Circuit   128

CHAPTER 8
OPPORTUNITY COSTS: THE DOWNSIDE OF THE UPSIDE   131

Missing Out on Memorable Moments   131

Stress Test: When Being a Superhub Is Not So Super   133

Married to Their Jobs: Work-Family Life Imbalance   135

Media Madness: Living Under a Microscope   136

Super-Sick: Paying the Ultimate Price   137

Clash of the Titans: Close Combat and Coups d'État   139

Triumph and Defeat: A Turbulent Career   141

CHAPTER 9
"WOMENOMICS": THE MISSING LINK   147

The Gender Gap: Women Missing in Action   147

The Access Gap: Exclusive Means Excluding   148

The Networking Gap: Schmooze or Lose   151

The Assessment Gap: Performance versus Potential   152

The Wage Gap: Selling Women Short   153

The Failure Gap: Demoting Promotions   154

The Mentoring Gap: Missing Out on Mentoring   154

The Sexism Gap: The Wolves of Wall Street on the Prowl   155

The Resilience Gap: Male Might and Female Feebleness   156

Closing the Gender Gap: Superhub Christine Lagarde   158

CHAPTER 10
REVOLVING SUPERHUBS: CREATING NETWORK
MONOPOLIES   163

Psychological Kidnapping   163

The Revolving Door   164

The Oscillating Megahub: Robert Rubin   165

Open Doors: Tony Blair   170

Cross-Connections: Cooperating Constructively in
Times of Crises   172

Launching a President   173

"Legalized Corruption": The Best Democracy Money Can Buy   175

   Purchasing Political Protection   175

Relationship Power: Diffusing the Euro Time Bomb   176

Super-Entity: The Capitalist Network That Runs the World   178

CHAPTER 11

DE-LINKED: EXPULSION AND COMEBACK   181

Sent into Exile: Dick Fuld   181

Shock-Resistant: Larry Summers's Network   184

   Meteoric Rise   185

   Against All Odds   186

   The Bull in Charge of the China Shop   187

Den of Thieves: Mike Milken   190

Complete Network Collapse: Dominique Strauss-Kahn   193

Ponzi Schemes and Sex Scandals: Buddy Fletcher and Ellen Pao 196

Omni-Connected: Michael Klein   203

CHAPTER 12

SUPER-CRASH: "EXECUTIVE CONTAGION"   207

The Crash of a Titan: John Meriwether   207

The Big Picture: Capitalism in Crisis   209

   Debt and Financialization   210

   Wealth Gap and Inequality   210

   Globalization Winners versus Globalization Losers   211

   Approaching the Tipping Point   212

When an Irresistible Force Meets an Immovable Object: Brexit   213

The Next Crisis: Systemic Failure and Contagion   214

   The Culprit: The Superhubs or the System?   214

   Disequilibrium: Superhubs Preventing the System from
   Correcting Itself   215

"Executive Contagion": Executives Becoming Super-Spreaders of Risk   216

Averting Collapse: Thinking Differently   218

The Growth Premise: A Paradox?   219

Culture: The Value of Our Values   220

Recalibrating the System: Revolution or Evolution?   221

The Law and Ethics   222

Corporate Culture: Psychological Detachment and Willful Blindness   223

Incentives   224

A Sense of Purpose: Creating Value for Society   225

An "Evolving Revolution"   226

Acknowledgments   229

About the Author   233

Notes   235

Index   263

Foreword

by Nouriel Roubini

Professor of Economics and International Business,
Stern School of Business;

Cofounder, Chairman, and Chief Economist
of Roubini Global Economics

I HAVE KNOWN SANDRA NAVIDI FOR SEVERAL YEARS, and have had the pleasure of working with her in my capacity as Chairman of Roubini Global Economics, a global macroeconomic research firm. $uperHubs is a natural extension of Sandra's academic background and her vast professional experience in law, investment banking, macroeconomic consulting, and the media. In her capacity as an expert, insider, and observer, she has gained the respect and trust of the global industry leaders she writes about and has obtained firsthand access to their international power circles.

In interacting with and advising key industry players, Sandra has acquired a keen, almost intuitive understanding of how they think, communicate, and operate. These fascinating encounters with the global financial and economic policy elite in combination with her knowledge of how the system operates inspired her to apply the analytical framework of network science to the world of finance and global financial policy. By doing so, she shows how networks and their nuclei—the "superhubs"—drive our financial system, our economy, our economic and financial policies, and our society.

Her personal anecdotes from the front lines of international finance provide important context and help familiarize readers with otherwise abstract concepts. By connecting the dots between theory and practice in an original way, and underpinning them with psychological, sociological, and anthropological explanations, she illuminates how human nature and systemic forces impact the course of history. While Sandra's in-depth analysis is substantiated by exhaustive research, she conveys her theories in an entertaining and user-friendly language, giving readers an intriguing insider's view of many exclusive networking platforms.

$uperHubs$ breaks down the complexity of networked systems into easily understandable parts, and while the focus is on finance, its sub-themes on network mechanics are applicable to virtually all areas of life. First, the book identifies and characterizes the most powerful people in global finance, economics, and economic and financial policy; it then exposes their interlocking relationships and their individual as well as collective influence on the system—for better or for worse. Moreover, $uperHubs$ explores the links that connect them: money, information, and opportunities. It also offers insight into how mere mortals become "masters of the universe," how they connect and transact within their own homogeneous circles, and why women struggle to seize a foothold in the executive ranks of the financial and business world. She also shows that the worlds of academia, economic policy, and global finance are interconnected as a number of individuals—throughout their careers—straddle these three interlocking networks and have played varying key roles in several of them over their professional and business careers.

Notably, $uperHubs$ also uncovers how the elite and their networks contribute to systemic weaknesses—the overconcentration of economic and financial power, the widening income and wealth gap, gender and racial disparity, social fragmentation, and the overall systemic fragility—and how they affect all of us. And just as these phenomena are not independent of one another, neither are the networks that govern them. As in every other network, the overwhelming influence of a few key players makes our system increasingly imbalanced and unstable—and therefore susceptible to failure and disruption.

This book provides an intimate glimpse into the obscure world of high finance and global economic policy, and while it will undoubtedly appeal to those outside of the inner circle, it should be voraciously consumed by anyone in business. Elite business schools often advertise their network potential to attract new students; however, they do not teach relationship and network building in their MBA programs. *$uperHubs* ought to be prerequisite reading material, as it provides an indispensable primer in network science and a master course in the intangible art of networking.

Sandra's balanced yet critical analysis of the financial power elite neither glorifies nor vilifies, nor does it absolve or blame. It warns that we must understand complex systems not only to think differently but also to pose different questions, because the longer the current unstable disequilibrium of power is allowed to exacerbate, the harder it will be to resolve, and kicking-the-can-down-the-road will make such problems like rising inequality even worse.

We should expect increasing national and global disruptions to come from technological innovations that are capital intensive, skills biased, and labor saving. Growing trade and globalization trends challenge workers, firms, and entire industries and economies. Booms and bubbles lead to crashes, busts, and financial crises with severe economic and fiscal costs. And geopolitical conflicts become geoeconomic conflicts thanks to the rise and decline of global powers. Thus, enlightened policies are needed to reduce inequality and provide greater opportunities for more people; otherwise, social and political instability will seriously rise over time within countries and across borders. Given their power and influence, superhubs—which increasingly connect the centers of economic, financial, and policy power—have a special responsibility to make the system fairer and stable. The alternative is economic, social, political, and geopolitical conflict and dystopia.

There are other books about Wall Street, about the power-elite, and about networks, but *$uperHubs* uniquely combines these three aspects, along with thoughtful—and thought-provoking—critique from someone who has enough access within the network to acquire valuable information and yet who is sufficiently outside of it to remain objective and reflective.

$superHubs is an incredibly timely book precisely because it's not only about the people within the system but also about the *system* itself. The financial world can only be fully comprehended by understanding all three strands—how Wall Street and global financial policy making operates, the superhubs who push its levers, and the networks that form within it. This is not a passing phenomenon. Superhubs will *always* form within networks, making this an evergreen topic and an invaluable, insightful book for generations to come.

Introduction

GENESIS

$uperHubs is the result of four years of research and the insights gained in the course of my work at the intersection of international law, finance, and the economy. As an attorney admitted to the New York and German Bar, my professional journey began at Deloitte in Germany almost two decades ago, where I advised institutional clients such as insurance companies and pension funds on alternative investments. Subsequently, I moved to New York for a position as general counsel at an investment firm, then transitioned to investment banking and, lastly, worked with noted economist Nouriel Roubini at his global macroeconomic advisory firm before launching my own consultancy, BeyondGlobal.

When I moved to New York, I had to proactively set out to develop connections. As I knew relatively little about networking and the world of finance, this was an organic rather than a strategic process. It was during this time that I came to wonder how a small number of executives, policy makers, and thought leaders manage to rise to the absolute top, lead their institutions to continuous success, and have unprecedented access to power. Eventually my own connections evolved and began to extend to global leaders and other elite decision-makers. My work, which had begun at the micro level of individual transactions and culminated at the macro level of the global economy, has provided me with a bird's-eye view that has enabled me to recognize different patterns of network formation and certain behavioral principles. I began to realize that in a world where everything can be commoditized and automated, and in which human interactions are increasingly digitized, these select few preside over the most exclusive and powerful asset: a unique network of personal relationships that spans the globe, the cultivation of which cannot be delegated or outsourced.

I have directly interacted with most of the superhubs written about in this book at invitation-only conferences and events, which I routinely attend because of my work as a macroeconomic consultant and strategic relationship manager.

ABOUT THIS BOOK

$uperHubs tells the story of our seemingly impervious financial system with a specific focus on the executives at its very top and their unique personal networks. It introduces the main protagonists, the "superhubs," who pull the levers of finance and are by far the best-connected and most powerful players. The narratives paint a picture of the human beings behind big institutions, capital, and macroeconomic events; their relationships; and their rarefied world of power, luxury, and privilege. *$uperHubs* takes you behind the scenes to their exclusive platforms: the World Economic Forum (WEF); the meetings of the International Monetary Fund (IMF); and think tank gatherings, power lunches, charity events, and private parties.

We learn how the superhubs' alpha personalities, inexorable quest for power, and desire to leave a legacy propel them to top network positions that come with access to unprecedented opportunities. We see the core characteristics most of them seem to share, such as a high degree of emotional intelligence, charisma, and charm. Molded by similar backgrounds within elite schools, the old boys' network, and exclusive social circles, they understand and trust each other, form deep and resilient alliances, and employ their relational capital to maximize the return on their relationships.

$uperHubs also draws the curtain on the personal sacrifices, pressures, and struggles that come with power and privilege. Women are grossly underrepresented in the highest ranks of finance despite the clear business case in their favor, because they are largely excluded from the predominantly male networks. Superhubs increase the efficiency of their networks

exponentially by weaving a tightly-knit fabric of relationships by way of the "revolving door," lobbying, and campaign financing.

Expulsion from these elite networks is exceedingly rare, but it does happen if legal, ethical, or societal rules are gravely violated—as in the case of the former chief of the IMF, Dominique Strauss-Kahn.

Lastly, *$uperHubs* examines the instability of the financial system by focusing on the interconnections of individuals rather than those of institutions, the consequences of this instability, and the measures that should be taken to make our system more resilient.

THE FINANCIAL INDUSTRY AND
THE POWER OF NETWORKS

Finance is the operating system of our society because it is essential for everything we do. Our dependence on it gives the captains of the financial industry pervasive power. Their decisions influence everything from industries, to jobs, currencies, commodities, food prices, and much more.

With their "network power," people such as Jamie Dimon, CEO of JPMorgan Chase; Larry Fink, Chair-man and CEO of Blackrock, the largest asset management company in the world; and billionaire hedge fund honcho George Soros shape history, transform the world we live in, and determine the future of our financial system, economy, and society.

Heads of central banks—such as the U.S. Federal Reserve, the European Central Bank and the Bank of England—directly impact the interest yield of our savings, the price of our mortgages, and the performance of our pension plans.

Every action of any one of these financiers directly affects the lives of each and every one of us. Through their interconnections with the corporate sector, they increase their individual power exponentially. According to a study by the Swiss Federal Institute of Technology, a select few financial institutions control a large part of the world's biggest companies through cross-holdings and board seats.[1] Because financial institutions consist of individuals, this ownership structure provides these individuals with enormous influence.

APPLYING THE LENS OF NETWORK
SCIENCE: SYSTEMS THINKING

Understanding our complex financial system can be an intellectually overwhelming exercise, and this book will make it more accessible by exploring the underlying personal relationship patterns through the lens of network science. Network science mathematically substantiates the structure and behavior of networks, thereby demonstrating how seemingly amorphous webs of relationships form. Networks consist of "nodes," which are connected by pathways called "links." All networks, whether natural or man-made, behave in the same manner. According to the law of "preferential attachment," all nodes prefer to attach to other nodes with the most connections, because a greater number of connections increases the chances of individual survival. The best-connected nodes at the center of networks are called "superhubs." Superimposing network science onto the financial system allows us to see how people become superhubs by instrumentalizing status, access, and the transaction potential of social capital.

As you will see, finance is a complex, self-organizing system—like an ant colony, for instance—where the interactions of individual players can produce large-scale effects. Yet individuals have no control over the whole system, as they themselves are subject to its laws and systemic forces. Recognizing the power of the elite few is all the more important as there is no one controlling force, no real checks and balances.

Physicist Stephen Hawking termed the twenty-first century the "century of complexity." Indeed, technologization, financialization, and globalization have created a level of complexity that we have a hard time keeping up with. To tackle contemporary problems, traditional linear, cause-and-effect thinking is of limited effectiveness. We should rather approach them with systems thinking, which focuses on the interlinked components of the entire system—particularly their connections. The superhubs of finance are amongst the most successful precisely because their advantageous position at the center affords them a wide-angle view, which enables them to see the system in its entirety. This superior perspective allows them to cultivate their extraordinary connections for tremendous actionable advantages. For instance, hedge fund magnate John Paulson made billions with a bet against the subprime mortgage market in 2007. Others—such as Larry Fink, Steve Schwarzman of the Blackstone Group, and Ray Dalio of Bridgewater Associates—have capitalized on their unique understanding by building billion-dollar fund empires.

CRISIS ALERT

Networks can be used as a force for good, but they can also have detrimental consequences. Interconnectedness is an indispensable component of our financial system, because the exchange of goods and services for money by its very nature presupposes connections. In fact, our ability to cooperate within networks distinguishes us from other primates and has made us the most successful species on the planet—so much so that scientists have proposed calling our current time period the "Anthropocene," the epoch of the human.

However, over time certain network dynamics—such as the "rich-get-richer phenomenon" and self-perpetuating feedback loops—will cause any system automatically to become more interconnected, homogeneous, and complex. Most systems are adaptive and self-correcting, so when they become too lopsided, circuit-breaking feedback loops kick in, restabilizing the system. Systems that fail to correct themselves ultimately self-destruct.

As the events of 2007 and thereafter have shown, networks can trigger and exacerbate financial crises. Yet it is the people at the top, rather than abstract institutions, who make decisions with enormous implications for millions of lives. In order to optimize the system for themselves and their organizations, they build ever more personal connections, driving further technological and geographical interconnectedness and thereby increasing complexity. Potentially corrective shocks—such as the most recent financial crisis—have so far not triggered the necessary "circuit breakers," because in an effort to protect their vested interests, superhubs have successfully resisted change. The resulting systemic fragility manifests itself in increasing opportunity, income, and wealth gaps and social corrosion. If the system does not self-correct and balance itself out, it will eventually become so lopsided that it will likely collapse.

AUTHOR'S NOTE

This book, while being critical and raising controversial issues, is not a "bank bashing" book. It seeks to provide a balanced and unbiased analysis of the network dynamics that govern the financial system as the result of the cooperation of a small number of people at the top, so that readers can form their own opinions. Naturally, since I am part of this world, my account is filtered through my experiences, but it is this perspective that I would like to share with you.

By viewing the financial system through the lens of network science, zooming in on the connected elite with the most influence, I hope to inform and educate readers and stimulate a constructive discussion. Ideally, my approach will help empower readers to advocate for change and, taking a page from this book, to possibly build their own "counternetworks" to transform a skewed system into a more equitable and stable one.

I have focused mainly on the U.S. financial industry because the Anglo-Saxon approach is still, at least for the time being, the dominant driver of global finance, while also taking into account international interconnections. Since the top executives are too numerous to mention, I have featured a select group with greater name recognition to make it easier for the general reader to relate. I use "superhubs" as an umbrella term for the best-connected people at the network's center, such as bank CEOs, fund managers, billionaire financiers, policy makers, and the like. While they have much in common—their relationships, pervasive network-power and high social standing, they differ greatly with regard to individual positions, personalities, and motivations. Accordingly, where applicable I may only make reference to a specific group, whereas in other more general sections I may use "superhubs" as a catchall term. But what these superhubs all have in common is that they are human, and—as you will soon see—finance is, above all, a human system.

CHAPTER 1

The Financial Universe
An Innately Human System

THE STRATOSPHERE OF POWER: DAVOS

It was a gray January day in New York. The frenzied holiday season had passed, the tourists departed, and the traffic deadlock dissolved. The city's famed energy seemed frozen and its residents hibernating. I, however, was engaged in a flutter of activity, preparing for my most important trip of the year—to the World Economic Forum (WEF) in Davos, Switzerland.

The exclusivity of the event and its high-profile attendees have shrouded "Davos," as it has become known, in legend. Set in a small ski resort in the Swiss Alps, the Annual Meeting attracts 2,500 global leaders, including heads of state, billionaire investors, managers of trillion-dollar funds, multinational CEOs, and elite academics. There they discuss the world's most pressing challenges, cut deals, and, most importantly, network. Attendance is by invitation only, and competition over tickets is fierce. The conference has limited capacity, and every year people pull all kinds of strings and call in favors to be admitted, despite the steep price tag. I had first been invited based on my capital markets expertise. Among other contributions, I served on the Council on Systemic Financial Risk, co-authored a study on international financial reforms, and have subsequently remained engaged with the WEF network through the people and firms I have worked with over the years.

Upon arrival at JFK Airport, I checked in at the provisional Swiss Airlines counter that had conveniently been established right beyond the revolving entry doors, exclusively for Davos travelers. Ground staff, clad in stylish dark-gray uniforms, was particularly accommodative and eager to cater to this special clientele. The airport lounge was filled with a cross section of Davos attendees: here George Soros, there Credit Suisse CEO Brady Dougan, and in the back *Washington Post* heiress Lally Weymouth. They, among many others, relaxed on the heavy leather armchairs, nibbling on delicatessen from the buffet to allow for uninterrupted sleep during the flight. The panoramic windows opened the view on the deepening dusk and a fleet of planes featuring the red-and-white Swiss cross. Conversations among the passengers continued on the plane until seats were reclined and eye masks pulled down. Eight hours later we disembarked in Zürich, where the highest-profile attendees rushed to their $10,000 helicopter rides, bank executives were collected by shiny chauffeured cars, and I, along with the rest, boarded the WEF shuttle bus.

The winding, snowy mountain road was a bumper-to-bumper convoy of limousines, their passengers obscured behind darkly tinted windows. As we reached higher altitudes, the snow deepened and powdered pine trees glistened in the sun. Almost three hours later, we arrived at the alpine resort. Any expectations that Davos might bear some resemblance to Thomas Mann's description of a timber-chalet-dotted ski resort in his classic novel *The Magic Mountain* are doused as soon as the village's dull, flat-roofed concrete buildings come into sight. Luckily, most of the architectural eyesores are covered in snow and dressed up with large event banners announcing the WEF.

Davos is a study in contrast. More basic than sophisticated, it presents a curiously juxtaposed backdrop for the power and riches of the participants. Many hotels are rather outdated—it's a bit like being caught in a time warp. Only a couple of years ago, rotary phones, which are particularly inconvenient when dialing lengthy international numbers, and faxes in the form of endless paper rolls were still the rule rather than the exception. Amenities generally taken for granted, like Wi-Fi, were more a function of luck than a matter of course, and the stoic Swiss hoteliers met complaints mostly with an indifferent shrug. Even the ultrawealthy must tolerate rooms they would ordinarily consider below their standards. I once witnessed a billionaire complain, in an exasperated mien, that his room at the five-star Steigenberger Belvédère was like a casket with a light attached to its lid.

In the last couple of years, however, the village has grudgingly given in to progress. It now even features a futuristic luxury hotel, the Intercontinental, which is owned by Credit Suisse and has been compared to a golden spaceship. Guests who prefer more privacy and space rent chalets; prices start at $150,000 for the duration of the conference—not including staff. A friend of mine, a Swiss investor, rents out his enormous chalet to "the Russian government" every year because they pay him any price he asks. Other friends rent out their two luxury apartments for $6,000 each.

I checked into my cozy, family-run hotel, a fifteen-minute walk from the conference center. Generally, the conference organization assigns hotels, and participants have little or no say in the decision. However, if attendees dole out extra money for a high-level membership, their chances of being assigned accommodations closer to the Congress Centre increase. VIP guests—along with several dozen heads of state—reside at the Steigenberger Belvédère Hotel, which—other than the Congress Centre—is the most important hub of activity during the event, where many major networking parties take place. The less fortunate might be assigned hotels in neighboring villages, requiring a time-consuming and expensive commute.

Despite being sleep-deprived, jet-lagged, and at the brink of exhaustion, I did not want to miss a single second of mingling at the event. After checking in, I trudged through deep snow in mind-numbing, subzero temperatures to pick up my badge. The precious conference badge gives attendees access to restricted and highly secured areas. During the WEF, Davos is the number-one terrorist target in the world: 5,000 heavily armed police officers and soldiers guard the village and man barbed-wired checkpoints. Masked snipers parole the rooftops, and fighter jets sit on alert to protect the no-fly zone. The security team controls the chaos with Swiss precision. Only officially credentialed participants are granted access, all of whom—except heads of state—must leave their bodyguards at the door and wait in line with everyone else. There is no preferential treatment for the upper echelons here.

Equipped with my new badge, I headed for the modern Congress Centre—a big, bright, state-of-the-art concrete maze of a building—where most of the WEF's formal activities are held. On my way, I crossed paths with Bill Gates, who gave me a friendly nod; IMF chief Christine Lagarde, who said hello; and private equity billionaire Steve Schwarzman, with whom I exchanged pleasantries. At the coat check, where I replaced my messy boots with elegant dress shoes, I ran into Larry Summers, former U.S. treasury secretary and Harvard economics professor, and Robert Shiller, Nobel laureate and one of the most influential economists in the world. Although I have attended the WEF several years in a row, I am still regularly amazed by the fact that everyone around me is famous, and that every financial titan who is regularly featured in prime-time news and on the front pages seems to have materialized simultaneously in front of me.

I was familiar with many who were there, and after some meet and greet, I withdrew from the babel of languages into a quiet corner, where I scoured the database, deciding on which of the roughly 300 sessions I would attend. The choices ranged from talks on the global economic outlook to more unconventional topics, such as the importance of being happy and the human brain. The multitude of opportunities, choices, and people is both invigorating and draining at the same time, and over the years I have learned to allocate my energy prudently. Every first-time attendee is completely overwhelmed, and although the village is small, it takes time to acclimatize and figure out how everything works. Initially, the density and approachability of powerful and famous attendees feels surreal, but as if by gravitational force, people are sucked into this parallel universe before being released into the world again five days later.

THE ORBIT OF THE FINANCIAL ELITE: THE GRAVITATIONAL FORCE OF NETWORKS

The official purpose of Davos is to foster critical discussions to find solutions for pressing global problems. In the past, the meetings have been described as the world's largest focus group, a method for taking the global geoeconomic temperature. With dozens of Nobel laureates and hundreds of the world's most esteemed academics and industry leaders, the intellectual firepower is nothing short of breathtaking, with hundreds of sessions, workshops, and interdisciplinary exchanges. Although I can rarely pinpoint at the time what exactly I have taken away from the meetings, I feel that shortly thereafter the information and ideas form a bigger picture, a better understanding and a clearer sense of what lies ahead.

But the real reason why heavy hitters spare no effort or expense to attend? The endless peer-to-peer power-networking opportunities. The WEF is one of the most famous and efficient fora for connecting leaders in the financial industry, with seven hundred journalists present, who broadcast their importance to the world. Contacts made here ripple through professional and personal lives like concentric circles. As the Davos saying goes, "Three days of attendance saves three months of travel." This is a key benefit for people who can always make more money but can never make more time.

Among the Davos attendees are many titans of finance who pull the levers of the global financial system. This system is not simply interlinked by institutions and transactions, but it is fundamentally a human system, because on the most basic level it is the result of human interaction. Understanding the interconnections of the key players is vital if we want to understand the system as a whole.

Why should we care? Because the actions of a relatively small group of individuals influence everything from national economies to the stability of the system as a whole. The heads of banks, private equity firms, hedge funds, and central banks make fundamental strategic decisions that directly impact industries, jobs, and living standards—*our* industries, *our* jobs, *our* living standards. Yet, despite their pervasive power, these moguls are still simply human. They make mistakes, and they get lucky. They are motivated by honorable or less than honorable goals. And they are driven by ego and emotion, not dissimilar to the rest of us.

Who are these people who reside at the center of the network? How have they achieved their status, and how do they retain it? What are their weaknesses, and what are their strengths? What kind of power do they wield within the global financial system, and what does that mean for the rest of us? These are the questions I set out to answer. Based on four years of research and many more years of personal experience, I realized that network science paired with stories from the lives of influencers can help us understand the complex structure of relationships in the financial world—and what they mean to the overall system.

The Financial System: Applying the Lens of Network Science

What do the brain, ant colonies, and the financial system have in common? They are all complex self-organizing systems. The brain is a network consisting of billions of neurons connected by synapses that cooperate with one another in a way that creates consciousness.[1] The brain does not have a master cell that tells it how to work—it self-organizes out of millions of electrical and chemical interactions. Another example is ant colonies, which function on the basis of collective, decentralized behavior. An individual ant, through communication with other ants, receives instructions on how to behave. There is no "leader-ant" that determines the dynamics of individual interactions or the colony as a whole; together, all ants contribute to a well-functioning and efficient system.[2]

By the same token, in the global financial system, the actions of autonomous individuals lead to collective activity. Who are the players in this system? They are executives at financial institutions, such as banks and investment funds; leaders of public-sector institutions, such as central banks and the International Monetary Fund; and many other formal and informal actors who interact in complex transactions across national borders. There is no global "central command" that determines how the system works. It self-organizes out of countless connections, interactions, and decisions.

Decision makers influence the system's dynamics with their actions, but they have no control over the system itself. No one person can change the price of commodities or the fluctuations of the global economy. But by their interconnections and interactions, they produce large-scale effects. For example, the individuals who lead major financial institutions have enormous network power. At the same time, they are subject to systemic forces and governing rules. Essentially, the "game" of finance has rules that influence how they play. In turn, the way they play impacts the rules and the nature of the game itself.

The Human Factor: The Power of Personal Connections

Previous analyses of the financial system and its risks have focused primarily on the interconnectedness of financial institutions, the validity of macroeconomic theories, and the power of quantitative models, while giving less consideration to the networks of people who preside over the institutions that comprise the system. Yet, in the end all comes down to people, because it is they, not abstract entities, who make decisions on institutions' behalf, who devise theories and decide which models to use. This human dimension adds another level of complexity, because the dynamics of human relationships that result in seemingly amorphous and elusive networks, are not strictly formulaic, and difficult to quantitatively measure.

However, since human networks are also subject to the laws of network science, we can use these laws to help us understand how relationships form and how they are structured. A better understanding of those who have the greatest influence on the system and their connections to each other will help us understand the system itself.

Network science explains the organizational structure of all systems.[3] It has gained popularity in recent years, mainly because of the growing importance of social networks. But it can also help explain how some investors have made billions of dollars, such as hedge fund superhubs George Soros and John Paulson. Or why it seems like no one has been held accountable for the events or decisions that led to the Great Recession.

In network science, "[it's] the pattern that matters, the architecture of relationships, not the identities of the dots themselves."[4] The key players understand that the ultimate competitive advantage relies on the extent and depth of personal bonds and alliances—the network of links or connections that gives a person influence. They understand the system itself, the complex relationship architecture, and the "magic formula" of developing powerful connections. From their superior perspective, they can see how their networks provide them with unprecedented opportunities, resources, and support, and thus a greater ability to influence the system as a whole. The better they understand it, the more successful they are within it. This is exactly why *we* should try to understand it, because, as Douglas Rushkoff poignantly notes, "If you don't know how the system you are using works, chances are the system is using you."[5]

Hence, we will take a look at the financial world through the prism of networked systems, because our interconnected world requires a more comprehensive perspective. Technologization, financialization, and globalization have created an intricate web of interconnections within the financial world itself and between the financial world and other sectors such as the economy and politics. While new linkages are formed at an unprecedented speed, our capacity to fully grasp the resulting complexity has not quite caught up with the new system we have created—as was evident in the miscalculation of the impact of Lehman Brothers' failure or the challenges of dealing with the eurozone crisis.

Introduction: Meet the "Superhubs"

Davos epitomizes the principles of network science as they apply to human beings. These meetings tangibly demonstrate that similar people attract each other—and that those who already have the most connections attract even more. The Davos success formula? The resort is hard to reach, isolated, and difficult to navigate. Deprived of their usual environments, infrastructure, and privileges, leaders are crammed into a vacuum with nowhere else to go. Constantly caught in bottlenecks of security controls, coat checks, bus lines, and traffic jams, they have no choice but to become engaged in conversation. You literally cannot escape mingling, and it is this inefficiency that actually drives the über-efficient networking dynamics. Other conference organizers have tried to compete with similar concepts, yet so far none have succeeded.

In Davos, the movers and shakers are relaxed and completely approachable, ready to casually mingle and strike deals in the hallways that will make headlines shortly thereafter. More than half of the attendees participate as speakers and panelists, and they—along with their audiences—bond over shared experiences. Many participants take advantage of the opportunity to hold informal bilateral meetings over a cup of coffee or in one of the designated private meeting rooms off the main corridors. Serendipity often creates the most valuable opportunities. You may run into a person who is or could be immensely important for your business, receive an invite to a circle that was previously inaccessible, or have a conversation that opens up new perspectives. At a recent Davos, I was sitting in the Congress Centre café when an unfamiliar man asked if he could join my table. Of course, I said yes, and eventually he was joined by two billionaires and two prominent fund managers. Thirty minutes later, I had made five new contacts.

Parties hosted by countries, companies, and individuals add an extra layer of networking benefit to the forum. Every year, JPMorgan hosts a glamorous cocktail reception at the Kirchner Museum opposite the baronial Belvédère Hotel and just minutes from the convention center. Even amongst the events in Davos there is a hierarchy, and this stylishly catered affair is considered a must-attend. At the entrance, JPMorgan's top brass forms a receiving line, which in the last few years has included Tony Blair, the former prime minister of Great Britain. Blair is a highly desired "anchor" who draws other influential guests. At the head of the receiving line is CEO Jamie Dimon, who graciously shakes hands with several hundred high-caliber guests in a row for three hours nonstop. He shines, poses for pictures, and engages in lively conversations. Meanwhile, guests roam around with their eyes set not so much on the extraordinary expressionist artwork but on the other attendees. Here, Ehud Barak, the former Israeli defense minister, mingles with the president of Iceland, Ólafur Ragnar Grímsson; private equity tycoon Steve Schwarzman; Russian oligarch Oleg Deripaska; and many of the more than one hundred billionaires of all nationalities at the WEF. This is a microcosm of the world's elite, and everyone eagerly takes advantage of the opportunity to meet with as many peers as possible.

These financial titans derive their elite status not only from their privileged position in the network, but also from the importance of the network itself. The financial system is the bedrock of our society and touches everyone's life, because we are a financial society and every activity we engage in requires finance, whether it is building a business, a house, or an educational background. This close interconnection between our culture and finance can be seen in some of the descriptive terms that finance borrows from our everyday language to express underlying concepts, such as "credit," which is derived from the Latin word *credere* and means "to believe," or the words "equity," "bond," "share," and "trust." Financial institutions like banks intermediate between savings and investments and allocate resources between different societal groups. This intermediation has created access to capital and opportunities for millions of people, especially those from lower- and middle-class income backgrounds. Moreover, these institutions provide payment systems, without which our highly interconnected world would likely come to a grinding halt.

The shadow banking system—financial intermediaries that do not have a banking license, such as investment banks, hedge funds, and money market funds—provides a variety of financial services. Financial regulators safeguard the system. Central banks are in charge of monetary policies. Think tanks develop new perspectives, offer expert advice, and advocate special interests. Academics and thought leaders provide innovative views and substantiate or invalidate practices in the financial system.

Leaders of financial firms impact the economy in any number of ways. They decide who gets business loans, influencing which industries will thrive and where jobs will be created. They provide mortgages and buy companies or take them public. They can move markets through the assets they control, the capital they direct, and the currencies they trade. The prices of basic necessities, such as energy and food, are impacted by bets they make on commodities, industries, and geographies—potentially fueling booms and busts. When countries are under pressure, their speculation can contribute to downward spirals. The political landscape is shaped through their financial contributions, direct interactions with politicians, and lobbying. During the financial crisis of 2007 and thereafter (hereinafter referred to as the "crisis" or "financial crisis"), they were a driving force behind the bailouts.

Relationships between the private and public sectors are solidified through the phenomenon of the "revolving door"—in which players oscillate between the two worlds. In good times, personal relationships among the superhubs of finance lead to ever more and greater transactions in a favorable regulatory environment. During financial crises, these relationships often tip the scale toward either the success or failure of an institution. In 2008, when the financial system teetered on the brink of collapse, strong personal bonds in both the public and private sectors became an important factor in the bailout of individual institutions and the stabilization of the system as a whole. For instance, Ben Bernanke, Tim Geithner, and Hank Paulson formed an effective trifecta that succeeded in preventing the financial system from collapsing in part because of their good personal relationships. In the midst of dramatic and chaotic circumstances they constructively cooperated, because they respected, trusted, and understood one another. A group of people who did not know and trust one another would likely not have been able to successfully work through such a crisis.

In terms of network science, the people who preside over these private and public institutions or have otherwise prominent positions are "superhubs," as they are the most well-connected nodes in the financial network. They are the few hundred executives who set the agenda, dominate the dialogue, and leverage their power on their organization's behalf. Often, they are in charge of tens of thousands of employees in dozens of countries. They may not be as visible or well known as politicians, yet like a global supragovernment, their power comes close to and sometimes even exceeds that of democratically elected officials. Many financial titans have risen from obscurity to become the wealthiest and most powerful people on the planet. Examples of major superhubs include bank CEOs like Jamie Dimon of JPMorgan; George Soros, the billionaire hedge fund manager; Christine Lagarde, the managing director of the IMF; and economist Nouriel Roubini.

Boasting a myriad of influential interconnections all around the world, all of these "human superhubs" have one characteristic in common: They have successfully built and navigated personal networks based on shared trust, experiences, and backgrounds. While their individual relationships make them powerful, their combined power is exponentially higher and leaves its imprint on the world. Because these relationships are invaluable in regard to access to resources and crucial information, they constantly travel around the globe to cultivate them, despite the significant investment of time, energy, and money. These leaders can outsource all kinds of professional skills, but they cannot outsource the interpersonal skills needed build deep and resilient relationships.

Fault Lines: The Fragility of Our Financial System

From the vantage point of ordinary citizens, finance has become increasingly abstract, impenetrable, and disconnected from their worlds. One of the main reasons for this disconnect is that the powerful self-reinforcing dynamics of the financial system have led to financialization of our economy. Finance has assumed an increasingly disproportionate share of the GDP,[6] and its rise has led to a gradual disconnect of the financial sector from the real economy. Rather than producing items of sustainable value for society, the financial services sector has created ever more artificial financial instruments supported by growing household credit—particularly residential mortgages—whose main purpose was to generate fees for the institutions that issued them. This dynamic greatly contributed to the financial crisis, which triggered a systemic breakdown that almost led to a collapse of the global economic system.

Finance has also been one of the key drivers of the growing wealth gap and inequality. While extreme global poverty has consistently fallen over the past decades to the lowest levels ever, the wealth gap has widened significantly. It is now at an all-time high and set to increase further: Today eighty people hold the same amount of wealth as the world's 3.6 billion poorest, and the combined wealth of the richest 1 percent will soon overtake that of the other 99 percent.[7] Many in this group of super-elites are financiers. This development has been exacerbated by the fact that the wealthy can capitalize on returns on ownership rather than solely on labor, a practice known as "rent-seeking." In other words, they can let their money work for them, and over time these investments yield a higher rate of return than the economy's rate of growth. In contrast, salaries derived from labor don't rise as quickly as the returns on capital.[8]

The opportunity gap has also increased. Rather than perfect competition, our system creates superstars—or superhubs—and amplifies their rewards in a reinforcing feedback loop where the winners of the competition receive the means to win further competitions, so that all but a few competitors are eliminated.[9] Tight interpersonal networks contribute to the unequal access to opportunities, and—as a consequence—people lose trust in the system. Yet, cooperation and trust are part of the social contract that binds us together.[10] Unequal societies function less well as people's willingness to cooperate declines. The wealthy want to protect their wealth and use their political connections to do so, while the rest fight for a larger share of the pie. The interests of the 99 percent conflict with those of the 1 percent. Moreover, the interests of those within the 1 percent begin to clash, because as elites grow bigger, they increasingly compete with each other. Ideological polarization leads to fragmentation and instability, as also evidenced in growing political disruption in many regions of the world.

The dangers of these developments are not lost on those of the 1 percent who discomfitingly warn of inevitable impending upheaval. Serial entrepreneur, superinvestor, and billionaire Nick Hanauer has cautioned his fellow zillionaires that the pitchforks are coming. An unapologetic capitalist, he argues that the U.S. is changing from a capitalist to a feudal society. In his opinion, this wealth accumulation is socially destabilizing and will inexorably lead to a revolution, which will likely be triggered by a sudden and unforeseen event.[11] Hedge fund billionaire Paul Tudor Jones echoes that view, opining that "income inequality will end in revolution, taxes, or war." While he also praises capitalism, he feels "we've ripped the humanity out of our companies . . . threatening the very underpinnings of our society."[12] And Rob Johnson, who is now executive director of the Institute for New Economic Thinking and previously worked with George Soros on his billion-dollar bearish bet on the pound, revealed that he knows "hedge fund managers buying airstrips in New Zealand in case they need a quick getaway."[13]

*   *   *

In this chapter, we have been introduced to some of the world's most influential bank CEOs, managers of trillion-dollar funds, and billionaire investors, who pull the levers of our global financial system. We have seen the incredible power they yield due to the role finance plays in our society.

They control multinational corporations, influence the political landscape and further multiply their power exponentially by virtue of their exclusive networks. In Chapter 2, we will take a look at the financial system through the lens of network science to provide a more structured explanation of the dynamics that propel a select few into the very center of networks, where they become the so-called superhubs.

CHAPTER 2

Superhubs

The Financial Elite and Their Networks

THE SUPERHUB PROTOTYPE:
HEDGE FUND TITAN GEORGE SOROS

Billionaire and hedge fund legend George Soros has built one of the largest and most powerful global networks in the world. It is so vast and complex that it is almost difficult to fathom. Soros has attended the World Economic Forum (WEF) in Davos for the last two decades and, as a veteran, truly knows how to optimize his time in this surreal place. He is meticulously scheduled for nonstop bilateral meetings with prime ministers, presidents, central bank governors, and billionaire businessmen. Some slots are allocated to interviews with the world's most important media outlets. And, of course, he is featured on several WEF discussion panels, along with Nobel laureates, senior policy makers, and CEOs.

What is so special about George Soros? What is the secret of his success? What has propelled him to the center of global networks? He literally transformed himself from someone who had neither money nor contacts to one of the most powerful men in the world. He is a prime example of a network "superhub," and chronicling his rise can teach us more about the inner workings of the financial system.

Soros was born to a Jewish family in Budapest. At fourteen years old, he survived Nazi and Soviet occupation under an assumed identity and in hiding. After the war ended, he moved to London and later made his way to the United States. Soros has repeatedly stated that his traumatic experience during the war profoundly influenced his thinking and, thus, his life. It made him realize that sometimes normal rules do not apply and risks must be taken. When he arrived in London in 1947 as a seventeen-year-old foreigner, he began studying at the London School of Economics and supported himself with odd jobs. Though eager to land a position in the financial industry, he had trouble finding employment as a distinct and definite outsider in London's class-conscious society.

In his quest, he wrote personal letters to managing directors at all the merchant banks in London, despite the fact that at that time, it was not customary for job seekers to directly approach prospective employers they did not know personally or through introductions. Getting a foot in the door proved close to impossible, and one banker bluntly told Soros that the city was a club and the only way to get a job was through personal connections. He added mischievously that the London establishment practiced "intelligent nepotism." Every family had at least one intelligent nephew who would get the job. Since Soros lacked school ties and wasn't even from the same country, his case was seemingly hopeless.[1] Eventually Soros did land a job through fellow Hungarians and subsequently found his first job in America through a colleague whose father owned a small brokerage firm in New York. He made the leap across the pond and, after successfully establishing himself in the new world with his old-world connections, founded one of the first and most successful hedge funds ever. In 1992, he acquired worldwide fame when he "Broke the Bank of England," forcing the British government to pull the pound from the European exchange rate mechanism.

Soros first built a reputation as an extraordinarily successful investor. However, in a world where countless people make a lot of money, financial success alone did not sufficiently distinguish him from others in finance. His efforts to obtain meetings with President Bush, Margaret Thatcher, and Gorbachev in the late eighties to discuss political issues went nowhere, and International Monetary Fund and U.S. Treasury Department staff dismissed him as just another rich, self-aggrandizing person. So he set about establishing himself as a thought leader. First, he created content. He always had a strong desire to make an impact on the world and from a young age had spent much time developing his philosophical, economic, and political ideas. Yet, until the early nineties, his attempts to publish opinion pieces in the *Wall Street Journal* and the *New York Times* remained unsuccessful. With dogged persistence and amid heavy criticism, he continued to publish his writings and books. Most notably, he devised the theory of "reflexivity," which is in part based on the ideas of philosopher Karl Popper and which he credits for much of his success.[2] Even though his views were still mostly dismissed, he slowly began to establish himself. His media exposure helped to gradually cement his reputation and, along with it, his power. By his own account, he was suddenly able to influence governments.

Focusing on making money is regarded as somewhat one-dimensional, but giving it away is an effective method for increasing one's standing in society. In 1979, Soros began engaging in philanthropy with his Open Society Foundations, which work to build tolerant societies with accountable governments and support education, health, and justice systems, among many other causes. They now have offices all over the world, and their networks are interlinked with other Soros and non-Soros-related networks. Moreover, in the nineties Soros helped establish the International Crisis Group, which is committed to preventing and resolving deadly conflict, and Transparency International, which monitors and publicizes international corruption. All organizations are independent, nonprofit, and nongovernmental.

Soros has aided in setting up many other initiatives, including political ones. In 2007, he assisted in launching the European Council on Foreign Relations (ECFR), an independent think tank on European issues. It consists of more than one hundred politicians, decision makers, thought leaders, and businesspeople. In 2009, he founded the Institute for New Economic Thinking (INET), which is dedicated to reforming academic research and teaching, and whose board consists of a "who's who" in economics.

Being a well-known philanthropist has given Soros access and helped his business, although he argues that he does not need philanthropy for business purposes and, quite to the contrary, worries that it may cloud his judgment.[3] What George Soros does understand is the importance of creating a vast network of personal relationships, which is what has helped catapult him into the realm of the financial elite, and has made him a "superhub."

A BLUEPRINT FOR NETWORKS:
NODES, HUBS, AND SUPERHUBS—
BANKERS, EXECUTIVES, AND CEOS

We all have an idea of what it takes to be successful: Get an education, work hard, and network. There are plenty of successful people in the world, but only a few become so disproportionately successful that they operate the very levers of the financial system. This extreme power concentration has given rise to conspiracy theories. However, it is not a nefarious plot that launches people into these places of power but instead laws of nature—as network science has proven. Network science helps us trace the formation of these elite networks and understand what it takes to become a highly connected and powerful nucleus, or "superhub."

Networks govern every area of human activity—social, economic, or political—and all aspects of our lives are interrelated via these overlapping webs.[4] Our financial system is simply one of those networks. When humans began settling into communities, they devised norms of exchanging labor and goods; with these, the network economy was born including the beginnings of financial systems.

Even before we are born, we are attached. As we grow, we are driven to connect in order to survive and thrive. Our fates are determined by the place we occupy within networks. While one person's network may be limited in reach, it indirectly provides almost infinite exposure through its connections to other networks. I'm sure you've heard of the six degrees of separation theory, according to which every person on this planet can be connected to any other person by an average of six links. It was popularized by social psychologist Stanley Milgram in 1967 to prove that the world was in effect quite "small," and later by John Guare in a play with the same name.[5]

All networks, regardless of whether they are natural or man-made, have the same underlying architecture: individual nodes connected via links, or pathways. Each node is a component of the network. It could be a neuron or an electrical substation or a person, like George Soros, for example. Nodes "always compete for connections because links represent survival in an interconnected world."[6] In human relationships, those links are the connections between two people and what they are based on: business deals and the exchange of information and favors.

In every network, the nodes exist in a hierarchy: The majority of nodes have only a few connections. Some nodes, which have several connections are known as hubs.[7] Only a select few nodes, the superhubs, have so many connections to other nodes, hubs, and superhubs that they are virtually connected to the entire network.[8] Superhubs tend to break the standard rules of exposure. Rather than six degrees, for instance, human superhubs, with greater professional seniority or social stature, might be separated from any other human by only a few degrees.

In our global financial network, anyone who works in the financial sector represents a node. More senior people, for instance, who are well connected due to their position and corresponding station in life are hubs. They typically have many subordinates and a fair amount of influence within their institutions and communities. The superhubs are the people in the very center of the financial sector, like CEOs of major banks. They occupy central network positions and have a large number of quality relationships and connections across different networks.

Every network—be it the universe, an organism, or a financial network—has a natural tendency to expand. Expanding networks do not follow a normal distribution; nodes prefer attaching to other nodes that are already more connected, because the more links a node has, the greater its chances of survival. Thus, it is advantageous for one to be connected to a stronger, healthier, more robust node. As a result, a few nodes, so-called hubs, attract a disproportionate number of links and become central connections. This dynamic has been coined the "rich-get-richer" phenomenon, because in the competition for new connections, those who already have more, get more.[9] (I explore this in more detail in Chapter 5.) According to physicist Albert-László Barabási, "If a node has twice as many links as another node, then it is twice as likely to receive a new link."[10] Thus, a few hubs—superhubs—will be connected to almost all nodes.[11] This is

called a "power-law distribution." The behavior of a network is governed
by the interactions between nodes, hubs, and superhubs. The interactions
are primarily determined by the network's purpose and to some degree
by randomness.[12] Due to power-laws, you can anticipate that the behavior
of the network will be influenced by many nodes trying to create links to
hubs and especially to superhubs. Thus, a few nodes, the superhubs, will
have the most influence within the network, and their actions and interactions will have broad effects throughout the network. That is certainly
true in our financial system.

Hubs can make networks more efficient by creating a high degree of
connectivity, but they also tend to make networks more vulnerable. The
failure of a hub can cascade through the network and cause a total system
failure. An example is the electrical grid, which is so interconnected and
sensitive that a single disturbance can travel through the system and cause
failures thousands of miles away. Electricity is like blood in the human
organism; without it, the system fails.[13] In August 2003, several states in
the United States experienced the largest blackout in American history.
Office buildings were evacuated, 800 people had to be freed from elevators, failed traffic lights paralyzed transportation, and 350,000 subway
passengers had to be rescued from dark tunnels. Hospitals had to switch
to generators, and airports experienced grave disruptions due to rerouting,
delays, and cancellations. More than seventy fires were reported. Nuclear
plants automatically shut down, and telephone service was interrupted.
No electronic equipment worked, and cash registers, ATMs, water supply
systems, and even toilets were nonoperational. New York City emergency
command operations were instituted to avoid looting, which had occurred
in previous blackouts.[14]

Another example is the Lehman debacle, commonly considered to
have been one of the triggers that caused the financial crisis to go global.
The U.S. Treasury Department and Federal Reserve underestimated how
intertwined Lehman was with other institutions around the world. When
they announced that Lehman would not be bailed out, markets crashed
and the global financial system came to a halt. Therefore, a network that
consists of nodes with only a limited number of connections is more
robust, because fewer connections will make it harder for failure to trigger

a domino effect and spread. Our financial system consists of many human superhubs with high connectivity and is most definitely not immune to the failures of those with the greatest influence.

Financial Superhubs: Network Equals Networth

At the WEF in Davos—like everywhere else—Soros is in high demand. He hurries back and forth between the modernist Congress Centre and various quaint hotels at which meetings and sessions are held. As he makes his way through the crowd, he is continuously approached by people who either know or want to know him; not having the time to speak to everyone, he politely brushes off most of them.

Human superhubs can often be easily recognized. You can literally observe network science in action when they enter a room: All those other nodes in black suits automatically turn toward them like magnets, eager to connect. Soros is the quintessential financial superhub, with countless strong connections to powerful people and institutions and broad influence through his words and actions. Any other node in the network would be ecstatic if they could develop a connection with George Soros. Why? He, like all other superhubs, has status and access that he can transfer to others.

In any human network, the value of a person's position is determined by the number and the quality of his connections. In the global financial system, a central network position has actual economic value,[15] and your network is quite literally your net worth. Their high connectivity, access, and status gives superhubs unique power to capitalize on opportunities by cross-fertilizing and executing profitable ideas. That power makes connecting with them desirable, because status can be transferred by association and, thus, be leveraged to further one's interest.

Network Geography: Location Matters

Status is an intangible and somewhat imprecise unit of measurement of an individual's rank or position in society, largely based on other people's perceptions. It reflects prestige, authority, and dominance and represents the influence and power a person has in the community relative to others.

In fact, studies on how our brains process certain rewards reveal that we may value social standing more highly than monetary rewards,[16] and being respected makes us feel good. Status has economic value as well; it can be transacted to acquire other things of value such as favors, information, and promotions. Superhubs may bestow status by association on others, because they like and trust them, feel that they are a good complement to them in some way, or that they can help them realize their interests. Improvement of position in a network and an increase in status are synonymous.

The very concept of status implies hierarchy. Hierarchies are an outflow of evolution, because structured groups operate more efficiently than egalitarian organizations. Hierarchical structures encourage high-ranking individuals to spend effort and energy competing with their peers, which creates progress that benefits everyone. The work of those at the top is essential to the success of their communities or organizations—and that positive influence gives them status.[17] As we moved from agrarian societies to industrial ones, social hierarchies became organizational hierarchies. Today, prestigious job titles such as CEO or chairman are status markers, and achieving higher professional positions is one of the most direct ways to increase your status.

Another way to gain more status is to increase your wealth. During the course of the debt-fueled global growth over the last thirty years, the status resulting from jobs that carry a social value—such as the medical or educational professions—has been overtaken by the status money provides. People in finance have made increasingly more money and seen their status rise as a result. Salaries in the financial industry are typically significantly higher than salaries in other sectors. Executives can capitalize on those salaries through rent-seeking—returns on ownership rather than from labor or production—as they have access to investment opportunities to put that money to work for them.

Location: Reputation Matters

Reputation is an important facet of status, reflecting integrity and competence. We automatically assess other people based on their reputations and consider good character a precondition for doing business.

In the world of high finance, a stellar reputation within the industry is an indispensable requirement to becoming a superhub. Yet what might seem reputation-destroying to many of us sometimes appears not to matter much in the business world. Jamie Dimon, CEO of JPMorgan, oversaw the loss of $6.2 billion, yet his reputation as a competent leader in global finance did not suffer. A larger-than-life reputation tends to become self-sustaining due to a cognitive bias known as the "halo effect,"[18] in which everything an individual does is viewed through the frame of his assumed excellence. In other words, once opinion leaders in the network deem someone to be extraordinary, the network assumes it as an eternal fact. Even in the event of a massive failure, the superhubs' tight network connections often prevent peers from falling through the cracks.[19] Loyalties and social capital are a strong base on which relationships are cemented, and most of the executives who lost their jobs during the financial crisis later resurfaced elsewhere.

Reputation: Access Matters

Anthony Scaramucci, the youthful, sunny founder of SkyBridge Capital—who bears a resemblance to life coach Tony Robbins—leveraged the access he found at Davos to make the move of his career. In 2010, in the corridors of the Belvédère Hotel, Scaramucci, a relative newcomer by Davos standards, engaged in a dialogue with Vikram Pandit, then CEO of Citigroup. He convinced Pandit to sell him Citi's $4 billion portfolio of hedge funds, which overnight brought SkyBridge's assets under management up to $6 billion. It was a coup that would not have occurred if he had been unable to converse with Pandit. This is precisely why access is so important.

Scaramucci has the quintessential megawatt smile and exudes sweeping enthusiasm in everything he does. He grew up in a working-class family on Long Island and, after graduating from Harvard Law School, joined Goldman Sachs—the source of many financial superhubs—before starting his own investment management firm. Several years ago, he finally landed a coveted invitation to the WEF, where I first met him. His folksy, backslapping, high-fiving demeanor is not everyone's cup of tea, but those who dismiss him grossly underestimate his intelligence and strategic prowess.

Scaramucci is a talented schmoozer with a knack for self-promotion, yet his consistent energy makes it all seem authentic. He cleverly product-placed a large SkyBridge banner in Oliver Stone's *Wall Street II*, and even landed a cameo. He further enhanced his profile with his well-received book, *Goodbye Gordon Gekko*, which was a timely self-critical reflection on Wall Street's culture of greed. His rise has been extraordinary, and Davos has played no small part in it.

While many of Scaramucci's most valuable contacts stem from the WEF, he has since spread his wings far beyond the WEF and built his own wildly successful forum, the SkyBridge Alternatives Conference (SALT). Within only a couple of years, SALT has become the premier hedge fund gathering in the world. This no-expenses-spared event features the best speakers (Bill Clinton, George W. Bush, Nicolas Sarkozy), the best par-ties—the best everything. A vital part of SALT's success is based in Scar-amucci's deep relationships and alliances. Hedge fund titans such as Steve Cohen, Ray Dalio, and David Tepper genuinely like and trust him and lent their support as he established SALT.

Scaramucci's network position, like that of every superhub, provides him with a most coveted and valuable asset: access to any other superhubs. Having calls answered, emails read, and the ability to obtain meetings is the decisive first step to achieving any business goal. The most senior people in the financial world, who are inundated with requests, care-fully allocate their most precious and finite resource—time—to those they like and deem important to their own interests, particularly other powerful people. Building and maintaining a large network is challeng-ing—the larger the network, the greater the time and effort required. So superhubs prioritize quality over quantity and discriminate.[20] According to "Dunbar's Number," our minds only have the cognitive capacity to retain approximately 150 true connections or relationships.[21] This natural limitation makes access all the more valuable. The concept of Dunbar's Number is widely recognized in business circles, particularly in client-oriented professions.

By leveraging their status and access, superhubs also have "convening power": the power to congregate networks of individuals working together toward a common goal. Convening power is a power multiplier. Superhubs are already powerful, but by linking up with other powerful and like-minded individuals, they increase their influence exponentially. Their power is twofold: By virtue of their status and reputation they have access to the most powerful people, and with their credibility they have the authority to convince those powerful people to join their cause. Klaus Schwab, the founder of the World Economic Forum, and George Soros are good examples. When they call, people line up, eager to join the cause whatever it may be. That convening power, in turn, increases their status.

Furthermore, superhubs have a great amount of control over network flows because they reside in its nerve center. They can open up access to one node by another, control the distribution of information, and limit access of other nodes, essentially playing the role of gatekeeper with regard to coveted opportunities.[22] That control in turn fortifies their network power.

In financial networks, the most important outcome of access to powerful people is access to the network currencies they control: information, financial capital, and opportunities. These are the essential links in the global financial network, and we'll explore them in the next chapter.

Access: Social Capital Matters

Elites in the financial sector leverage a common currency: social capital. In a sense, it is a form of accumulated labor expended for the benefit of another. Human networks are based on the exchange of social capital, which acts as a glue that cements relationships and facilitates cooperation. The metaphor of capital implies that one can invest in their social connections and expect a correlated return—an expectation of reciprocity based on trust and shared values.[23] We all feel obligated to return favors and keep track of them.[24] In the networks of the superhubs, every request for a favor is a complex negotiation, and favors are like loans collateralized by the status of the borrower. The higher the status, the more value is attached to the favor. As a person's status and access grow, so does his social capital, creating a potent combination of power that attracts other nodes. Social capital complements financial and human capital and is one of the forces that drive economic growth. Human capital—the sum of a person's intelligence and experience—has long been recognized as a measure of productivity. In contrast, social capital—the extent and depth of a person's network—has been neglected in assessing productivity output.[25]

Trading favors has always been an integral part of Wall Street culture. Financiers follow an unwritten honor code when it comes to relying on someone's word, so the exchange of favors balances out most of the time. When it does not, the obligor is in danger of being penalized with status-lowering gossip or, worse, expulsion from the network.

Financial superhubs have access to everyone and everything, and when they make requests, others are all too happy to oblige. The attendance of high-demand superhubs upgrades the prestige of every event, and people are eager to exchange thoughts with, befriend, and work with them. Through their status and access, they have massive power in the financial network.

Superhubs inevitably form in all communities, be they among students in school, tradespeople in a small city, or actors on a global stage. Their formation follows the laws of network science, and with gravitational force they attract a disproportionate number of connections. Superhubs in the financial system are particularly powerful due to their access to capital and globalization. They do not procure their prominent positions by accident; rather, they decipher the DNA of a network and abide by its rules until they are in a position to influence them, thereby perpetuating the system. When they link directly to each other and form clusters, their power multiplies and becomes pervasive, touching the lives of each and every one of us.

One of the greatest advantages of being a superhub is easy access to other superhubs, a feature that particularly applies to George Soros. Whenever he starts a new venture or engages in a cause, he does not have to ask for support; the highest-caliber people from all over the world, including former heads of state and senior policy makers, offer their help, as they are eager to be associated with his ideas and endeavors. In the same vein, he does not simply provide ideas and funds to his contacts and causes. His own powerful networks serve as a crucial resource and when Soros calls, people respond.

Soros's eightieth birthday party was a testament to the deep personal relationships that he has built throughout his life. Friends from all over the world flocked to celebrate the occasion with a big bash in Southampton, New York. In a white gazebo-themed tent, economist Nouriel Roubini chatted with Byron Wien, vice chairman of Blackstone. Under the palm trees, Caio Koch-Weser, vice chairman of Deutsche Bank, sipped champagne with Min Zhu, deputy managing director of the IMF. Meanwhile, Pete Peterson, cofounder of the Blackstone, and Charles Dallara, then managing director of International Institute of Finance, searched for a quiet place to sit down and talk.

Soros's wedding to business consultant Tamiko Bolton in 2013 was even more extravagant. Since the event had been scheduled to take place on the weekend preceding the United Nations General Assembly and the Clinton Global Initiative, many world leaders were in New York. The festivities were held at the Caramoor Estate near Katonah, New York, an hour's drive from the city, and I looked forward to attending. Approaching the venue, we joined a long convoy of black limousines and were greeted by the Budapest Festival Orchestra playing a composition created solely for the occasion. In a splendiferous tent, at the center of which loomed a life-sized sculpture of a hot air balloon made entirely of flowers, a microcosm of the financial elite mingled. IMF chief Christine Lagarde; World Bank president Jim Yong Kim; former UN Secretary-General Kofi Annan; House minority leader Nancy Pelosi; Senator Chuck Schumer; Iceland's President, Ólafur Ragnar Grímsson; Estonian President Toomas Hendrik Ilves; Liberian president Ellen Johnson Sirleaf; Albania's prime minister Edi Rama; Italian foreign minister Emma Bonino; former Greek prime minister George Papandreou; hedge fund titans Paul Tudor Jones, Julian Robertson, and Stan Druckenmiller; Lord Adair Turner; Lord Mark Malloch-Brown; Charles Dallara; and the singer Bono from the rock band U2 were all in attendance, to name just a few. George's and Tamiko's friends had come from near and far to celebrate this joyous occasion—and to reinforce existing social bonds.

* * *

In this chapter, we have superimposed network science on the relationship structure of the best-connected and most powerful people in the financial system to explain how superhubs emerge. More concretely, we have revealed the dynamics that make some people superhubs, such as status, access, and social capital. How are superhubs connected, what makes their connections so valuable, and what is actually exchanged in these networks? In the following chapter, we'll examine more closely the main links that connect them: money, information, and opportunities.

CHAPTER 3

The Links That Connect Superhubs

Money, Information, and Opportunities

NETWORK NUCLEUS: LARRY FINK

Every year during the World Economic Forum in Davos, the *Financial Times* and CNBC cohost the "Nightcap" at the majestic Belvédère Hotel. The reception is a must-attend for the captains of the various industries. It was there that I first met Larry Fink, who I had only known from his media appearances. With his narrow-set, tense eyes, prominent forehead, and almost exaggeratedly brainy appearance, I had expected him to act like a socially awkward genius. Yet, that evening, he effortlessly worked the crowd and was open, friendly, and approachable. Most fascinating was watching guests gravitate toward him, eager to engage in a conversation. Even if I had not known who he was, I would have sensed that he was someone "important"—a superhub—by the way other important people pursued him.

Fink is the founder, chairman, and CEO of BlackRock, the largest asset management company in the world. Institutional investors entrust him with record amounts of money derived from "regular people's" savings and pensions, and governments around the world ask him for advice. Fink is a prime example of how superhubs are linked to other players in the system via money, information, and opportunities. Moreover, he has all the usual superhub prerequisites: brilliance, a top education, and an alpha personality. After graduating from UCLA with an MBA, he joined First Boston in New York and made the bank hundreds of millions of dollars in a decade. Used to extraordinary success, he felt humiliated when fortunes reversed and he lost a hundred million dollars. His subsequent departure from the bank had the appearance of a firing and was the talk of Wall Street.

Fink drew several lessons from his failure, the first of which turned out to be groundbreaking: He realized that asset managers have an incomplete understanding of risk, especially when things are going well. He concluded that building risk management systems was one of the most fundamental necessities of successful portfolio management. In 1988, he cofounded his own company under the umbrella of the Blackstone Group, a private equity firm established by Steve Schwarzman and Pete Peterson, which extended a $5 million credit line to Fink and his partners in exchange for a 50 percent stake. Within only a few months, his business flourished. However, in 1992, Schwarzman and Fink, likely two of Wall Street's biggest personalities, clashed over compensation and ownership issues and parted ways. Fink set out for bigger and better things and, accordingly, called his new firm BlackRock, a step up from Blackstone.

Fink has built an unparalleled global network. His bipartisan Washington ties and increasing involvement in political discourse have given him particular cachet. Fink further expanded his network by hiring high-profile former policy makers such as Philipp Hildebrand, the former governor of the Swiss National Bank, and Kendrik Wilson, a former U.S. treasury official. He is also said to have a close relationship with former U.S. treasury secretary Timothy Geithner, whom he reportedly had hoped in vain would join BlackRock at the end of his term. With all of his connections to those in power, Fink is now himself immensely powerful. He dedicates much of his time to developing and maintaining relationships and spends half of the year flying around the world to visit clients.

BlackRock's financial links are ubiquitous. It controls trillions of dollars, more than most countries' GDP and at times exceeding the Federal Reserve's balance sheet. Through its management and advisory mandates, BlackRock is connected with most sovereign wealth funds, pension funds, central banks, endowments, and foundations. By the time of the financial crisis, BlackRock essentially had a monopoly on risk management and Fink had become known as "Mr. Fix-It." Several governments retained BlackRock firm to help sort out the mess, and U.S. treasury secretary Geithner mandated it to analyze and sell $30 billion of risky mortgage securities. BlackRock was then retained to proceed in a similar fashion with AIG's mortgage securities, a deal that eventually yielded a profit for taxpayers.

In line with Fink's original idea, the firm's core expertise centers on risk management. Thousands of computers operated by "rocket scientists" monitor tens of thousands of investment portfolios with proprietary quantitative programs. These systems process information input and, in turn, churn out even more valuable information with the help of sophisticated algorithms. The fact that BlackRock advises, analyzes, and manages so much money for so many institutional investors across the world gives it unique insights into the condition of the financial system as a whole. In addition, Fink himself is an information hub. His hyperconnectedness provides him with a high degree of valuable "information currency," and his access to a vast personal network, capital, and information creates a wealth of opportunities.

NETWORK POWER: MONEY

The very fabric of the financial system is money. Money has transformative power and profoundly influences the way we organize our society and culture. The financial system, the economy, and markets are networks, with money connecting all three. Because it is one of the most ubiquitous links that connects nodes, hubs, and superhubs, money has serious network power. The flow of capital creates a web of transactions between market participants and links a wide network of financial institutions such as central banks, banks, and other financial firms. It creates relationships through credit, commerce, and trade; company shareholdings; and political contributions.

Money, as a means of exchange and store of value, exhibits typical network properties. For instance, paper currency travels in patterns and at a speed similar to viruses. When the money flow stops, economies grind to a halt, financial systems freeze, and markets become prone to collapse, as was evident throughout the crisis. Money is mostly created by banks offering loans.[1] Central banks control the amount of money in an economy through the setting of interest rates and purchase of assets.

The network power of money extends to executives at the top of the financial system, who make decisions about its creation, allocation, and flow. The links created by money in turn form the base of the executives' network power. Thus, networks create and impact money, while money creates and impacts networks. One of the most basic ways in which money connects people is through different types of institutions. The global financial system rests on several key pillars: central banks, "regular" banks, nonbank financial firms—the so-called "shadow banks"—and other financial institutions such as the Bank for International Settlements and the IMF. Many of these entities hold regular conferences where their executives maintain their ties.

The Printing Presses: Central Banks

Today almost all countries have central banks, which are independent government agencies, such as the Federal Reserve, the European Central Bank, or the Bank of England. Their mandate is to attain stable growth at low inflation and maintain the stability of the financial system. To achieve these goals, they use monetary policy: setting interest rates, regulating and supervising financial institutions, and providing liquidity in times of crises.

The European Central Bank (ECB) regularly holds conferences on its home turf in Frankfurt. Those meetings are usually matter-of-fact and technical. Leading central bankers and academics deliver presentations and papers on monetary policy, and participants have the opportunity to casually mingle. Guests frequently include the ECB president, ECB board members, the heads of the Bundesbank and the IMF, top executives from the European Commission, and many other central bank governors, senior policy makers, academics, bankers, and fund managers. These conferences usually coincide with the European Banking Congress, which most European bank CEOs attend. Policy makers such as the chairman of the U.S. Federal Reserve and finance ministers from around the world shuttle back and forth between conference venues and deliver talks to enlighten their audience of bankers. Speeches of senior policy makers are the highlights of any commercial event, yet another manifestation of how various different networks—in this case public and private ones—interact and reinforce each other.

Since 2008, central banks have pumped trillions of dollars into the global financial system to give politicians time to create more fundamental solutions. They now rank among the biggest investors in world markets.[2] Central banking has become a quasi "asset class in and of itself" as they move global markets with their decisions. Because of their independence from politics, central banks are relatively unconstrained with regard to their actions as long as they maneuver within their mandate. In contrast to political institutions, they can make quick decisions and execute them. As a result, central bankers are now among the most powerful people in the world—in many respects more so than elected officials—due to the sheer scale of their financial firepower and their ability to quickly pull the trigger. They co-determine the course of the global economy and have a huge impact on all of our lives.

Central bankers live in a rarefied and peculiar world. Due to the length of their terms and frequent meetings throughout the world, they know and trust one another and communicate on the same frequency. Highly educated and with a deep passion for economics, this small group of experts tends to be friendly, unpretentious, and approachable, though somewhat reserved, because they must be careful of what they say. Most of them are men, and many of them have known one another throughout their lives. Various central banks also hold international conferences, with Jackson Hole being one of the most well known. And, of course, many central bankers gather at the Annual Meeting of the WEF in Davos. In between all those meetings, they are in constant contact and consult with each other. The increased interconnectedness of our world and constant crises and emergencies have shaped a transnational central banker identity, further homogenizing an already fairly uniform group.

Federal Reserve Chairman: In Charge of the World's Reserve Currency

The chairman of the central bank of the U.S., the Federal Reserve, is perhaps the most powerful person in the country besides the president. Unelected, independent, and accountable to Congress and the public, she or he has immense power with implications for both the U.S. and the world as a whole. Former Fed chief Ben Bernanke has been a superhub in the financial system as he steered the United States through the largest crisis since the Great Depression. His words moved markets, and his actions were of unprecedented consequence for all our lives. For years, he has been at the center of all key policy gatherings around the world.

I once visited him at the Fed with Nouriel Roubini. Upon entering the Eccles Building, I was struck by its austere classical elegance. Perhaps buildings somehow do take on and reflect the history that they witness throughout the years. Beyond housing the Fed, it also hosted the Arcadia Conference during World War II, at which Franklin Roosevelt and Winston Churchill coordinated their war efforts. The monumental white marble edifice is a modernist interpretation of the Beaux-Arts style, which reflects the spirit of the Depression, during which it was built. It comprises four stories designed in the shape of the letter H, with the empty spaces arranged as courtyards. Doric columns and grand dual staircases frame a two-story atrium, its floors and walls decked out in rich Georgia and travertine marble. A surreal, magic light emanates from the ceiling's frozen skylight, which is decorated with a majestic eagle. The halls exude a dignified quiet and in the background a hint of classical music lingers.

The Fed chair's high-ceilinged office is decorated with art from the Fed's Fine Arts Program's permanent collection, whose director described Bernanke's taste as creative and innovative and his choices as unpredictable and unconventional. In person, Bernanke comes across as a genuinely nice and regular guy. He is always friendly, albeit slightly reserved, and markedly different from other financial top executives. He lacks the typical alpha male trait of a big ego, which might have interfered with his sober and prudent decision making.

Regrettably and somewhat unbelievably, the Fed completely missed the developing crisis buildup. Bernanke later conceded that he had failed to realize the scope of the credit bubble and that he did not understand "the interconnections to off-balance sheet vehicles and complex credit derivatives,"[3] meaning the highly technical and nontransparent financial vehicles created for abstract and practically incomprehensible financial instruments. A sociological analysis has confirmed that the similar backgrounds of the top central bankers created an echo chamber and narrow mind-sets that failed to connect the dots.[4] However, once Bernanke grasped the severity of the situation, he intervened forcefully and with great determination. Under his guidance, the Fed orchestrated the $700 billion Troubled Asset Relief Program (TARP) rescue package for the U.S. Treasury and instituted a lending program of virtually unlimited, unconditional financing to banks totaling $7.77 trillion in commitments. These programs were kept top secret even from lawmakers and top aides and only became public when Bloomberg LP prevailed in a lawsuit that requested disclosure of the emergency measures.[5]

The mild-mannered, soft-spoken, and unassuming Bernanke, who had overnight acquired almost unfathomable power, had suddenly taken a strong and courageous lead. Some of his measures may have lacked democratic legitimacy,[6] but while in normal times democracy is effective, in times of an existential crisis, a more imperial style may sometimes be expedient. Bernanke warned that monetary policy was no panacea, but he was forced to step in to compensate for political inertia. Taxpayers may not have been adequately compensated for the risks taken with their money,[7] but the system was saved, at least for the time being.

In terms of network dynamics, Bernanke is an outlier because he obtained his positions primarily based on academic credentials rather than through a network of well-established contacts. Although he was a star in academic circles, he did not have the airtight old boy's network to propel him to the top, never having worked on Wall Street or participated in the Washington political establishment. He was an introvert, not known for being a suave networker, and who for the most part shunned the Washington cocktail circuit. Although Bernanke lacked the strong relationship portfolio possessed by his well-connected predecessor, Alan Greenspan, once he became Fed chief, he actively embarked on developing relationships with members of Congress and the White House, while also relying on the much better connected Hank Paulson and Fed board member Kevin Warsh.[8]

Bernanke's background is anchored in the values of Main Street rather than Wall Street. He grew up in modest circumstances in a small town in South Carolina, where his parents owned a drugstore. During his university years, he worked typical student jobs in construction and hospitality. He excelled at academics, graduating from Harvard University and earning a PhD at the Massachusetts Institute of Technology (MIT). Stanley Fischer, who later became the governor of the Bank of Israel and thereafter Vice Chairman of the Federal Reserve, was his thesis adviser. While at Harvard, his path crossed with many who would later become key figures in the crisis: Lloyd Blankfein, CEO of Goldman Sachs; Kenneth Rogoff of Harvard University; and Paul Krugman, Nobel laureate and Princeton professor. Both Bernanke and Larry Summers earned degrees at MIT.

Bernanke went on to become a professor at Stanford Business School and a visiting professor at New York University before receiving tenure at Princeton University. His studies focused on the Great Depression, and his papers and speeches eerily foreshadow the crisis management job that awaited him years later in his career. As his academic footprint grew, he was recognized in Washington circles and became a member of the Board of Governors of the Federal Reserve. His background was all the more serendipitous in view of the fact that, at the time of his appointment as Fed chair, the administration had no idea of the financial system's impending implosion.

Bernanke was well suited to steer the U.S. through the crisis not only because of his expertise but also because of his personality. Despite the chaotic environment, he proceeded in a methodical manner; when markets were panicking, he exuded calmness and successfully collaborated with the diverse parties involved. His unassuming demeanor was a refreshing antithesis to the Greenspan personality cult, and in contrast to his predecessor's convoluted and opaque "Greenspanese," Bernake explained complex issues in simple terms in an effort to promote transparency. Bernanke also possessed the diplomatic and political skill to deal with the supersized egos he had to bring to the table during this time.

Bernanke worked tirelessly throughout the seemingly endless crisis, and eventually the stress of carrying the weight of the world on his shoulders took its toll. The curse of knowing too much coupled with great responsibility began to show. At meetings he sometimes appeared detached, almost robotic, and the vociferous criticism regarding his policies likely added to the pressure. Yet, he had made a deliberate choice to devote his career to public service, even serving a second term.

Central Bank of Central Banks: The Bank for International Settlements

Every other month, central banks meet at the Bank for International Settlements (BIS) in Basel, Switzerland. The oldest international financial institution in the world, the BIS is the bank for sixty central banks around the world and counts among its members the Fed, the ECB, and the Bundesbank. As the nerve center of the international financial system, it acts as a prime counterparty for central banks, supporting monetary and financial stability and conducting research and analysis. In addition, it provides a platform for the Basel Committee on Banking Supervision, the Committee on the Global Financial System, the Committee on Payment and Settlement Systems, and the Financial Stability Board (FSB).[9] Set up in 1930 primarily to manage Germany's World War I reparations, the BIS's unusual history has to a large extent been driven by the strong personalities of central bankers.[10] Its offices are located on sovereign soil not subject to Swiss law, and its employees enjoy quasi-diplomatic status and Swiss tax exemption.

A Primer on Banks: Regular and Shadow Banks

"*Regular*" *banks* take deposits and in turn pay interest to depositors. Then they put the deposits to work to generate revenue, usually by giving loans for which they receive interest or by investing.

Savings banks are focused on accumulating money, *commercial banks* on working with businesses, and *private banks* on servicing high-net-worth individuals.

Investment banks do not have banking licenses and do not take deposits from savers. Rather, they invest on their clients' behalf, render investment advice, and engage in corporate transactions such as mergers, acquisitions, and initial public offerings. Their deals are usually a bit riskier because they deal with sophisticated clients.

Shadow banks is a catchall term for all financial service providers that lack a banking license, such as investment banks, broker dealers, investment funds, and money market funds. Shadow banks have recently come into focus as much business has fled from heavily regulated banks to the lightly regulated and nimbler shadow banks. In fact, they have received such large capital inflows that they are now considered a potential risk for financial stability.

Bank CEOs are amongst the most powerful individuals in the financial system due to the indispensability and pervasive power of their institutions. Because they are located in the center of a web of highly valuable connections, they are superhubs.

The Perpetual Crisis Manager: The International Monetary Fund

The International Monetary Fund (IMF) promotes global monetary cooperation, financial stability, international trade, employment, and economic growth. Established at the Bretton Woods Conference in 1945, today it has 188 member countries[11] and holds regular Conferences around the world for its staff to meet with central bankers, finance ministers, policy makers and representatives of the private sector. Over the years, I have regularly attended the Annual Meetings and other IMF events, and they have given me an interesting glimpse into a world that is otherwise largely inaccessible.

One such meeting was the "High-Level Conference on the International Monetary System." It was cohosted by the Swiss National Bank and the IMF at the storied Baur au Lac Hotel in Zürich, located in the center of the city with scenic views of Lake Zürich and the Alps. A relatively small event, it had a couple hundred participants, among them central bank governors, other senior policy makers, leading academics, and commentators.

They included Philipp Hildebrand, governor of the Swiss National Bank; Dominique Strauss-Kahn, then managing director of the IMF; Christine Lagarde, French finance minister; Mark Carney, governor of the Bank of Canada; and Larry Summers, head of Barack Obama's National Economic Council and former U.S. treasury secretary. By invitation only, the meetings were governed by the Chatham House Rule, meaning that information could be used but not attributed to any particular person.

Amidst a worsening crisis in Europe, the meetings featured tense debates on the reform of the international monetary system. Panel presentations on capital flows, reserve currencies, and global liquidity provisions were followed by controversial discussions between speakers and the participants. Christine Lagarde, elegant and energetic, keynoted during the luncheon, and Michel Camdessus of the Banque de France spoke during a traditional Swiss dinner at Zunfthaus zur Meisen in the old part of town.

From Zürich, I traveled to Germany for business meetings where I received a text message from Nouriel Roubini with shocking news. Four days after the conference in Zürich, Dominique Strauss-Kahn, who had been en route to Germany to meet with Chancellor Angela Merkel, had been arrested in at JFK Airport. He was charged with rape, perp-walked in handcuffs, and imprisoned in Rikers Island. We were incredulous, but more on that later.

NETWORK CURRENCY: INFORMATION

In finance, the most valuable currency is actionable information that can be converted into monetary gain. People with access to the right information to capitalize on business opportunities have an invaluable advantage—and the most efficient and reliable way to obtain information is to get it directly from the source.

All networks are systems of communication and feed off information. Evolution itself has been a continuous exchange of information between organisms within their networks.[12] As the decisive catalyst for our thoughts and actions, information has enormous network power because its movement holds together the links and nodes that comprise the network and determine its operation.[13] The times when obtaining information was the goal or challenge have long passed. Through the information revolution, more high-quality information is freely available than ever before. The Internet, the nerve center of modern society, contains any information that can be digitized. In the next few years, billions of more people will receive access to it and feed in even more information and insights. The Internet has become a democratic platform,[14] and as Eric Schmidt, executive chairman of Google, notes, "We've gone from a hierarchical messaging structure where people are broadcast to, and information usually had local context, to a model where everyone's an organizer, a broadcaster, a blogger, a communicator."[15] As a result, we are suffering from information overload, which makes filtering relevant information all the more challenging. Big data showing statistical correlations only adds to the inundation.

The challenge in finance is that—more often than not—it does not deal with tangible objects or straightforward services that are easily understood, but with abstract derivatives thereof. Since the results of these often elusive constructs only materialize in the future, verifiable information is all the more critical. However, publicly available information gives an incomplete picture at best and a skewed or inaccurate one at worst. The media covers finance from all angles, as do bloggers, tweeters, and other social media users, in addition to experts, pundits, and thought leaders. The research that financial institutions publish is naturally biased, because it is a vehicle for them to sell their products and bolster their reputations. Warren Buffett stated in a 2014 investment letter that managers' top priority—trumping everything else, including profits—must be to "zealously guard Berkshire's reputation."[16] In the information war, public relation agencies and corporations spend exorbitant amounts of money to surreptitiously invade traditional journalism. They have hired legions of journalists at attractive salaries, who often—under the guise of serious journalism—combine compelling storytelling with stimulating and entertaining multimedia content to present the company in the best light. Perception is reality, and the line between favorable reporting, spinning, and outright manipulation is blurry.

Another currency in financial markets is misinformation. Spreading rumors to induce others to trade has long been a tool of market manipulation and profiteering. A prime example is the fall of Lehman Brothers. Rumormongers, mostly short sellers, spread whispers that Lehman would be the next Bear Stearns, which led to a self-fulfilling prophecy: a run on the bank, a precipitous fall in share price, and the institution's eventual demise. Today, rumors are ever more prevalent, with many more outlets and much faster travel routes. In a complex environment and crisis atmosphere, distinguishing fact from fiction can prove near-impossible, especially when there is a good chance—as in the case of Lehman—that enough fiction over time will be perceived as fact.

Hence, personal contacts as key conduits for information have become more valuable than ever. Firsthand knowledge is the needle in the haystack of information. The glue that binds original sources together is homophily—social ties based on shared backgrounds, personalities, and qualities that facilitate communication and trust. (More on this in Chapter 5.) Whereas people with strong ties are reliable and easily accessible sources, weak ties are equally important because they open up access to new information outside of established business and social circles. Another valuable source is dormant ties, longtime contacts that may have been neglected but are easily resuscitated. Communication is a crucial means of forming network power. By virtue of their centrality, superhubs are nerve centers and information brokers, because they have access and control over the information flow. The information inundation, which makes it increasingly difficult to filter the signal from the noise, has only amplified their information power.

The Influence of Personal Connections

According to a Harvard Business School study titled *Assess the Value of Your Networks*, personal ties based on social, educational, employment, and gender backgrounds strongly influence the flow and quality of information. Often people distrust public information and prefer familiar and trusted sources. Particularly in recruiting and job searches, executives rely on each other's opinion and discretion, which ensures better results and lower search costs.[17]

Another Harvard study called *The Power of Alumni Networks* examined how information flows affect stock prices by comparing the performance of investments into connected firms, where senior officials had common school ties, to nonconnected firms without such ties. Their results revealed that managers place larger and more successful bets on companies whose executives attended the same schools. They know and understand each other better, have long-standing relationships with a high degree of interaction, and because of their similarities are able to more accurately assess each other.[18]

Information Access and Proximity

Proximity to decision makers—particularly central bankers—is invaluable because information on monetary policies can be directly converted into profits. Central bankers often mix with financial industry executives to explain their policies and inform themselves on the state of the financial sector. The 2007 crisis caught central bankers by surprise because they had been unaware of the degree of leverage in the system and the scope of subprime mortgages. Staying in touch with the "real world" helps them to form a more complete picture of markets and design more efficient monetary policies.

However, at the same time, as guardians of the currency, central bankers are subject to strict guidelines and must provide equal and public access to information to ensure that no one gains an unfair advantage by trading ahead of the market. But central bankers are human, and lines can be blurry, which in the past has led to leaks and suspicion that well-connected financiers had monetized confidential information. Conflicts of interest are exacerbated by the revolving door as numerous central bankers eventually join the private sector. Former Fed chief Alan Greenspan has advised Deutsche Bank, PIMCO, and Paulson & Co., and his successor Ben Bernanke has acted as senior adviser to PIMCO and Citadel following his departure from the Fed. Similarly, the former head of the German Bundesbank, Axel Weber, went on to become chairman of UBS, and Philipp Hildebrand of the Swiss National Bank took on the position of vice chairman of BlackRock.

Anecdotes of inappropriately cozy relationships between central bankers and financiers are numerous. Such a relationship may even have cost Paul Tucker the job of governor of the Bank of England. As a respected and well-liked senior Bank of England official, he had been Mervyn King's heir apparent. However, when investigations into the Libor-rigging scandal unearthed emails between him and Bob Diamond, the CEO of Barclays, evidencing their close relationship, Tucker was questioned by a parliamentary committee. The job ultimately went to Mark Carney.

Many research and consultancy firms unabashedly advertise their close relationships with the public sector. For instance, Medley Global Advisors, a macroeconomic and political research firm that provides research to the financial sector, proudly states that its network includes central banks and other public bodies. Though likely exaggerated, word on the street was that its founder, Richard Medley, had built the firm's business model on being an "intelligence agency" for Fed measures. The firm came under scrutiny after it published details on Fed deliberations a day before the Fed made them public in 2012. As a result, Congress probed the Fed on the leak. Medley, which was purchased by the *Financial Times* in 2010, defended itself with the claim that it is a media organization, entitled to special protections under the law.[19] At the time of this book's completion, the investigation was still ongoing. Two years prior to the investigation, Ben Bernanke had warned policy makers about leaks of inside information to the press and consultants. He specifically stated that "there may be leaks to nonmedia outsiders, including market participants, former officials, consultants, and others, some of whom stand to make money by their inside access either to participants or to staff."[20]

Another incident causing controversy was a conference sponsored by Brevan Howard, a hedge fund with $27 billion under management. The event was hosted by the Centre for Financial Analysis, the Centre for Economic Policy Research, and the Swiss National Bank at the posh Berkeley Hotel in London and attended by hedge fund managers, traders, and bankers. During the dinner, Benoît Coeuré, a member of the executive board of the European Central Bank, announced that the ECB would buy extra government bonds in the coming weeks. When his remarks were published on the ECB's website over twelve hours later, the euro fell sharply and government bonds experienced increased volatility. Coeuré's mentioning the ECB's plans to a select group of financiers led to accusations that he had leaked confidential information. The ECB's president, Mario Draghi, countered in Coeuré's defense that increase in government debt purchases had already been obvious from the figures published on the ECB's website over several preceding days but promised to improve the bank's communication policy.

Asymmetrical or unequal access to information regarding the bailouts during the financial crisis gave rise to the suspicion that Wall Street capitalized on an unfair advantage. Particular attention was paid to the Fed's 2008 hiring of four private asset management companies—PIMCO, Black-Rock, Goldman Sachs, and Wellington—to help implement its quantitative easing program. Lacking the necessary expertise and infrastructure to implement the enormous program itself, the Fed had to rely on third-party managers and provided the retained firms with nonpublic information so they would understand how to proceed. That posed a potential conflict of interest, because those firms traded in the same securities on behalf of their clients that they bought for the Fed. To avoid those conflicts, confidentiality agreements, "Chinese walls," audits, and other control procedures were instituted.

But PIMCO's large bets, "confidence in its trading," and consistently outsized returns attracted attention, particularly in view of the fact that it enjoyed close relationships with the Fed through its advisers, specifically former Fed chairman Alan Greenspan, New York Fed advisory committee member Mohamed El-Erian, and Bernanke confidante Richard Clarida. During the time in question, Greenspan had two confidential meetings with then Fed chairman Ben Bernanke. Bill Gross, CEO of PIMCO, used his close Fed connections as a selling point. He stated that his goal was to "shake hands with the government" and bragged about his access and foresight. Transactions were subjected to retroactive scrutiny as far as possible and no evidence of illegality or impropriety was found.

The Benefit of Connections in Tumultuous Times

Former U.S. treasury secretary Tim Geithner is one of the best-connected executives on Wall Street. As the head of the New York Fed, the young-looking, affable, and athletic Geithner was popular with subordinates and superiors alike. Although he had never worked in banking, he possessed a privileged background and began his career at Kissinger Associates, run by policy gurus Henry Kissinger and Brent Scowcroft. At the venerable New York Fed, located at the heart of the financial district, he oversaw many of the U.S.'s biggest financial institutions, including Citigroup. He often communicated with Wall Street executives, as evidenced by his official calendar, in an effort to gather intelligence on the market. His personal life also overlapped with many executives of the institutions he oversaw. Later, he was criticized for his failure to realize that so many institutions under his watch were sliding into crises, along with the entire financial system. In the opinion of renowned economist Willem Buiter, the New York Fed under Geithner was compromised by the financial industry.[21]

An MIT study titled *The Value of Connections in Turbulent Times*, coauthored by noted Wall Street critic Simon Johnson, examined the financial firms with ties to Tim Geithner during his term as U.S. treasury secretary to see if they derived any special benefits during the crisis. Johnson defined connections as friendships, professional associations, and other interactions such as charity collaborations. The study revealed that in the run-up to his appointment, shares of financial firms whose executives had connections with Geithner increased significantly in value relative to the firms with no such connections. When Geithner's nomination became less certain due to his personal tax issues, the same firms saw abnormal negative returns versus unconnected firms. However, the study found no evidence that these jumps in stock price were due to any illegal or unethical collusion between Geithner and those firms.

There were no indications that Geithner was in any way corrupt. He has been widely criticized for his policies but not for a lack of integrity. He did not need to bribe financial firms to obtain lucrative positions in the private sector because all doors had already been open to him when he left the New York Fed. Since he did not seek political office, he did not need to court donors. Rather it turned out that in times of crisis when fundamentals were skewed, panicked investors looked for any clues that would give them an edge. Accordingly, the study found that price jumps resulted merely from the market's *expectation* that connected firms would have better access, the so-called "social connections meets the crisis" interpretation. This expectation was correct because Geithner did hire people whom he trusted since "during times of crisis and urgency, social connections are likely to have more impact on policy."[22] Urgent situations necessitate sidestepping bureaucratic processes and relying more heavily on trusted established personal connections. So Geithner's hiring choices were the result of an established pattern of human behavior, according to which people prefer to work with those whom they know and trust. Most likely, anyone in a job with extraordinarily high stakes would prefer hiring familiar and loyal people with whom they are comfortable rather than total, albeit perfectly qualified, strangers.

Due to Wall Street's and Main Street's tight interconnections and complexity, policy makers seek advice from Wall Street peers who have relevant expertise, are informed, and have decision-making power. While this seems expedient, especially since there are few alternatives, it is doubtful if anyone—even given their best efforts—can completely escape the bias of self-interest or cultural capture. "Cultural capture" in this case means that the financial industry indirectly influences regulators by subtly convincing them that the interests of the financial sector are identical to those of the general public. The assumption is that if policy makers hang out long enough with Wall Streeters, they begin to relate to them, subconsciously adopting their viewpoints and giving them preferential treatment. Politicians will always be influenced by the people they talk to; hence the success of the thriving lobbying industry. The study concludes that the benefits for connected firms were temporary and a result of the crisis atmosphere: "Once policy discretion declines and the speed with which important decisions have to be taken slows down, these connections become less important."[23]

Thought Leaders—Superhubs of Valuable Information

Thought leaders are their own individual think tanks. They provide analyses on various aspects of finance and the economy and, as a result, influence the way we view the world. What exactly do they do, how great is their influence, and why have they become so popular?

I had the privilege of working with such a thought leader during the height of the financial crisis: Nouriel Roubini, a noted economics professor at New York University's Stern School of Business and chairman of the consultancy firm that bears his name. Of Jewish Iranian heritage, he was born in Turkey and grew up in Italy. After earning a PhD in economics at Harvard University, he worked at the IMF, served as senior economist for the Council of Economic Advisers, and subsequently became a senior adviser to Tim Geithner at the U.S. Treasury Department. He has authored numerous books and been granted various honors and distinctions. Roubini was prominently featured in the Oscar-winning documentary *Inside Job*, and in a cameo in the movie *Wall Street 2* by famed film director Oliver Stone, which earned him a coveted invitation to the Cannes Film Festival.

Roubini is a professor right out of central casting: Not particularly vain, he is usually dressed in a slightly disheveled shirt, with collar and tie perennially askew. In an otherwise rather dry industry, he is one of the more colorful characters, making headlines with both his professional and personal life. His connections encompass the academic, policy, financial, and corporate world, and he is influential not only because of his academic credentials but also because of his central network position.

Working with Roubini was a fascinating learning experience and provided exposure to some of the most interesting and powerful people in the world. At the same time, it was also exhausting due to the never-ending financial crisis and his extremely busy schedule.

He was one of the few forecasters who had presciently and accurately predicted the U.S. subprime crisis and its dramatic consequences for the global financial system several years in advance. If the system was on the brink of failure, you would not have known it at the WEF in Davos in the beginning of 2007. There, blissful optimism prevailed.[24] For instance, Laura Tyson, then dean of the London Business School and former chief of the U.S. Council of Economic Advisers, said that she was betting on "another Goldilocks year." Jacob Frenkel, then vice chairman of AIG International, said that the "perma-bears"—those who were negative about the future of the economy—would be proven wrong in the course of the year.[25] Critics such as Roubini were in the minority, regarded as attention-seeking doomsayers and subject to vociferous criticism. However, when the dominos began to fall, the pendulum swung to the other extreme: Suddenly, the previously dismissed were feted as sages. Roubini quickly became a sought-after adviser and was flown around the globe to speak to presidents, central bank governors, and CEOs of global companies. Many of these meetings were return trips to the inner sanctum of power where he had once worked: the White House, the Treasury, and the IMF.

In Roubini's view, networks are less relevant in academia than in other professional areas because accomplishments there are primarily based on merit. He made the transition to the policy world only after establishing himself as a scholar and authority. Although Roubini has high-level access, he believes that external experts have only limited influence. In order to truly affect policy, he explains, you must occupy a formal full-time position and be involved in the information flow and granular details. Getting access to policy makers is hard work. Contrary to what some may think, policy makers such as the Fed Chair Janet Yellen and ECB president Mario Draghi are extremely cautious and reluctant to talk about confidential matters. In addition, the heads of institutions typically do not have sole decision-making powers but act as part of a committee, which makes outcomes even harder to predict. For example, Janet Yellen is one of twelve members of the Federal Open Market Committee, and Mario Draghi is one of twenty-four persons on the ECB Governing Council. Generally, policy makers do not know what decisions will be made well into the future because those decisions hinge on uncertain, conditional developments across the world. In addition, their views and assessments are subject to major changes over time.

Roubini concedes that being plugged into a network of policy makers does provide a better understanding of the logic behind their thinking and decision-making processes, but he reiterates that it is no substitute for thorough analysis. My own view is that, being well aware of the ramifications of confidentiality breaches, policy makers will not disclose any "state secrets." However, in personal meetings you may still be able to read between the lines from the tone of their voices, their body language, or choice of words and thus get a sense of where things might be heading. Of course, such intuitive impressions can never replace the hard, nose-to-the-grindstone analysis, but they can give you an edge.

Roubini agrees that possessing emotional intelligence is helpful but argues that the power of his ideas is what established him as a thought leader. His business consultancy has likely benefited from both his intellectual and social skills. Consulting is a competitive field as research is generally considered a cost and not a profit center, and the market is flooded with gratuitous high-quality analyses. There are no barriers to entry as it is not a licensed profession, and anyone can call him- or herself a consultant. Therefore, having top academic credentials, policy experience, and access to high-caliber networks provide thought leaders with distinct competitive advantages that propel them into the league of superhubs.

Most thought leaders in finance are economists. A select few have become academic celebrities, such as Thomas Piketty, Nassim Taleb, and Paul Krugman, because they have touched the zeitgeist. They are their own brands, with rock star status and almost cultlike followings. Inundated with media requests, exclusive invitations, and offers to join prestigious boards, their work surpasses the insular world of academia and becomes the center of public attention. They often contribute to the public discourse by translating their abstract and complex analyses into layman's terms. Governments, institutions, and corporations take their views into account when making decisions. Meanwhile, the thought leaders' market value increases, enabling them to bill top dollars for their services. Their centrality affords them superhub status. For U.S. thought leaders, the rate for a one-hour speech usually starts at $75,000 in addition to first-class tickets and five-star hotel accommodations. An overseas speech can exceed $150,000 depending on the remoteness of the location.

Thought leaders typically challenge conventional thinking. Economic, financial, and political developments in the last few years have invalidated many existing paradigms. When they produce transformational research, thought leaders contribute to the collective thought process. However, their contrarian views often become controversial as many people are uncomfortable with change and resist challenging traditional norms. Thus, thought leaders stir heated debates, enrich the dialogue, and inspire innovative approaches.

The great demand for them is remarkable, considering that most economists' forecasts have been notoriously incorrect. The spectrum of their misjudgments ranges from the movements of the stock markets to the breakup of the euro. Prakash Loungani, a senior economist at the IMF, analyzed various economic forecasts and found dismal results: In line with the saying "It is difficult to make predictions, especially about the future," forecasts from the public as well as the private sector were equally incorrect—especially at inflection points such as the run-up to a recession or a return to growth.[26] Perhaps that's why economics has been called the "dismal science" and some segments of the academic world have made profound efforts to drive fundamental reforms. In a 2013 graduation speech at Princeton University, Ben Bernanke noted that economics is superb at explaining to policy makers why their past choices were wrong, but that its predictions for the future left much to be desired. However, he stated that economic analysis is at least helpful in eliminating the most logically inconsistent ideas.[27]

Why do experts have such a hard time making predictions, even in relatively predictable scenarios? One reason is that the future is inherently uncertain; it is impossible to connect the dots going forward[28] and model it mathematically. Another is the fact that human thinking is limited by cognitive biases. As a consequence of our evolutionary development, we are wired to draw inferences, particularly in uncertain situations, as mental shortcuts to make judgments and arrive at conclusions. We presume our beliefs to be a permanent reality and tend to interpret events within our own frame of reference, believing only what supports our views. Biases save valuable time in the fight for survival, but they also keep us from accurately processing new information and adapting our views. Therefore, experts who demonstrate a capacity to think beyond biases add valuable dimensions to the dialogue and serve as key information links.

CEOs must constantly innovate and develop long-term visions and strategies. In times of concurrent revolutionary paradigm shifts across many parts of the world, decision parameters become more uncertain and complex. In a different world of low global growth, increasing political instability, and incalculable macroeconomic risks, CEOs look for unbiased guidance and innovative perspectives. Jamie Dimon once said that CEOs are terrible forecasters who can only see the recent past.[29] High-level executives often operate in an echo chamber of homogeneous thinking, which can lead to tunnel vision and "analysis paralysis." Thought leaders are the signals among the noise of groupthink, and they can help CEOs generate fresh ideas and see the big picture. By influencing the influencers, thought leaders' ideas become part of the economic and financial evolution, providing them with "expert power." Some argue that, figuratively speaking, CEOs give these advisers their watch so that they can tell them the time. Others criticize that consultants only provide CEOs with cover and justification for poor performance or unpopular measures such as layoffs.

NETWORK INVESTMENTS: SOCIAL CAPITAL

As already alluded to in Chapter 2, another commodity that superhubs exchange within networks is social capital, which consists of resources such as information, services, and the leveraging of influence. Social capital is an investment that pays a return, as the analogy "capital" implies. The higher one's position in the hierarchy, the greater one's creditworthiness, meaning one's wealth in social capital and the ability to transact it.

Social capital can be accumulated by helping others and building goodwill. For instance, people can leverage their contacts and influence for the benefit of someone else or arrange for direct access. Perhaps unsurprisingly, the ultra-capitalist superhubs are as rich in social capital as they are in relationships, and in network commodities that they can exchange. In a sense, social capital serves as a vehicle for the transaction of other network commodities such as money and information.

The exchange of social capital is particularly important in the top ranks of finance, but sometimes the equation does not quite add up. At the height of the financial crisis, Goldman Sachs's clients worried that bank contagion could spread to the firm and render it insolvent. As a precaution they began to withdraw money in droves. A sentiment began to spread within Goldman that it usually instilled in others: fear. Gary Cohn, Goldman's copresident, personally tried to convince clients to keep their money with the firm. When Stanley Druckenmiller, George Soros's former star trader who then managed $3.5 billion of his own, withdrew his money, Cohn tried to activate the social capital he had built with Druckenmiller over the years professionally as well as personally and asked him to return the money to the bank. Druckenmiller refused, which prompted Cohn to respond that he was making lists of his friends and enemies—and that Druckenmiller's lack of support would change their relationship for a long time.[30] By not projecting his confidence in Cohn and Goldman, Druckenmiller not only withdrew all his financial capital, but his social capital as well.

MONEY + INFORMATION + SOCIAL CAPITAL = INFINITE OPPORTUNITIES

Through their networks, the financial elite are ideally suited to create circumstances favorable to advancing their interests. Opportunities are both the cause and the effect of inextricable links between people, money, and information—with social capital serving as a conduit. They are also subject to power laws, according to which the more you have, the more you get. The sociologist Robert Merton described this phenomenon as the "Matthew Effect," since Matthew states in the Bible, "For unto every one that hath shall be given, and he shall have abundance; but from him that hath not shall be taken away even that which he hath."[31]

The more quality connections you have, the greater your access to additional connections, capital, and information, which in turn leads to more opportunities. These properties—social capital, financial capital, and information—are interdependent, meaning that the more you have of one of them the more you can get of the other.

George Soros had the prerequisite network, capital, and information to bet on the British pound, a trade that is rumored to have netted him a $1 billion profit. His global connections, especially in the political realm, provided him with information that was not generally known. Because he had access to so many pieces of the puzzle, he was able to zero in on the opportunity and convert his insights into monetary gain. Of course Soros is brilliant, but speculation is always, at least in part, based on information. The better the network, the better the information; the better the information, the better the analysis; and the more money bet, the more profit yielded. In 2016, Soros's net worth amounts to $24.9 billion.

Larry Fink, founder of BlackRock, has created sophisticated, world-leading risk analysis systems that build upon existing information to yield even more valuable insights. Beyond merely having access to information, he produced new information, thus becoming an information hub. The more sophisticated information he produced, the more capital he attracted, the more his network grew, and the greater his opportunities became. In 2015, BlackRock managed $4.72 trillion.

When Steve Schwarzman cofounded Blackstone with former U.S. treasury secretary Pete Peterson, they were able to convert Peterson's network of CEOs and senior policy maker contacts into deal-making opportunities. The information that their network yielded, greatly contributed to Blackstone's success. The firm has seen its assets under management rise to over $344 billion in 2016.

Bill Gross, founder and former manager of PIMCO—the world's largest bond fund—capitalized on his close network connections to the Fed, which provided him with valuable information, creating better opportunities, which in turn attracted more capital. When Gross joined Janus Capital in 2014, he was able to raise $1.4 billion from his network during the first year.

If Anthony Scaramucci had not had access to Citi CEO Vikram Pandit, he would not have learned of the opportunity to acquire Citi's hedge fund portfolio at a discount, thereby growing his fund and attracting further capital. In 2016 SkyBridge's assets under management stood at $12.6 billion.

* * *

In Chapter 3, we have seen that the access to people, money, and privileged information provides an invaluable advantage, as it opens up unique business opportunities inaccessible to those outside of this exclusive circle. But what exactly creates these superhubs? How do some people wind up on a trajectory that catapults them into the career stratosphere? In Chapter 4, we'll take a closer look at the superhub personality profile and the important characteristics that set them apart to succeed.

CHAPTER 4

The Matrix

Decoding the Superhub DNA

INDIVIDUAL CHARACTERISTICS ARE IMPORTANT in the financial universe because while financial capital creates the links that connect superhubs within a network, it is ultimately the superhubs themselves who decide how capital is created, transacted, and invested. Personal traits and skills are the drivers that propel players into the center of networks. There are countless successful people, but only a few reach the pinnacle of power where they operate the very levers of the financial system. What are the essential characteristics of superhubs that lead them to become so well connected? In this chapter, we will explore their most common traits and skills.

THE ALPHA PERSONALITY: JAMIE DIMON

Superhubs are extremely competitive and continuously challenge themselves to take the lead and stay ahead of the game. Their innate desire to have impact and power, and to leave a legacy, is either driven by an extremely strong self-confidence or by deep insecurities that cause them to overcompensate in an effort to prove themselves. The quest for power on the most basic level is fueled by the need for survival. The motivation to acquire it is correlated with high testosterone levels,[1] and its possession is shown to cause pleasure-inducing neurological responses. In addition, power provides control over one's life, which demonstrably increases happiness, health, and life expectancy. The quest for power is an indispensable aspect of the superhub personality.

On a busy fall day in New York, Nouriel Roubini and I met with Jamie Dimon for an exchange of thoughts on his turf, JPMorgan's world headquarters at 270 Park Avenue. After registering with security and passing through the vast, high-ceilinged marble entrance hall, we were accompanied to the secluded Holy Grail: the executive floors at the top of the building. Dimon welcomed us in a bright, modern conference room with breathtaking views of New York City. Roubini's and my stance on big banks had been rather critical, and I had the distinct feeling that Dimon had planned a charm offensive to convince us otherwise. He dominated the room with a highly amusing, profanity-laced monologue. The conversation was not particularly profound, and we gained no new insights, but by the end of the meeting I felt that Roubini was quite taken with Dimon. I was left with the uncanny sense that if Dimon wants to accomplish something, he will find a way to psychologically arm-wrestle his counterpart until he prevails.

Dimon stands out even among superhubs. A profile in *Vanity Fair* described him as charismatic and handsome,[2] and noted bank critic and former FDIC chief Sheila Bair characterized him in her book *Bull by the Horns* as the smartest executive in the room with towering height as well as leadership ability.[3] A *New York Times* article headlined "America's Least-Hated Banker"[4] pointed out that many of his counterparts did not survive the crisis, such as James Cayne of Bear Stearns, John Thain and Stanley O'Neal of Merrill Lynch, Chuck Prince of Citigroup, and Richard Fuld of Lehman Brothers, among others. By his own account, he has emerged from the financial crisis "battered and bruised but still standing and fighting."[5] Under Dimon, JPMorgan became one of the biggest financial institutions in the world with $2.4 trillion in assets and a quarter of a million employees.

Dimon, like most other financial top executives, has a type A personality. Throughout his life, he has had a tendency to be irreverent and to speak up to authority. In high school, he once left the classroom in protest after a history teacher commented on an African American student acting out with a racially inappropriate remark. He also earned the respect of his classmates at Harvard Business School when he challenged an intimidating professor on a case study, only for the professor to concede that Dimon was right. Neither did Dimon shy away from antagonizing his superiors. He refused to back down in a power struggle with his almighty mentor Sandy Weill, which eventually culminated in Weill's firing of Dimon.

Dimon even got into a physical scuffle with one of his top lieutenants at a black tie dinner when the latter supposedly snubbed a colleague's wife.[6] And he has no problem snapping at his peers in front of fellow CEOs: When Tim Geithner and Dimon cohosted a conference call to discuss JPMorgan's takeover of Bear Stearns, Vikram Pandit, the CEO of Citigroup, delivered a barrage of highly technical questions, which prompted an annoyed Dimon to bark, "Stop being such a jerk." He added snippily that Citigroup should be grateful that JPMorgan came to the rescue.[7] Such a public snub of a fellow CEO was unheard of and prompted jaws on Wall Street to drop.

A few months thereafter at a Harvard MBA graduation speech on leadership, Dimon advised graduates to skip anger, because "it is a bad thing that always backfires, hurts people, and then you have to apologize." Ignoring his own advice, a couple of years later he managed to offend Mark Carney, then the governor of the Central Bank of Canada, during the Annual Meetings of the IMF by implying that Carney was anti-American. The bank CEOs in attendance were baffled by Dimon's attack and worried that his confrontational style would hurt their interests. Dimon later apologized for his tirade. Carney accepted his apology, which was lucky for Dimon because Carney subsequently became even more powerful as governor of the Bank of England and chairman of the Financial Stability Board. In interviews, Dimon can get belligerent as well, especially when arguing against financial reform and in favor of higher remuneration.

Neither does Dimon have any qualms to openly fight for his power. After JPMorgan suffered its record $6 billion "London Whale" trading loss in 2012, investors opposed Dimon's dual role as CEO and chairman, arguing that his overseeing himself obviously hadn't worked so well. Amongst much media attention, Dimon threatened to resign if forced out of his chairman role and in the end prevailed against his critics.

As Wall Street's unofficial ambassador in Washington, Dimon also became the leader of the pack among big bank CEOs. He impressed the bureaucratic establishment with his business acumen and charm, quickly becoming the Beltway's darling. For a long time, he was even considered to be President Obama's favorite banker. The president repeatedly praised Dimon publicly, and the presidential cufflinks Dimon wore during his testimony at the Senate Banking Committee in connection with the London Whale loss were rumored to have been a present from the president himself.

EQ: CONNECTING EMOTIONALLY

One of the most indispensable skills leaders must possess is emotional intelligence. Finance is a Darwinian environment, where only the strongest survive. Most firms render similar services without any intellectual property to protect, and in general all top-level managers are smart, educated, and hard working. Therefore, executives who possess emotional intelligence—self-awareness and the ability to understand and relate to others—have a decisive competitive advantage. Evolved leaders run institutions more smoothly and successfully because they are more comfortable facing their shortcomings, their limitations, and criticism from others. Their ability to see issues from other people's perspectives helps them align subordinates and deal with customers. In a globalized world, empathy, which is part of emotional intelligence, is of particular importance because it facilitates cross-cultural dialogue. Even if people from different backgrounds speak the modern-day *lingua franca*, English, they must stay attuned to cultural subtleties and sensitivities, which otherwise can be a minefield.

The good news for someone not blessed with a particularly high degree of emotional intelligence is that it can be learned and that it increases with maturity. The higher executives rise, the greater the demands on their leadership skills, which also entail social skills to attract and retain talent. In Jamie Dimon's opinion, emotional intelligence is more important than IQ when it comes to success, because social skills make all the difference.[8]

As an added benefit, emotional intelligence provides job security. According to a recent study, the jobs of chief executives, particularly in finance, are safe from automation due to the importance of personal human relationships in that sector, which cannot be formed by soulless robots.[9]

MASTER CLOSERS: STEVE SCHWARZMAN

Successful executives possess extraordinary communication and sales skills. In order to generate revenues in a low-growth environment, they must attract prospects and be able to close deals. Selling ideas and products requires social and persuasion skills. Since finance is abstract and intangible, and its performance only materializes in the future, it is vital for executives to build trust and create convincing narratives for transactions. Only people who manage their own money—such as family office hedge funders like George Soros, Stan Druckenmiller, and Steve Cohen—are free from such pressures and constraints.

Having a premium brand is an invaluable competitive advantage; it facilitates sales and can be a precondition for obtaining access to desirable client segments. Accordingly, most superstar CEOs are "brand masters," marketing billion-dollar companies as well as their own personal brands, which in many cases are synonymous with the firms they represent. Dimon has established his own brand to stand for leadership, strength, and a fortress-like balance sheet.

Today the perception of performance has become even more important than performance itself. In contrast to the nineties, most careers today fail due to adverse perception regarding performance or personalities. Therefore, executives must actively manage perception through communication.[10] Reputation, or the perception of others, results from integrity, performance, and consistency. Once a reputation of integrity is ruined, it is difficult—if not impossible—to rebuild. As Warren Buffett cautioned, "It takes twenty years to build a reputation, and five minutes to ruin it."[11] In other words, your present reputation determines your future success. Warren Buffett's uniquely stellar reputation stands for integrity, investing excellence, and stability. It is so valuable that it commands a premium in and of itself, and businesses associated with him appear automatically endorsed. Indeed, Buffett plans to license the Berkshire Hathaway name to estate agencies to turn his good reputation into a consumer brand.[12]

Steve Schwarzman, the founder of Blackstone, is a superhub who could sell sand in the desert. Once the world's largest private equity firm, Blackstone has since morphed into one of the most diversified investment companies in the world with more than $344 billion in assets under management. In Davos, he seemed omnipresent. I bumped into him several times on the snowy streets, his geeky ski cap pulled wide over his face, and only recognized him by the brown shearling jacket he wears every year. What Schwarzman lacks in height, he makes up for with a big personality and charisma. He shone on panels, rushed to bilateral meetings, and appeared to enjoy the famed Davos parties.

In fact, if anyone knows how to throw a good party, it is Schwarzman. The mainstream media headlines on his sixtieth-birthday party were as ubiquitous as his presence in Davos. He celebrated this personal milestone, which would soon become a public one with an over-the-top gala at the New York Armory on Park Avenue. Virtually the entire cast of global superhub characters flew in to fete the financier. Even in America, where displays of wealth are acceptable to a much larger extent than almost anywhere in the world, the extravagant affair—with estimated costs ranging in the millions—caused quite a stir. Characterized by the media as ostentatious and decadent, this exposure arrived at a politically inopportune time as private equity funds lobbied for preferential tax treatment and were heavily criticized for their business practices. The birthday-party hype was soon eclipsed by Blackstone's immensely successful initial public offering, which yielded Schwarzman personally over $10 billion. He was now officially the "king of capital."

Schwarzman is one of the best-connected financiers in the world. Always on duty, he tirelessly circles the globe, building and maintaining relationships for the purpose of maximizing business. He has a nonchalant demeanor that makes others feel comfortable in his presence. In his frequent interviews and speeches, he displays his ability to explain complex issues in simple terms, and to disarm audiences with his dry wit. With a straight face, he mercilessly tells hilarious stories and delivers a killer imitation of German Chancellor Angela Merkel. Social by nature, he and his wife are popular staples on the party circuit.

Born into a middle-class family in Pennsylvania, Schwarzman was a self-starter from an early age. He earned his undergraduate degree at Yale University and, like so many of his peers, subsequently graduated from Harvard Business School. During his time at Yale, he took on leadership positions, such as class president, and joined the elite Skull and Bones secret society, which counts President George W. Bush and numerous other prominent figures among its members. In the mideighties, Schwarzman left Lehman Brothers, where he made partner at age thirty-one, to start Blackstone with his boss Pete Peterson, who was a couple decades his senior. Peterson, a former secretary of commerce, brought with him a portfolio of stellar corporate and political connections, which he successfully used to raise assets and close deals.

Private equity firms have become a powerful force in the economy. They raise equity capital and employ debt to buy companies, take management control, and subsequently sell them at a profit. In contrast to public companies, private equity companies can focus on long-term profitability as they are not under pressure to produce quarterly results. The industry has been criticized in the past because in the course of turning around companies, they often laid off employees and borrowed heavily against the company's assets, sometimes disassembling it and selling it piecemeal. Although private equity firms suffered from a lack of liquidity during the 2008 financial crisis, they did not require any bailouts. On the contrary, the government sought to consult their turnaround expertise, for instance in the auto industry. Although private equity firms and banks compete in parts, they are also intertwined by business relationships as private equity firms give banks much business and pay them billions in fees.

Schwarzman went on to hire strong partners who brought both their business acumen and networks along with them. According to colleagues and business partners, he is incredibly driven, has an uncompromising work ethic, and is as demanding of others as he is of himself. Blackstone did not merely survive the crisis; it flourished, largely due to Schwarzman's cautious risk management and low tolerance for mistakes. The government even sought his advice because of his turnaround expertise. Despite occasional tone deafness, Schwarzman's self-awareness and persuasive sales skills have been instrumental in building an empire and elevating him to superhub status.

INQUIRING MINDS

High intelligence and academic achievements at top schools are indispensable to becoming a network's nucleus. In addition, superhubs are typically open-minded, intellectually curious, creative, and receptive to considering new opportunities. If they weren't in finance, many superhubs would probably be inventors, engineers, or entrepreneurs. They are equipped with mind-sets that can cope with and even thrive on times of uncertainty and change, since they understand how our complex, nonlinear world operates. In the course of their careers, they typically develop a strong intuitive sense, because complexity is difficult to grasp with intellect alone.

Contextual intelligence—the ability to understand evolving environments and capitalize on trends—is another important aspect of cognitive ability. Being connected and understanding interconnections are an important source of relevant power.[13]

In *Soros: The Life and Times of a Messianic Billionaire*, Soros described his total absorption in managing his fund. His primeval instincts of fear and greed made him sense impending downturns way in advance, as if he had his nerve endings in his fund. This manifested itself in backache problems, which flared up whenever he sensed impending doom.[14] His unique life experiences as a survivor of the Holocaust most likely contributed to his ability to recognize and monetize inflection points far in advance. With their ability to look beyond facts and think outside of conventional parameters, superhubs are better able to anticipate change, develop a vision, and execute.

To keep their minds crystal clear, the newest trend among superhubs is thousands of years old: meditation. Hedge fund bigwigs Ray Dalio and Paul Tudor Jones, as well as many Goldmanites, invest time and money in introspection to clear their minds and gain a competitive edge.

INVENTING IDEOLOGIES

Another common characteristic of intellectually curious superhubs is that they often construct their own theories or ideologies, rather than follow those of others. In their quest to crack the code of the world's operating system, they fine-tune their intellectual discipline and intuition, and posit their own framework of successful strategies.

For example, Robert Rubin, former secretary of the treasury, developed an intellectual construct that he describes in his best-selling book *In an Uncertain World: Tough Choices from Wall Street to Washington*. He shares how a philosophy course at Harvard inspired him to base his thinking on the assumption that nothing is provably certain. The daily decisions he made on Wall Street were based on probability: "Success came by evaluating all the information available to try to judge the odds of various outcomes and the possible gains or losses associated with each."[15]

This creation of a thought construct is reminiscent of George Soros's theory of reflexivity, developed while he was a student at the London School of Economics. Within this conceptual framework, which Soros credits for much of his success, he focuses on the relationship between thinking and reality.

Klaus Schwab pioneered the stakeholder principle, "according to which the management of an enterprise is not only accountable to its shareholders, but must also serve the interests of all stakeholders . . . who may be affected or concerned by its operations." He later built on this theory to create the concept of "global corporate citizenship."[16] The stakeholder principle is the ideological foundation upon which the WEF is built and gives it legitimacy.

Ray Dalio, founder of the world's biggest hedge fund, developed an ideology that views the economy, businesses, and people as operating like machines. A manifest outlining his belief system, titled *Principles*, is published on the Bridgewater Associates website.[17]

Mike Milken, the bond king of the eighties, billionaire investor and philanthropist, also created a philosophy as the basis of his thinking and doing. He devised a formula, $P=EFT (DHC+ESC+ERA)$, according to which prosperity is the sum of financial technology times the sum of human capital plus social capital plus real assets, a mantra that he has repeated throughout his life.[18]

Larry Fink, the founder of BlackRock, is the rock star of risk management. After reflecting upon his own monumental trading losses, he theorized that according to which asset managers have an incomplete understanding of risk, especially when things are running smoothly. He came to the conclusion, therefore, that developing risk management systems is a fundamental necessity of successful portfolio management and proceeded to build the world's most reputable and comprehensive systems.

These theories often reflect an understanding of the psychology of human nature, markets, trends, and turning points—in short, the system and the mastery thereof. The theories themselves may not be the most important factor—and, indeed, are not always that innovative—but they reflect the typical superhub's underlying skepticism, intellectual discipline, and intuition, which lead to clarity of thought and result in prudent decision making. Structured thought parameters also seem to provide orientation and a focal point that helps superhubs stay in control of their emotions. However, it is not always entirely clear which came first, the theory or the experiences on which the theory is based. Such discipline unfortunately does not make a person's judgment infallible as all of these superhubs have experienced failures regardless. For many superhubs, having their own intellectual creation is also a matter of prestige and a way to distinguish themselves.

THE CULT OF FAILURE

Financial executives almost without exception abide by the "cult of failure" and stress the formative nature of failures, setbacks, and disappointments, because in their opinion we learn the most from them. At a graduation speech at NYU, Fed Chair Janet Yellen pointed out the importance of grit, commitment, and perseverance.[19] Indeed, many of the most successful people on Wall Street have experienced significant failures on their journey to the top, and they would likely not be where they are today if it had not been for their perseverance.

For example, Jamie Dimon was fired from Citigroup by his long-time trusted mentor, Sandy Weill. The highly publicized move came as a complete shock to Dimon, who until then had consistently enjoyed great success. After taking some time off, he picked himself up and accepted an offer to become CEO at Bank One, whose value he doubled within a short time and thereafter successfully merged with JPMorgan. Dimon became JPMorgan's CEO and chairman and subsequently made *Time* magazine's list of the World's 100 Most Influential People several times, and *Institutional Investor* named him the best CEO in America.

Another example is George Soros, who against all odds and through his own initiative was already one of the most successful money managers when he tried to establish himself as a serious intellectual and philosopher. Since childhood, Soros had expressed high ambitions regarding intellectual accomplishments and recognition. In 1998, due to perceived urgency on his part, he stitched together a book, *The Crisis of Global Capitalism*, with a red-hot needle and had it published shortly thereafter. Not only did his predictions of impending economic collapse fail to materialize, but his overall intellect and basic reasoning were ridiculed and derided by distinguished academics in the most respected publications. The *Economist* and the *Financial Times* characterized his writings as "incoherent," "ramblings," and "embarrassingly banal."[20] In the face of such scathing reviews, most people would have been happy to quietly fade into the background—but not Mr. Soros. On the contrary, he took the criticism to heart and tried even harder to hone his thinking and writing skills. Frequently, the most burning motivation and passionate perseverance result from perceived injustice, humiliation, and the desire to rehabilitate oneself and prove doubters wrong.

CEOS—CHIEF EGO OFFICERS: BILL GROSS

A small degree of deviation from the norm in terms of personality can bode well for success in the financial world.[21] Some research even claims that executive floors house three times more psychopaths than the general population.[22] While this is likely an exaggeration, top executives in the financial world generally have big egos, a phenomenon that seems more pronounced in the commercial sector than in the policy world. However, due to the financial crisis, the zeitgeist has changed in recent years. As a result of political and shareholder pressures, the imperial and hard-charging celebrity "chief ego officer" has fallen out of favor and been replaced by "boring is the new sexy": low-key, risk-conscious, and conciliatory personalities.

Top performers often have a distinct need for attention and praise, which motivates them to achieve extraordinary results. However, overly strong self-confidence and a sense of invincibility lead to a greater inclination toward risk taking. Often, people with a slight psychopathic touch have excellent political skills, which they use to finesse others in order to further their goals. Their attitude of entitlement, some argue, also manifests itself in the size of their pay packages.[23]

An exaggerated sense of self can in some instances border on narcissism and hubris.[24] In these cases, executives lack empathy, are excessively arrogant, and feel superior. Extraordinary boldness and risk-taking behavior often conceals deep-seated insecurities: Many of the most successful people make it to the top because they have a chip on their shoulder, be it their backgrounds, past failures, or negative experiences. This is slightly disconcerting because a leader's personality has a direct effect on their company's performance. For instance, if too many psychopathic character traits are too pronounced, they may lead to increased volatility. If that is an indicator of where the system is headed, it may not be a good omen. I would like to believe that none of our financial institutions are headed by psychopaths, but it definitely is an environment rich in eccentric characters, and Bill Gross is one of them.

Bill Gross (net worth $2.3 billion), the founder and former chief investment officer of the world's largest bond fund, PIMCO, has some entertaining idiosyncrasies. He possesses many prerequisite qualities to be successful in investing, but his interpersonal skills—or lack thereof—are said to have eventually caught up with him. The world of investment funds is pretty cut-and-dried and, except for hedge funds, has produced few publicly known superstar managers. However, the lanky seventy-year-old yoga devotee with a high-pitched voice is one of them. In the stuffy investment community, his unorthodox remarks and offbeat sense of humor garnered much attention. A few months prior to his exit from PIMCO, he spoke at an indoor investment conference wearing black sunglasses and comparing himself to twenty-year-old bad-boy pop star Justin Bieber. Then, in a riff on *The Manchurian Candidate*, he proceeded to ask journalists to repeat after him that he was "the kindest, bravest, warmest, most wonderful human being you've met in your life." The joke left the audience baffled and prompted a *Wall Street Journal* journalist to tweet: "Something weird is going on with Bill Gross."[25]

His highly respected and widely read investment outlook in 2014, the year of his departure, was essentially an ode to his recently deceased cat, Bob. Fittingly, it was simply titled "Bob" and contained such interesting tidbits as, "Aside from sleeping, Bob loved nothing more than to follow me from room to room making sure I was OK. It got to be a little much at times, especially when entering and exiting the shower."[26] One might wonder how Bob's stalking might have been relevant to the bond markets, but if nothing else, Mr. Gross's remembrance served as an indicator of his sophisticated ability to build rapport with cats. In contrast, his interactions with humans, at least in the later stages of his career, left much to be desired.

Gross founded PIMCO, which is located in Newport Beach, in 1971 and was instrumental in its spectacular growth to $2 trillion under management. The bulk of investments came from institutional investors, and he has managed many ordinary Americans' money via pension funds and insurance plans. Gross, driven by a desire to beat the system, revolutionized bond trading and generated unprecedented profits. He combined quantitative skills with the ability to make accurate macro calls on the economy, including the subprime mortgage crisis of 2008, and managed to consistently predict interest rate movements ahead of his peers. Over the course of the financial crisis, however, as central bank actions skewed the markets, his bets turned out to be increasingly incorrect. Performance slipped, and investors withdrew billions of dollars.

For the "bond king," who had been spoiled by extraordinary success throughout his career, the experience was sobering, and confrontations between Gross and his staff grew more acrimonious. Reports from inside the firm described his management style as authoritarian and autocratic. Purportedly, he grew hostile toward more successful traders, and colleagues were forbidden to question his trading strategies. A derisive email to senior colleagues was leaked in which he openly berated one who had executed a decision that he himself had made. He voiced irreverent statements such as, "I've made you all rich . . . see how you do without me," and repeatedly threatened to do the unthinkable: quit.[27]

Perhaps most significant, Gross became more confrontational with his designated successor, Mohamed El-Erian, a highly respected, soft-spoken economist, who in many respects is his antithesis. When Gross accused El-Erian of trying to undermine him, people began to perceive him as paranoid. Such airing of dirty laundry is a violation of the implicit code of conduct and pretty much unprecedented among superhubs. El-Erian, who had until then been assumed to take Gross's leadership, abruptly resigned in early 2014, which caused a medium-sized earthquake among investors. He subsequently explained his move by claiming a desire for a greater work-life balance and more time with his family.

After the popular El-Erian's departure, the animosity and alienation between Gross and the rest of the team escalated, and management asked him repeatedly to return to a more amicable demeanor. Eventually, colleagues staged a coup d'état. A couple days before the planned announcement of his ouster, he beat management to the punch, giving his resignation and joining Janus Capital, a much smaller and lesser-known company. The fallout was humiliating for Gross, and the fact that billions of dollars immediately followed him out the door likely did not lend much satisfaction. The sudden withdrawal of huge amounts of money placed PIMCO in crisis mode, and regulatory authorities were concerned about a potential destabilization of bond markets. Their concern illustrated the power that one person can have over entire markets.

Gross successfully cultivated an image of a celebrity investor, primarily by the canny use of the media and particularly business TV. In a sea of monotonous suits, Gross's casual, zenlike, Californian style coupled with his unconventional remarks (in 2007 he compared the appeal of mortgage-backed securities to that of "six-inch hooker heels" and a "tramp stamp") provides great entertainment value.[28] Over time, he achieved gurulike status with a significant following. His word became law, and since his fund was so enormously big, it did not simply invest in the market but was a major part of the market itself. Being a superstar-brand/invest-ment manager makes it much easier to raise assets because of the name recognition and the fact that, from a professional investor's point of view, if one's peers all are investing in PIMCO as well, it provides cover in case something fails. But having a branded star manager who is synonymous with the fund also highlights the perils of key-man risk. So what is the moral of the story? Even the most talented fund manager must employ a minimum of interpersonal skills and build a network of loyal support-ers to call in favors, accumulated in the form of social capital, when the time comes.

ON A MONOMANIACAL MISSION: RAY DALIO

Another common superhub trait is an ability to focus excessively on one idea. Perhaps Elon Musk's ex-wife, Justine, put it best when she said that "extreme success results from an extreme personality." But their chief characteristic, according to Justine, can be summed up in two words: Be obsessed. "People who are obsessed with a problem or issue can work through all the distractions and barriers that life puts in their way. And that obsession needs to be your own, to the point where it borders on insanity."[29]

One superhub with an extreme focus is eccentric money manager Ray Dalio. At the WEF in Davos, banks, corporations, and countries all host parties on Friday night, competing for high-profile guests. Over the last few years, the party of Russian oligarch Oleg Deripaska, who in 2015 was the fifteenth-richest person in Russia, has become a staple on the party circuit. The invitation-only event attracts all the elite WEF attendees. Deripaska's blue-lit chalet is inconveniently located off the beaten track on the top of a hill, so guests must make an extra effort to get there. Once inside, they are greeted with endless streams of the finest champagne, vodka, and Russian caviar amidst dancing Cossacks and beautiful Russian models. It was there that I first met Ray Dalio, who was standing to the side, all by himself, serenely observing the scene. We chatted for a while and exchanged business cards before he hurried off to his private plane jetting back to New York.

The tall, slightly gaunt, and friendly-looking Dalio is not well known to the general public, although he should be, because he runs the largest hedge fund in the world, with over $150 billion under management. Bridgewater's investors are institutions such as pension funds, insurance companies, and endowments, which in turn manage the savings of millions of ordinary people, therefore indirectly exposing them to Dalio. Mention his name to Wall Streeters, and their eyes begin to glow. His long track record of success, idiosyncratic investment approach, and pursuit of excellence evoke great admiration and respect amongst his peers and those who aspire to rise to his station. Unlike many of his fellow asset managers, Dalio has until recently chosen to remain under the radar.

Dalio invests on the basis of macroeconomic trends. His rigorous analysis, disciplined investing, and consistent performance have garnered the attention of many sophisticated investors. Dalio showed great foresight when he warned of the financial crisis well in advance and throughout it outperformed the market when many other funds faltered. Like many successful billionaire money managers, he is not primarily motivated by money, and unlike most of them, he lives rather modestly. Bridgewater's offices are located near his home in Westport, Connecticut, surrounded by old trees and lush bushes. He recently joined the Giving Pledge started by Bill Gates and Warren Buffett, committing at least half his fortune to philanthropic causes.

What Dalio lacks in material pretensions, he makes up for in intellectual ones. He does not want to be seen as merely a speculator or trader, but instead—driven by the desire to make a social impact—as a philosopher and educator, explaining how the world works to make it a better place. He credits much of his success to transcendental meditation, which he practices religiously. As is typical for overachievers, he loves to pursue challenges in his quest for personal evolution, and he focuses on his mission with intense passion. Dalio developed an ideology that compares the actions of the economy, businesses, and people to the operation of machines. He identified cause-and-effect patterns and chronicled his insights in a manifesto titled *Principles*, in which managers who talk about subordinates behind their backs are called slimy weasels.[30] When the document leaked, it created a slew of negative publicity.[31] An article in *New York* described his rule book "as if Ayn Rand and Deepak Chopra had collaborated on a line of fortune cookies."[32] The popular Wall Street website Dealbreaker had a field day with a section that it interpreted as Dalio comparing Bridgewater to a pack of hyenas feeding on a young wildebeest.[33] The *Financial Times* called his musings "billionaire financier drivel"[34] and Dalio himself "deluded, emotionally illiterate, and weird."[35]

Around the same time, reports from inside the firm began to leak. One former employee compared it to a cult, given its charismatic and isolated location. Some described the culture as bizarre, totalitarian, and demoralizing. Others characterized it as a mind-control operation and a human behavioral experiment. The stories made Bridgewater sound like the Pyongyang of hedge funds, although with much better food and compensation. According to one ex-employee, everyone gains ten pounds in the first year due to the great cafeteria and long hours in an isolated environment. All emails are monitored, and conversations as well as phone calls are taped, except for the most personal ones. Everyone can listen to the recordings, which are stored in a "transparency library." Overhead cameras document employees' every move. "Issue logs" and "believability matrices" track mistakes, and gossip is strictly prohibited.

It is perhaps unsurprising that in view of such comprehensive surveillance, some people might become a little paranoid. Yet even fewer employees are able to deal with the practice of "radical truth": In the pursuit of perfection, everyone's views are constantly challenged, questioned, and attacked in group discussions. The process of this "evidence-based meritocracy"[36] is rigorous, as virtually nothing is accepted at face value. Employees are asked to check their egos at the door and make judgments unencumbered by emotion. Equipped with iPads, they have to operate an app called Pain to track negative feelings. Another app named Dot Collector polls employees on all discussions involving at least three people. Yet another app called Dispute Resolver is used to mediate conflicts, or even form tribunals where both sides submit evidence.

Dalio wants to prevent his subordinates from being hijacked by their emotions, but one wonders about their psychological well-being. All employees must constantly evaluate each other—with their "believability index" ratings hanging over their heads. With the help of Palantir Technologies' "big data analysis" programs, former CIA and NSA officials administrate the myriad of employee data.[37] The company primarily hires college graduates, many of whom initially suffer from culture shock over the constant dress-downs. Accordingly, the turnover is extraordinarily high, with at least a quarter of new hires leaving or being fired within the first eighteen months. Obviously, the environment is not for everyone, but people are still lining up to be hired for what certainly appears to be a well-compensated learning experience and a stellar reference on one's resume.

The firm's radical culture once contributed to a duel at the very top involving Dalio himself and his top lieutenant and handpicked successor, Greg Jensen. Dalio purportedly heard that Jensen had shared his grievances about him behind his back.[38] According to the *Wall Street Journal*, Dalio asked the firm's management and stakeholders committees if they believed Jensen had integrity. Jensen, in turn, asked the group to decide if Dalio was fulfilling his succession plan.[39] At the time of this book's writing, the implications of this struggle were unclear.

Planning for a future without Dalio also involves hiring parts of IBM's Watson artificial intelligence team to perpetuate his intellectual DNA mechanically, thus decentralizing management and preserving the essence of the firm. By feeding in information about Dalio's and other top investors' thinking, the plan is to develop it into a decision-making tool that can learn and adapt to new information. Dalio's rules and management style may come across as strange, but in a world where only results count, his track record is extraordinary. Investor demand proves that his monomaniacal focus has succeeded.

* * *

This chapter examined the prerequisite traits and qualities for becoming a superhub. Now that we have a profile of superhubs and the common characteristics they share, we can begin to understand why they prefer one another's company. Many of them possess similar backgrounds and therefore trust each other more implicitly, creating a powerful network of a like-minded elite. Chapter 5 will explore why superhubs gravitate toward other superhubs and find comfort in their commonalities.

Homophily

Similarity Breeds Connection

THE CHARITABLE SUPERHUB
NETWORK: THE ROBIN HOOD GALA

Every year in May, the titans of finance unite at the grandiose Robin Hood charity gala in New York. It takes place at the Jacob Javits Convention Center, a massive, modern, nondescript building located near the Hudson River and of the sort that can be found anywhere in the world. Because the Javits Center is virtually devoid of any atmosphere, the organizers invest great effort in breathtakingly elaborate designs and decorations. The space has double the capacity of even the largest ballroom in New York City, which makes the entire event a bit overwhelming. The four thousand attendees, the technical displays, the stars, the entertainment—your head is spinning in sheer overstimulation. And before you can take it all in, the evening has ended and you must scramble to locate your driver amid the thousands of others all leaving at the same time.

Established by hedge fund manager Paul Tudor Jones III (net worth $4.3 billion) in 1988, the Robin Hood Foundation is one of the most successful charities in the financial world. Jones runs a $13 billion hedge fund, and since Robin Hood's inception, he has raised an incredible $1.5 billion to fight poverty in New York City. The event brings in major stars ranging from Michael Bloomberg to Elton John and Lady Gaga, and of course, virtually all of the titans of Wall Street. Attendees include George

Soros, Ray Dalio, Larry Fink, Ken Griffin of Citadel, Howard Lutnick of Cantor Fitzgerald, Jamie Dimon, Lloyd Blankfein of Goldman Sachs, Steve Schwarzman, and Henry Kravis of the private equity firm Kohlberg Kravis Roberts & Co. (KKR). They all lend their support; for example, in 2009 George Soros challenge-pledged $50 million to Robin Hood, meaning that the foundation would have to raise at least another $50 million for Soros's money to be released. Robin Hood not only succeeded in matching Soros's donation but far exceeded it. Tickets start at $3,000, and the silent auctions attract obscene amounts of money. In 2015, the event raised a jaw-dropping $101 million in one evening. Of all New York fund-raisers, Robin Hood brings in the most money. In comparison, the much-feted Metropolitan Museum of Art's Costume Institute Benefit (the "Met Gala") in 2014 raised "only" $12 million.

Robin Hood's board members, a who's who of Wall Street, have a combined net worth of $25 billion. They bear all the costs of the event, ranging in the millions, so that all donations can flow directly to funding projects. So far, Robin Hood has donated to 200 charities. Paul Tudor Jones has redefined the standard of fund-raising and is considered one of the pioneers of "venture philanthropy," a performance-based and results-oriented form of giving. His "anchor guests," or superhubs, have been an incredible draw for Wall Streeters; the charity provides an inroad to access for top executives, and if you want to "belong," you must pay up. It is peer pressure at its best for a good cause. In this parallel social universe, power players revolve around each other like binary stars, and the law of homophily—of similarity breeding connection—creates a gravitational field of attraction.

The ties that people possess say a lot about them; as Goethe stated, "Tell me with whom thou art found, and I will tell thee who thou art." Human networks continuously evolve in line with the laws of homophily—which translates to "love of being alike"—meaning that people tend to associate with those who resemble them.[1] While others who are different from us may seem more interesting, we generally find it easier to relate to, connect with, and be comfortable around people when we have something in common.[2]

A LAW OF NATURE: WHY THE
RICH GET RICHER

All networks have a tendency to grow, and new nodes prefer to attach to nodes that are already well connected. This "rich-get-richer" phenomenon disproportionally benefits the senior nodes, which over time become monopolistic.[3] The same dynamic applies to human networks, and it is particularly pronounced in the financial world. Those executives who are the best connected attract the most new contacts of the highest quality, and they all stick together. Their financial expertise optimally positions them to maximize preexisting wealth, which then makes them even more desirable links. Wealth in turn creates a vacuum of exclusivity and privilege that homogenizes the world's richest and most powerful financiers even more.

GLOBAL CONQUEST: THE
TRANSNATIONAL FINANCIAL ELITE

Major technical progress in combination with financialization have been the key drivers of rapidly increasing globalization and have created an exclusive microcommunity of financial top executives. Nearly all of them are male, and most are self-made. Though they may not share a native tongue, they speak the same language and use the same financial lingo, which sets them apart and leaves outsiders mystified. They attend the same schools, have similar careers, and think alike. Common experiences create common reference points, which facilitate relating to one another. They move in globally overlapping social circles and bump into the same people at conferences, clubs, and charity events in New York as they do in London or Singapore. Whereas early farmers spent their entire lives within a day's walk of their village, today's movers and shakers live across time zones. For them, the dimensions of time and space have shrunk as they continuously circle the globe on planes, zigzagging between cities and continents within the space of a few days. Often they spend more time in the air than on the ground, with jet lag as a constant companion. Being able to swiftly travel anywhere in the world allows them to take advantage of more opportunities than the average person, in business and otherwise.

These executives intermingle with top policy makers of central banks, the Bank for International Settlements, and the International Monetary Fund, along with corporate CEOs, as everyone is a potential client. They have similar lifestyles, living in the same neighborhoods and sending their children to the same private schools. Inevitably, they advance their mutual interests through their collaboration, even if they compete. The old adage that "the higher you climb, the lonelier it gets" rings true in that points of relation with regular people are few and far between: All menial work is outsourced, and chauffeured cars, private jets, and private elevators physically separate them from the rest of the world. Their personal and professional lives are closely intertwined, and friendships evolve over the course of time. Typically, financial executives do not work to live, but they live their work. Through their social interactions, they strongly influence one another, thereby homogenizing their sphere even more.

MEETING OF THE MINDS: CIRCLE OF TRUST

Superhubs conduct business with people they know and trust. To reduce uncertainty and ease the governance of large, unwieldy institutions in a complex financial system, executives generally prefer to work with people who are like them. Homogeneity facilitates communication, understanding, and comfort. It also plays an important role with regard to social capital. Individuals who "share a common employment history and educational backgrounds, gender, and social status" relay privileged information directly, which can provide an important advantage in identifying and exploiting business opportunities.[4] By the same token, a high number of contacts ensures quick dissemination of information. The financial elite tick the same way, and emit the same social signals. Knowing each other's history and reputation enables them to make better judgment calls. In contrast, out-of-network acquaintances do not provide any context and the parameters needed to calibrate one's decision-making process.

Moreover, working with a known entity reduces costs and hiring risk. Familiarity with leadership styles and cultural environments shortens the learning curve and increases effectiveness by saving time and money. In fact, a study revealed that by leveraging their own networks, chief investment officers saved money by hiring key decision makers who shared similar beliefs, work ethics, and philosophies.[5]

Also, when making decisions of great consequence in risky and time-sensitive situations, executives tend to sidestep formal protocol and connect directly with people they trust.

THE HEGEMONY OF HOMOGENEITY

Do you know the feeling when you join a group of people and feel immediately at ease? When you can talk in shorthand and express your thoughts with just a glance? When you are on the same wavelength and effortlessly relate to one another? Well, that's because of homophily.

One criterion that produces homophily is a shared background—be it social, educational, professional, or economic. Philosophers like Aristotle and Plato already studied the "force field" of similarity.[6] In the 1300s, financial firms were formed in Italy on the basis of family, guilds, and social class. By the same token, the French financial establishment was based on ties of friendship, neighborhoods, and political affiliations.[7] The Rothschilds had their own exclusive banking network, with different family members dispersed throughout Europe, which afforded them prime access to information, opportunities, and clients.[8] Personal bonds are an important factor in how financial decisions are made, which transactions are entered into, and what deals are abstained from so as not to damage an ally. Steve Schwarzman and Pete Peterson of Blackstone decided early on not to pursue hostile deals but to instead use their connections to partner with companies in their buyouts.[9] Today's leaders in finance do not have to be born into privilege to make it, although executives from connected families, such as Jamie Dimon, certainly get a head start. Homophily also extends to the choice of spouses with a comparable socioeconomic background in what is called "assortative mating," the pairing of like with like. Power couples lead prosperous lives, and they further perpetuate income inequality by facilitating their offspring's advantaged start in life.[10]

A perfectly just system should be meritocratic, but true meritocracy has proven elusive. In 1995, Newsweek featured a cover story titled "The Rise of the Overclass," which included numerous Wall Street stars—women and various ethnic groups among them. This was seen as evidence of a diverse meritocracy. But diversity has proven to be illusory in the world of high finance. At the entry level, human capital has indeed become more diverse, but the most senior positions are still primarily occupied by white males. In a 2014 Princeton graduation speech, Ben Bernanke suggested that no system is entirely meritocratic and that such factors as family and health skew the equality of opportunity.[11] In order to have a chance to climb the ranks, the safest bet is to adapt and try to pursue as many commonalities as possible. However, there is one commonality that is difficult to achieve without an advantaged socioeconomic background: sophistication. The vast majority of firms require a "cultural fit," which usually means having the right accent, being well-traveled, having similar experiences, and employing the same social etiquette—in short, characteristics that require an upbringing in a reasonably wealthy household and an investment of time and money. Interviewers are likely often not even aware of this subtle form of discrimination, which results in further similarity at the expense of diversity. Chemistry and the "airport test," the question of with whom you'd prefer to be stuck at an airport, prioritizes rapport over merit, excluding potentially more qualified and—since the class bias is overwhelmingly male—stereotypically feminine candidates.[12]

The personal backgrounds of top executives are also similar. They are expected to be married and have a stable home life.[13] Single or openly gay CEOs are a rarity. Thus, almost all leaders are married, and since most executives are male, most spouses are wives. Some have careers themselves, but the majority are homemakers. The more money available, the more complex life becomes, and since there is only so much one can outsource, managing social engagements becomes a job in and of itself. Spouses are an essential component in the executives' success, as they coordinate private and public activities such as entertaining and volunteering in charitable activities. They ensure that their children are accepted into highly competitive private schools, supervise various households on various continents, and keep the staff in check.

The IQ Elite: A Master's Degree in Networking

IQ and academic accomplishments are indispensable to climbing the financial Olympus. Studies have shown that leaders in finance are academically gifted and range among the top of IQ distribution. This correlation is especially distinct with regard to billionaires, whose higher cognitive ability and education is directly tied to higher compensation and net worth.[14] It seems obvious, but now we have scientific proof: Greater smarts help amass greater wealth.

Almost all leaders in finance have a college degree, and most have graduate degrees. So no matter how smart you are, you need formal qualification to prove that you have developed those smarts and put them to the test. Harvard, Stanford, and the Massachusetts Institute of Technology (MIT) are consistently ranked among the top business schools.[15] From the moment applicants are associated with these exclusive brands, their professional lives move on a steep upward trajectory. A prosperous career is virtually guaranteed; they can choose from a wealth of unrivaled opportunities, and almost every door will be open to them. The awareness of being accepted into an exclusive circle of current and future leaders provides students with self-confidence, a sense of identity, and purpose.

Top schools are not only "intellectual boot camps"; they also help develop interpersonal skills by engaging their extensive alumni networks. Beyond the education, students are eager to attend Harvard first and foremost for the invaluable relationships they can form there, which would otherwise likely be inaccessible. Chances are that in the future the resulting connections will prove much more valuable than anything taught in class. Students buying into that network learn how to interact with high-level professionals and how to maintain and grow those relationships. They form deep bonds for life by spending intense time with peers in classrooms, in libraries, and working together on projects, thereby learning to think along similar lines and developing similar world views. It is an exclusive club, with the default assumption that anyone who has not attended a top school is not quite on par, or—even if of comparable qualifications—at the least, very different. In 2015, hedge fund billionaire John Paulson donated $400 million to his alma mater, Harvard, the largest donation it had received up to that point. For him it wasn't just a charitable act, but an investment in his network. By elevating his status and reputation and increasing his social capital, he officially moved into the center of one of the world's most coveted networks, becoming a bona fide superhub.

Wall Street still heavily recruits from elite schools, although classic financial firms and banks have lost some of their appeal in the aftermath of the crisis. In 2007, almost half of Harvard graduates ventured into finance; although that number has since declined, in 2011 the financial industry was still the top employer of Ivy League graduates.[16] The prestige and high pay of these jobs are particularly attractive to graduates in view of high student debt and an uncertain economic outlook. Firms also link themselves to universities by financing research and engaging well-known academics for consultancy work and marketing events. Elite academic affiliations lend credibility and cachet to financial firms, serving as an implied endorsement. Critics view these financial ties as a major conflict of interest, corrupting the unbiased research process.

Network Plutocracy: "The Old Boys' Club"

Elite schools directly tie in with another aspect of career advancement: the old boys' network. The term originates from the connections formed at all-male private schools; indeed, to this day alumni associations of prestigious schools are a crucial component of the superhub network. Ivy League universities have seen record donations in recent years. In 2014, hedge fund executive Kenneth Griffin made a donation of $150 million to his alma mater, Harvard, and private equity guru Steve Schwarzman gifted Yale with $150 million in 2015. Over time, an informal system developed in which affiliations ensure that "members of the club" help one another in advancing their interests. They interact at work, golf clubs, think tanks, and any other platforms with high barriers to entry, be they financial, status-wise, or both.

The old boys' network is less conservative and stereotypical than it used to be, but it is still alive and well. Its members have similar social backgrounds and usually live in an exclusive bubble of privilege. Because of their influence, they determine the culture, define norms, and set the tone. The more-senior members recognize themselves in the younger ones and relate to their personal and professional struggles. Based on loyalty, they provide mentoring, introductions, and favors. Since both old and young club members share similar views, they reinforce one another, thereby becoming even more conformist. Although the financial system has gradually become more meritocratic, increasing focus on grades and performance, it still skews in favor of those with connections. In the insider-outsider dynamic, members of the old boys' network—without premeditation and perhaps subconsciously—exclude others merely by sticking together. They give special consideration to those of their ilk while passing over others who do not fit the mold. This results in the distinct lack of women and minorities in leadership positions. (We will take a closer look at this in Chapter 9.) Without any checks and balances, the system continues to self-perpetuate these biases. Decision makers often shape the organization in their likeness and tilt it in their favor, if only to subconsciously preserve their status. Through their crisscross connections, the fabric of their relationships remains tightly interwoven and robust. Developed over centuries, such patterns of power preservation will only evolve slowly.

The interconnections of the leaders in finance are so numerous, and they overlap in so many industries—in both the private and public sectors—that trying to diagram them is a tedious exercise. Here's one representative example: The vice chairman of the U.S. Federal Reserve and former central bank governor of the Bank of Israel, Stanley Fischer, was once the MIT professor of former Fed chairman Ben Bernanke and ECB president Mario Draghi. Fischer had previously occupied positions as deputy managing director at the IMF, chief economist at the World Bank, and vice chairman at Citigroup. His students also included former U.S.

treasury secretary Larry Summers and Greg Mankiw, who chaired the Council of Economic Advisers during the administration of George W. Bush. Fischer had also been in the running to become IMF chief when Dominique Strauss-Kahn resigned, and Fed chairman after the end of Bernanke's term. Fischer's, Bernanke's, and Draghi's aligned thinking was reflected in their similar approach to quantitative easing during the financial crisis and in its aftermath. The central bank governor of the Bank of England during the crisis was Mervyn King, who had also once taught in MIT's economics department. It is quite incredible how much our world has been shaped by the few who attended the same school.

The epitome of the old boys' network is Goldman Sachs. It is the most exclusive of all exclusive clubs and artfully illustrates how the power-laws of network science correlate with actual network power. Due to the fact that Goldman always seems to make money regardless of the circumstances, it has been vilified as the "great vampire squid wrapped around the face of humanity"[17] and alleged to have caused as well as profited from various financial crises. Goldmanites are everywhere, as the firm hires former high-level public sector employees, and partners leave the firm to take public office.

In the time leading up to the financial crisis, Robert Rubin, previously co-CEO of Goldman Sachs, served as secretary of the U.S. treasury under President Bill Clinton. During the crisis, Hank Paulson, then CEO of Goldman Sachs, became the next U.S. treasury secretary. The president of the European Central Bank, Mario Draghi, was once vice chairman and managing director of Goldman Sachs International. Mario Monti, prime minister of Italy from 2011 to 2013, worked as an adviser for Goldman Sachs. Robert Zoellick went from being Goldman Sachs's head of international affairs to president of the World Bank. From there he returned to Goldman and became chairman of the international advisory board. The German government awarded him the Federal Cross of Merit for his services regarding the German reunification.

Speaking of Germany, its government was heavily criticized for providing too much top-level government access to Goldman Sachs, which the political opposition labeled the "bonus program for investment bankers." Prior Goldman Sachs employees have also obtained high-level government positions throughout the world. Numerous other influential and famous Goldmanites include John Thain (former chairman and CEO of CIT Group, former president and co-CEO of Goldman Sachs), Jon Corzine (CEO of MF Global, former U.S. senator of New Jersey, former CEO of Goldman Sachs), Duncan Niederauer (former CEO of NYSE Group, former partner at Goldman Sachs Group), Joshua Bolten (White House chief of staff to U.S. President George W. Bush, former executive director for legal and government affairs at Goldman Sachs), and countless more.

That's Rich: Superhubs and Super-Riches

One thing that nearly all top financial executives have in common is great wealth, which is a measurable, publicly known yardstick for success. Together they can increase their financial muscle even more, be it for political influence, charities, or otherwise. Although they are active in different fields, they are united by the privileges and problems that wealth creates.

Policy makers are not part of this particular sphere, as they make substantially less money than hedge fund titans, private equity kings, or bank CEOs. For instance, Fed Chair Janet Yellen in 2015 received a salary of roughly $200,000, and Christine Lagarde, Managing Director of the IMF, was compensated with close to $500,000. However, since the lack of financial clout can be compensated for by other factors such as power and status, they remain firmly entrenched in the center of the financial network. Similarly, academics, intellectuals, and top service providers are part of the mix, because their commonalities outweigh their differences. Still, compensation remains a powerful common denominator among superhubs that allows them to perpetuate their exclusive microcosm.

CEOs in the financial industry continue to make headlines with their almost outrageously high remuneration, which outpaces overall Wall Street pay. Their ever-skyrocketing compensation is a manifestation of the superstar economy as well as the superstar CEO. The term "economics of superstars" was coined in the early eighties by Sherwin Rosen, an economist at the University of Chicago. He argued in a widely recognized paper that technological progress would provide the best performers with greater market access and, as a consequence, disproportionate pay.[18] This dynamic explains the megapay of successful athletes, actors, and musicians, and Sherwin's prescient theory also applies to similar trends in the financial world. As economies grew, banks morphed into monstrous global conglomerates, and investment funds began to manage trillions of dollars. Fierce competition for the best human capital ensued, and compensation increased to previously unimagined heights to meet the demand. CEOs developed superstar brands in their own right with public relations campaigns, TV interviews, and industry awards. Pay packages are exceedingly high on an absolute basis, as well as relative to other executives.

Financiers generally believe that compensation is purely performance based and, because it is measurable in terms of profits, well deserved. However, in the complex and opaque world of finance, objective performance measurement is challenging. There are many unknown variables beyond executive control, such as the blowup of a previously hailed asset class, like energy, or the bursting of a bubble like the Internet. A systemic financial crisis may even reveal that *all* asset classes are in fact negatively correlated. The application of performance metrics has been questioned in view of the recent billion-dollar losses and fines ranging in the hundreds of millions. Yet, CEOs still receive rising pay.

Proponents argue that winner-takes-all compensation is simply the result of market forces and freely agreed contracts, and that competitive salaries are necessary to obtain and retain top talent. According to them, paying finance executives handsomely is less costly and disruptive than losing them. Critics counter that financial CEOs are self-interested and biased toward perpetuating the upward pay spiral. They run the companies that pay them and often chair the boards that determine their own remuneration. The National Bureau of Economic Research suggests that rising salaries are the result of contagion, because boards are influenced by the higher pay awarded by other companies.[19] Rather than traditional compensation for services rendered, today's pay packages have aptly been described as resembling prizes won at tournaments.[20]

Of course, circumstances vary depending on the nature of the financial institution. A publicly traded bank is accountable to its shareholders. Hedge fund founders—such as George Soros, Steve Cohen, and Stan

Druckenmiller—manage their own multibillion-dollar fortunes and, therefore, are accountable to only themselves. Other hedge funds that manage billions on behalf of pension funds, insurance companies, and other big investors are often founder- or partner-owned. Their fees and compensation parameters are relatively clear-cut and transparent. The same generally applies to private equity, although the industry has recently come under scrutiny by the Securities and Exchange Commission (SEC) regarding hidden fees.

The international consulting firm McKinsey played a major part in legitimizing ever-growing pay packages. One of their consultants, Arch Patton, conducted a study on executive compensation in the early sixties[21] that was publicized in the *Harvard Business Review*. It received much attention and thereafter was revisited annually. This study provided rationalization and justification and, due to McKinsey's wide global network of CEOs, spread and became "the law."[22]

As David Mitchell points out in the *Observer*, one of the greatest skills top bankers possess is convincing us that they merit millions.[23] Despite criticism, the assumption that "the higher the remuneration, the more qualified the executive" is deeply engrained in people's minds and, barring a shareholder or social revolt, excesses will likely be reined in only very slowly, if at all.

Renumeration varies widely across industry lines—hedge fund titans make the most, followed by private equity kings. Both their remuneration is disproportionally higher than anyone else's, because they charge substantial management fees in addition to success fees. Hence while their actual payout may vary wildly depending on performance, their downside is limited, because they receive the management fee regardless of performance. Bank CEOs earn significantly less, as they head publicly-listed companies with utility-like character, who to a large extent deal with financially so-called unsophisticated investors. Also, their job has more of a corporate management nature, rather than solely an investment management one. The twenty-five best-paid hedge fund managers in 2013 earned a total of $21.1 billion, in 2014 $11.62 billion, and in 2015 $12.94 billion.[24] As the *Guardian* points out, the $1.7 billion that the two top earners, Kenneth Griffin of Citadel and James Simons of Renaissance

Technologies, made in 2015, is equivalent to the annual salaries of 112,000 people at a minimum wage of $15,080. In fact, Simon's earnings were so large in 2015 that if he were a country, it would rate as the world's 178th most productive nation.[25]

In 2013, George Soros (net worth $24.9 billion) led the pack with an estimated $4 billion. Since converting his fund into a family office, he's no longer included in the hedge funder compensation lists.

David Tepper (net worth $11.4 billion) of Appaloosa Management in 2013 made $3.5 billion, in 2014 $400 million, and in 2015 $1.4 billion. Bridgewater Associates' Ray Dalio, in 2013 $600 million, in 2014 $1.1 billion, and in 2015 $1.4 billion.

Steve Cohen (net worth $12.7 billion), founder of SAC Capital, now renamed Point72 Asset Management, in 2013 took home $2.4 billion, in 2014 $2 billion, and in 2015 $1.55 billion.

John Paulson (net worth $9.8 billion), founder of Paulson & Co., in 2013 pocketed $2.3 billion, which was good for him, because in 2014 and 2015 he failed to make the list.

Jim Simons (net worth $15.5 billion), founder of Renaissance Capital, in 2013 earned $2.3 billion, in 2014 $1.2 billion, and in 2015 $1.7 billion.

In comparison, the titans of private equity made significantly less, though they will likely still be able to get by:

Steve Schwarzman (net worth $9.5 billion), cofounder of Blackstone, in 2013 made $374.5 million, in 2014 $690 million, and in 2015 $810.6 million. Leon Black (net worth $4.6 billion), founder of Apollo Global Management, in 2013 took home $369 million and in 2014 $331 million. Henry Kravis's (of KKR, net worth $4.2 billion) pay in 2013 amounted to $327 million, in 2014 to $219 million, and in 2015 $165.1 million.

Bank CEOs are poor in comparison: In 2013 Jamie Dimon (net worth $1.1 billion), CEO of JPMorgan Chase, in 2013 and 2014 respectively made $20 million and in 2015 $37 million. Lloyd Blankfein (net worth $1.1 billion), CEO of Goldman Sachs, in 2013 received a total compensation of $23 million, in 2014 $24 million, and in 2015 $23 million. And Michael Corbat, Citigroup CEO, in 2013 received compensation valued at $17.6 million, in 2014 at $13.1 million, and in 2015 at $16.4 million.

Unsurprisingly, CEOs have not been known to oppose their ever-rising pay packages. An exception is James Gorman (net worth $50 million), Morgan Stanley's CEO, who, in a 2012 interview with the *Financial Times*, lamented that compensation was too high and expressed sympathy with shareholders who viewed the industry as overpaid.[26] Luckily for him, this seems not to have negatively impacted his 2013 pay, as it almost doubled from the previous year to a total of $18 million; in 2014 he made $22.5 million and in 2015 $21 million.

The "Flocking Effect": The Superhub Habitat

Nowhere are the laws of network science more obviously reflected than in geography. Superhubs as a rule tend to cluster around one another. Like a swarm of birds, the titans of finance flock in the same direction and stay in close proximity. They live in the most expensive neighborhoods, in houses so enormous that they deserve their own zip codes. Living in the same areas, and even the same buildings, provides a sense of belonging, and by sticking with their kind, they de facto exclude those who are different. In line with the laws of network hierarchy, they often occupy the most centrally located houses or the top floors of metropolitan buildings—which tend to feature breathtaking panoramas of the city below. Trophy pieces of real estate in the "center of the center" are indispensable, because network location is one of the most visible signs of social status. The highest concentration of financiers in New York can be found on the Upper East Side close to Central Park; in Greenwich, Connecticut; in Bedford, Westchester County; and, of course, in the Hamptons on Long Island. While some more conservative financiers prefer "old money" New York addresses on Fifth and Park Avenue, others flock to the "newer" billionaire rows in Midtown. In the aggregate, those buildings literally house billions of dollars in personal wealth under one roof.

Private equity king Steve Schwarzman lives in one of the most pedigreed buildings in Manhattan: 740 Park Avenue. The magnificent limestone edifice, which sits on the corner of Park Avenue and 71st Street, has been home to many famous captains of industry. Its most spectacular feature is its storied history, which in a young country, is a hot commodity. Schwarzman is said to have paid $30 million in 2000 for an apartment that once belonged to John D. Rockefeller, a member of one of America's most prestigious families. The triplex, which occupies the top three floors of the building, is equipped with twenty-four rooms, servants' quarters, and every imaginable luxury. Other financiers who share the same address include hedge fund titans Israel "Izzy" Englander (net worth $5 billion) and David Ganek; the former CEO of CIT Group, John Thain; and Howard Marks (net worth $1.87 billion) of Oaktree Capital Management.

Among those who prefer Fifth Avenue to Park Avenue are hedge fund founders Marc Lasry (net worth $1.69 billion) of Avenue Capital Group, Glenn Dubin (net worth $2 billion) of Highbridge Capital Management, and legend George Soros. Soros resides in a sixteen-room duplex in a white-glove building on Fifth Avenue and 87th Street with gorgeous Central Park views. The seventh floor, with its sumptuous living and formal dining room area, is primarily for entertaining, while the personal rooms are located on the eighth floor. During the United Nations Week, many foreign dignitaries visit the building to make their overtures, much to the dismay of the neighbors, who must endure the inconvenience of having 87th Street blocked by barricades and hovering security details.

The price tag differs, but usually the top financiers spend upwards of $10 million on trophy real estate, with a few extra million allocated to renovation. A minimum of $100 million in liquid assets is required even to be considered as a potential buyer in these buildings, and financial records are scrutinized. But the price tag is not the only hurdle. The board, which functions as an admissions committee, is even harder to overcome. Many of Manhattan's most exclusive buildings are cooperatives, which means that they operate like clubs, and residents decide whether or not applicants are deemed appropriate. According to the adage "money can't buy you class," many wealthy and well-known applicants have experienced embarrassing rejections.

One of the newer and most prestigious addresses is the sparkly 15 Central Park West. The "tower of power" is located on the southwest corner of Central Park. Of modern and effortless elegance, it is the epitome of extravagance. It contains a seventy-five-foot sky-lit lap pool, a private restaurant, a wine cellar, a gym, and a screening room. The staff is highly trained and renders top service for top dollar, as monthly mainte-nance alone typically runs in the thousands. Many of the apartments are equipped with private elevators, spectacular terraces, and floor-to-ceil-ing windows that allow for sweeping views of Manhattan. One-bedroom apartments are available to accommodate the residents' staff. The build-ing has counted former Citigroup CEO Sandy Weill, CEO of Goldman Sachs Lloyd Blankfein, and hedge fund billionaire Daniel Loeb amongst its residents.

Townhouses on the Upper East Side of Manhattan are also popular with the billionaire crowd. They come with a backyard, which is the ulti-mate luxury in a city where space is such a finite commodity. Leon Black recently bought a $50 million townhouse in the tony neighborhood that requires another $20 million in renovations. It will serve as the perfect backdrop to Black's spectacular art collection, which comprises many masterpieces worth hundreds of millions of dollars.

On summer weekends, the power scene moves either to the Hamptons on Long Island or "to the country," lingo for north of the city. Virtually all financiers own McMansions, equipped with pools, tennis courts, and guesthouses, surrounded by lush formal gardens, tall privet hedges, and security features. The upkeep costs hundreds of thousands of dollars a year and often requires the employ of an estate manager. Even within clus-ters, supernuclei form. In the Hamptons, superhubs congregate around Meadow Lane, Gin Lane, and Dune Road. Leon Black owns a massive beachfront compound where he celebrated his sixty-third birthday with a spectacular private Elton John concert. Financiers David Ganek and Henry Kravis also reside in the neighborhood. Steve Schwarzman acquired a property in Water Mill that once belonged to an heir to the Vanderbilt fortune, and rebuilt the estate.

Luxurious weekend homes also serve as the perfect sites for entertain-ing and hosting glamorous parties, another way that the financial elite remain within their own social circles.

Every year on the Fourth of July, Lally Weymouth, the *Washington Post* heiress and author, hosts an elegant reception followed by a formal sit-down dinner at her classic Southampton estate. I had heard much about her annual gathering, one of the social highlights of the summer for the rich and famous. Invitations are highly coveted, and all the titans of finance and their glamorous wives are eager to attend: Steve Schwarzman belongs to that circle, as does Lloyd Blankfein, Leon Black, Henry Kravis, and Wilbur Ross. Outsiders are accepted as long as they bring something interesting, entertaining, or useful to the table. I was thrilled to be invited but was unsure about the decorum: what dress to wear, what kind of present to bring, and what to expect.

* * *

Chapter 5 has delved into the preeminent forces that empower the financial elite and make it so homogeneous: *homophily*—or the "love of being alike"—and the "rich-get-richer" phenomenon. Now that we have a clear sense of how homophily operates within the circles of the financial elite, Chapter 6 will explore exactly how these executives build networks to further their power.

CHAPTER 6

Executive Networking

Relational Capital

THE SUPERHUB OF SUPERHUBS:
KLAUS SCHWAB

Located in the French part of Switzerland, Geneva is a match for its French neighbor in terms of style and elegance. It has a quaint charm coupled with understated glamour. Majestic mansions and manicured gardens with a touch of patina have borne witness to its history as an exclusive and discreet enclave for the rich and their fortunes. Against the backdrop of the massive snow-covered Alps, life here appears deceptively serene, but it is like a swan on Lake Geneva—quiet on top, but paddling vigorously underneath. Many big and influential institutions are headquartered in Geneva, such as the World Health Organization (WHO), the European Organization for Nuclear Research (CERN), and the World Economic Forum (WEF). The WEF is most commonly associated with the Swiss ski resort of Davos, because of its renowned annual gathering, but the institution's headquarters are located in an exclusive municipality of Geneva called Cologny.

During one of my frequent business trips to Switzerland, I accepted an invitation to visit the WEF. A taxi ferried me across Lake Geneva to the Left Bank and up the hills along the old parts of town. As I took in the pretty view of the mountains and traveled the winding road lined with greenery and colorful blossoming flowers stretching toward the sun, it felt more like a vacation than a business trip to one of the world's most powerful institutions. The taxi eventually made a left turn and approached a heavy metal sliding gate. After passing the high-security clearance, the gate opened automatically and a sweeping circular driveway led to an ultramodern concrete-and-glass building. I made my way to the reception desk, where I ran into a couple of familiar faces and was led to a conference room. The architecture reflects the uniqueness of the institution it houses. A mix of Eastern and Western elements, it features an open design with glass walls offering magnificent views of Lake Geneva. A lively cosmopolitan mix of predominantly younger people dressed in business casual outfits congregated in the spacious and sun-drenched public areas, which are decorated with eclectic art from all over the world.

The WEF is one of the least understood and most controversial organizations in the world. Its mystique may result from the fact that it is the creation of only one person, and doesn't seem to neatly fit into any box. Even though the Forum was originally focused on economic issues, it now embraces a holistic approach that includes science, politics, and culture. It is perhaps the most effective and powerful network platform and incubator of our time. Like a giant think tank, it focuses on pressing issues and provides a framework for solutions, often by joining or brokering public-private partnerships. The convocation of power players in Davos has suffered criticism for undue collusion, but global problems require global solutions, and the WEF is uniquely positioned to bring together an eclectic mix of influencers. The WEF's status was significantly elevated in early 2015, when the Swiss Federal Council recognized it as an international institution for public-private cooperation similar to that of the Red Cross.

One of the greatest network creators is the WEF's founder, Klaus Schwab. How did an academic, from his start as a young economist and engineer, manage to attract the world's most influential people and establish the preeminent international interdisciplinary meeting platform? The bald, bespectacled, and earnest German professor speaks slowly in a baritone voice with a thick German accent. With his straight gait and head held high, he has the demeanor of a statesman, and by virtue of his superhub position, he is as powerful as many of his guests. Surprisingly, by his own account, he is an introvert and shuns the party circuit. Some mistake his shyness for arrogance. He may seem reserved, but his wide and deep network is a testament to his thoughtfulness and sincerity. He is known for his discipline, affinity for strenuous mountain hikes, and dry sense of humor.

Schwab established the forum in 1971 as a modest gathering of European business executives. With vision, intuition, a curious mind, and laser-sharp focus, he developed the Forum into an exclusive global brand. Now in his seventies, he is still the driving force of the organization and a continuous source of innovation. Critics—mostly those who have never been invited—perennially predict Davos's demise, and attendees complain about everything from the logistics to the fees. Yet they all return year after year, and the demand for tickets far exceeds available spots.

So what is the magic formula of Schwab's network power? Like many other top leaders, Schwab developed a theory at the outset of his career that would become the foundation of all his endeavors. According to the stakeholder principle, "the management of an enterprise is not only accountable to its shareholders, but must also serve the interests of all stakeholders, including employees, customers, suppliers and, more broadly, government, civil society and any others who may be affected or concerned by its operations." He later expanded this concept to include global corporate citizenship, which views "corporations as stakeholders in global society, together with government and civil society."[1] Companies that have benefited tremendously from globalization are encouraged to take a socially responsible approach and give back. Schwab's theory tapped into a worldwide trend, which at the WEF's inception was only beginning to develop: globalization and the emergence of transnational power elites. The declining power of nation states, the lack of global leadership, and the emergence of powerful conglomerates have increased the relevance of the stakeholder concept. Based on Schwab's theories, the WEF's mission takes an all-inclusive approach, inviting representatives of nonprofit organizations and young global leaders without charge. The stakeholder principle provides the WEF with legitimization, authority, authenticity, and a purpose for its platform—to improve the state of the world.

Schwab slowly developed from a node to a hub and then a superhub. Apart from creating a sound ideology and distinguishing himself academically in Switzerland, he also earned a master's degree in public administration from the Harvard Kennedy School of Government. There he gained international exposure, made numerous important contacts, honed his skills, and solidified his reputation. Among other innovations, he conceptualized the annual *Global Competitiveness Report*, which also includes sustainability considerations. Over the years, his brainchild has morphed into an authoritative research paper that commands global attention. Through his thought leadership, Schwab has cemented his status in the world community and accumulated an impressive fourteen honorary doctorates, seventeen national distinctions, and countless awards. He was also chosen to serve on the steering committee of the Bilderberg Group. He perfectly exemplifies the fact that every network needs a nucleus around which other nodes can circulate.

Schwab cleverly chose a secluded mountainous location devoid of distractions for the WEF's annual gathering, where he could assemble a high concentration of superhubs. Moreover, he chose neutral Swiss ground and focused on participants' commonalities rather than their differences. By stressing elements of homophily, he ensured a greater draw, as people tend to gravitate toward others with whom they have something in common.

For the longest time, the question of succession remained unaddressed, which prompted some to speculate that Schwab was either in denial or had simply not yet found anyone he deemed up to the task. Regardless of the fact that Schwab has no plans to retire, the official recognition of the WEF as an international organization in 2015 finally necessitated a formal succession plan and governance matrix to ensure the Forum's sustainability and long-term success. However, Schwab's iconic status, and the highly personal nature of his relationships, calls into question the future of the Forum should he one day resign. But until that day and forever thereafter, he will undoubtedly remain the superhub of superhubs.

FRIENDS WITH BENEFITS: CAPITAL
NETWORKS = NETWORK CAPITAL

Today more than ever, power is defined by who is the most connected and knows how to best use those connections. Network strength provides network power, and the most successful executives reach the top not solely based on their analytical skills, but because of their strong relational apti- tude. We all begin our professional lives with our own personal human capital, but at a certain level executives are expected to cultivate wide and deep professional networks. Relational capital is an intangible asset that reflects the value inherent in a person's relationships. The more high-level the relationships and the greater their strength, the more valuable the "relational capital". It is a prized asset, because in a knowledge economy where almost everything can be replicated, a person's relationships are unique.

"Relational capital" creates "network capital," which increases the "return on relationships." An executive's relational capital is considered most valuable, because it expands the institution's own network and, thus, its profitability. Particularly in view of globalization, networks have become a distinct area of competition. Globalization has exerted upward pressure on quality and downward pressure on prices, which makes it harder for firms to distinguish their products and services. This makes human connections, which by their nature are highly personal and unique, even more coveted. They can be the decisive factor with regard to which banks are chosen to orchestrate landmark IPOs, which funds see billions of dollars in inflows, and which firms receive access to megadeals.

One of the most valuable resources is network intelligence, as we explored in Chapter 3. The most crucial information comes from other people, not theoretical resources, and this serves as a strong link among superhubs. In an age of constant information overload, relevant, timely, and private information from original sources is now an indispensable commodity. As Klaus Schwab noted, contextual emotional intelligence cannot be acquired in reading papers, but only through interactions with other people.[2] Therefore, building a deep, diverse, and dynamic network is imperative for leaders, because in order to succeed they must remain informed, have access to opportunities, and the resources to be able to seize them. Strong networks enable superhubs to connect with peers and weak ties alike in order to weave an ever-tighter web that extends beyond the echo chamber of homogeneous thinking and covers any blind spots. Such alliances provide resources, support, and greater influence.

More an Art than a Science: Attraction + Interaction = Transaction

Human networks form according to laws that we can analyze and apply. But relationships also contain unknown variables, intangible aspects, elements that cannot quite be grasped. Why, when we enter a room, do we immediately click with or feel repulsed by some people? Why do we trust someone immediately while dismissing others right off the bat? Interpersonal chemistry is hard to grasp and more difficult to explain than the scientific laws of network science. But there are a few mechanisms that illuminate this invisible phenomenon, at least to some extent.

Throughout our lives, one of our innermost needs is to connect with other people. The degree of our cooperation and success differentiates us from other species. We are wired to build human rapport, and evolutionary history has fine-tuned our ability to do so. We have learned to assess others and discern subconscious signals by interpreting their voice, facial expressions, and body language. The more senses involved, the more accurate our assessment.

The face is the most expressive part of the human body; it divulges a wealth of visual clues about one's emotional state. When we meet someone new, we decide within thirteen milliseconds whether or not we like them.[3] People who are familiar make us feel comfortable, whereas foreigners put us on alert. These responses are triggered by the brain, which processes cognitive as well as emotional stimuli. The amygdala, which is part of the brain's "survival system," receives inputs from all senses and processes fear and emotional memories. Suspicious signals, which trigger distrust, activate the amygdala. In contrast, when we trust others, the brain's prefrontal cortex, which is associated with cognitive processes, is activated. These reactions confirm that we can really only build profound relationships in person, because it is the optimal way to assess and connect with people.

Digital Bits versus Human Touch

In an interview with the *Financial Times*, Klaus Schwab predicted that "in twenty, thirty years' time, people will not go to conferences any more," because "the digital dimension will change how people interact and how conferences are done."[4] How do new communication technologies impact the networks of leaders in finance? Do they make personal interaction less relevant or even redundant? Much has been made of the possibility to connect with people through the Internet. Revolutionary developments in telecommunications have reduced the dimensions of time and space, allowing connection with anyone anywhere at any time. Wireless technology added vastly increased capacity and connectivity at unprecedented speed. Nowadays, the Internet is the nerve center of communication.

While technology serves as a connector, it also establishes a barrier. Both the connecting as well as the separating aspects have value: Electronic networks can grow exponentially faster than personal ones, enable a dialogue with an audience unlimited in number, and assist the organization of social or political movements. At the same time, these networks can lead people to retreat from direct interaction. The harshest critics argue that technology degrades our being as an individual and deemphasizes personhood.[5] In their view, we embrace the illusion of having close relationships without making the requisite investments and sacrifices; we "give human qualities to objects and . . . treat each other as things."[6] Indeed, sanitized electronic communications make it more difficult to ascertain people's authenticity. They can misrepresent their identity, distort facts, and hide intentions without broadcasting any conventional warning signs, therefore manipulating human relationships. Subtle communication nuances such as tone and inflection often get lost in email. Video conferences are the next best thing to face-to-face meetings, but they cannot replace them as participants cannot engage in direct eye contact, exchange handshakes and other personal gestures, or interpret nonverbal cues. Thus, digitized interaction is superficial at best and fragile at worst. Internet-based social networks such as Friendster and Myspace are often fleeting. With no barrier to entry, users have little loyalty and move on when the next best thing comes along. If technology fails, or is blocked by governments, connecting becomes impossible.

According to the Pew study *Social Isolation and New Technology*, people still prefer face-to-face communication as the primary means to stay in touch.[7] A deep and trusting relationship is a privilege that must be earned with an investment of time and effort, tested through adversity, and fostered through mutual experiences. Also, the scarcer human interactions become, the more valuable they will be. That's why overscheduled financiers, time-pressed CEOs, and overstimulated billionaires invest time and effort to attend international gatherings around the globe. Thus, while algorithms can help support the maintenance of personal relationships, human interactions are so complex that digital bits will never truly rival or replace them.

Beyond Networking: How to Win Friends and Influence People

Networking is aimed at building, maintaining, and using informal relationships to facilitate work-related activities and gain access to resources.[8] The best networkers practice a holistic approach of "positive linking," because they are genuinely interested in other people, always want to learn through the mutual exchange of thoughts, and enjoy communicating and connecting. Malcolm Gladwell recognized that a small number of people, the connectors, have a truly extraordinary knack for making friends and acquaintances.[9] They are the threads that tie society together and are an extremely important component of our social networks.[10] Superhubs all have this network mind-set; they are the "chief network officers" of Me, Inc. Throughout their lives, they tirelessly and effortlessly cultivate a circle of influence. Everything they do promotes networking in a feedback loop of cause and effect. Networking feels natural to them, and they have a knack for placing others at ease. They value quality over quantity, connecting over collecting, and farming over hunting. Often, long-term relationships start out without any specific motivation or business purpose and mature over time, withstanding trials and tribulations before culminating in mutually beneficial relationships.

Having a networking mind-set entails being open-minded. Successful CEOs are curious, seek challenges, push boundaries, and are unafraid of risks or failures. In their lifelong quest to learn and expand beyond the status quo, they embrace the opportunity to meet new people. They usually have a positive view of humanity, seek out new acquaintances, and build relationships for the long term. Generally, when we meet new people, we quickly prejudge them in line with our biases to save time and stay within our comfort zone. Great networkers keep an open mind; with their high emotional intelligence, they create true connections and make others feel comfortable in their presence. That's important, because "people will forget what you said, people will forget what you did, but people will never forget how you made them feel."[11]

Top networkers are memorable. It is not simply who you know but, even more important, who knows you. It helps to stand out in a positive way, be it by way of charisma, intelligent contributions, quick wit, or acts of kindness. Pleasant, energetic people with appealing personalities and excellent social skills will always have an easier time obtaining support, information, and feedback. Josef Ackermann, longtime CEO of Deutsche Bank, coined the phrase "The right personality can learn anything, but you can't learn to have the right personality."[12] Deep and resilient relationships cannot be built on schmoozing alone; they must be based on content. Superhubs like to spend time with interesting people who bring conversational currency to the table. Klaus Schwab, the founder of the WEF, has emphasized that great networkers are not only seekers of knowledge but also catalysts in the exchange of ideas.

Powerful CEOs utilize the power of association with other powerful people. Networks are only as valuable as the caliber of people comprising them and as strong as the relationships within them. Since a specific network configuration can increase its effectiveness,[13] CEOs increase their connectivity if their contacts are well connected in turn. Exclusive networks by definition exclude the majority of people, often by instituting high barriers to entry. Superhub platforms are like invitation-only clubs where the demand for memberships exceeds the supply, and superhubs know how to overcome high barriers by way of status, reputation, and connections. The higher the rank, the more homogeneous the people who interact, and the lower the barrier is for peers. Homogeneity within a group facilitates familiarity—or at least the illusion thereof—and peers typically respect one another's achievements, even if they compete. Yet, on this level, their relationships are still subject to rivalries, resentments, favoritism, and peer pressure.

These pillars of finance may perhaps be blessed with more professional strengths than the average person, yet they are certainly not immune from human weaknesses and vulnerabilities. Networks can lend them psychological support during setbacks and times of stress. Who can better understand you than someone who has faced similar challenges and experiences? Personal alliances provide the support and caring that emboldens superhubs to overcome difficult situations. The various overlapping spheres of personal life, such as friendships, social circles, and charities coupled with the professional realm—are woven together into a tightly knit fabric.

The Alchemy of Chemistry: Charm Offensive

Truly effective leaders in finance not only possess technical skill and emotional intelligence but also other intangible qualities such as charisma and charm.[14] With their open attitude, charismatic people attract people and opportunities, giving them a distinct advantage when networking. They combine substance with personality and have the ability to focus on someone with undivided and genuine attention, which makes others feel special. They project a strong presence, draw attention to themselves, and enrapture audiences. With their self-confidence and ability to charm, they manage to persuade and align people, furthering their own objectives. Most people at the top have a great sense of humor—an expression of social intelligence that is supremely helpful in disarming and bonding with people. Their often self-deprecating quick wit bridges differences in culture, status, and interests.

George Soros is masterful in firing off unexpectedly dry tidbits. When reminded of something he'd rather avoid, he'd reply, "I do not remember the past; I only remember the future," and when asked about his work habits, he says, "When I have to, I work furiously because I am furious that I have to work." And Nouriel Roubini tirelessly cracks one economics joke after the next, such as, "The difference between capitalism and communism is that in capitalism, man exploits man, and in communism it's just the opposite;" "In capitalism, what is mine is mine, and in socialism, what is yours is mine;" and "God created economists to make weathermen look good."

The Lords of Networks and Their Creations

Many of the most successful networkers take the initiative to build big and bold networks. For instance, Steve Schwarzman initiated the Schwarzman Scholars program, which provides scholarships for international students at Tsinghua University in Beijing to help develop their professional networks. Schwarzman has stated that "his protégés would have access to some of the most influential people in the Chinese power structure" and many Davosians—such as Lawrence "Larry" Summers; Harvard historian Niall Ferguson; and Jack Ma, chairman of the Alibaba Group—are involved.[15] Paul Tudor Jones has created a vast and tight network of the world's richest financiers with his enormously successful Robin Hood Foundation. Klaus Schwab has developed the ultimate superhub network with his World Economic Forum. George Soros, who has started many think tanks and charities, knows that the best strategy to achieve access and influence within a network is to initiate its creation.

In China, where personal relationships known as guanxi are traditionally more important than in the West, many international financial firms have embarked on the popular strategy of hiring "princelings", the children of the "Yuan" percent. Buying directly into the networks of the Asian governing and corporate elite is a convenient shortcut to obtaining access to business opportunities. However, this practice isn't without pitfalls. Hiring in exchange for business violates U.S. anti-bribery laws, and many major banks have been implicated in this practice.

Negative Notions on Networking

Over lunch at the Four Seasons restaurant in New York, a French family office principal lauded my networking skills, for he abhorred the very concept of networking and seemed mystified by the enthusiasm with which Americans embraced it. Although he recognized its importance, he didn't want to be bothered with it himself.

Many people have an innate resistance to networking. They are uncomfortable with the concept of transactional relationships because they equate it to using people or, even worse, manipulating them. To them, forming bonds strategically on the basis of potential benefits seems disingenuous, artificial, or even unethical. Favors with strings attached are seen as offensive. According to a study from the University of Toronto, professional networking can create feelings of moral impurity and physical dirtiness. People included in the study felt conflicted when they were motivated by a selfish rather than an altruistic concern. However, those already in power are more comfortable with networking, which reinforces and advances their positions, thereby fortifying existing power structures.[16]

Others are uncomfortable with the act of networking itself, finding it awkward to work the room, approach people, or engage in small talk. Some executives, especially if they have strong technical skills and did not have to rely much on interpersonal skills, see networking as an undignified exercise at best and torture at worst—a nuisance that comes at the expense of spending time with family and friends. Introverts often have a harder time networking because it takes more effort for them to proactively connect with others. They are less prone to self-promotion and view making superficial connections as shallow and a waste of time.

Since the purpose of networking is to cooperate and exchange information, resources, and access for mutual benefit, by definition it must be reciprocal. In his book *Give and Take*, Adam M. Grant examines how the motivation, ability, and opportunity of successful people affects reciprocity. He distinguishes between three kinds of people: "takers," who take more than they give; "givers," who give more than they get; and "matchers," who maintain a balance between giving and getting. According to Grant, research demonstrates that givers rank both among the best and worst performers, whereas takers and matchers range in the middle. Givers tirelessly build deep networks and give to others without expecting anything in return. Givers who rank among the worst performers are too good-natured and get taken advantage of. Successful givers continuously work to create win-win situations for all, but also know when and how to set boundaries. Due to the goodwill built throughout their lives, they have access to support and resources whenever called for. Interestingly, when givers give, it spreads and cascades. People who only take are punished with negative reputational information, especially if they unfairly exploit others.[17] Kindness and generosity are rewarded, if not concurrently with the act of giving then as network capital deposited in the social capital bank.

At the end of the day every human being longs for deep and genuine connections. In today's world, we are all dependent on one another, and creating connections is not about deliberately taking advantage of people, but rather creating opportunities for all. If executed properly, it is mutually beneficial. Self-interested and predatory people repel others and will not get far. Only balanced relationships with real give and take will be sustainable and stand the test of time.

Think Tanks: Network Motherboards

Think tanks are more influential in the financial system than I had initially realized. The term sounds abstract and esoteric, but within think tanks there are real people with real power and real money actively exerting influence. They are seamlessly interlinked with the business, financial, and—perhaps most importantly—political establishment and, therefore, have all-encompassing access. These nonprofit organizations also bring together experts who conduct research, generate ideas, and advocate interests.

Nearly all top financial executives are engaged in think tanks. The Brookings Institution is considered the most influential one, counting the heads of Carlyle and Deutsche Bank as trustees. Another influential think tank is the Council on Foreign Relations, whose board of directors includes former U.S. treasury secretary Robert Rubin, Larry Fink of BlackRock, and Steve Schwarzman of Blackstone. The ones I am personally most familiar with are the Group of Thirty, the Bretton Woods Committee, and the Institute of New Economic Thinking (INET). The Group of Thirty[18] focuses on economic issues, and its board includes the heads of the ECB, the Bank of England, BlackRock, and UBS. The Bretton Woods Committee[19] examines international economic cooperation and counts Larry Summers, George Soros, Klaus Schwab, and many central bank governors on its board. Both the Group of Thirty and the Bretton Woods Committee congregate during the meetings of the IMF, therefore taking advantage of all the power players being in one place.

INET works on reforming economic theories to better serve economies. It was founded by George Soros, and the organization quickly found support from other financiers. Its gatherings are prime examples of executive networking, as they attract a truly mind-blowing assortment of Nobel Prize laureates and otherwise überaccomplished academics, central bankers, and top financial executives.

INET: Connecting the Connected at Bretton Woods

The first INET conference I attended took place in Bretton Woods, in New Hampshire's White Mountains. Together with George Soros and his team, I took a private plane from Teterboro Airport in New Jersey and arrived an hour later at Mount Washington Regional Airport. It was early April, and the majestic Appalachian Mountains were still covered in snow. A minibus picked us up and made a detour to an observation deck to let us take in the imposing, rugged landscape. Although the sun was shining, the cold was paralyzing, so we decided to skip lunch and drive straight to the white, red-roofed Spanish Renaissance–style Mount Washington Hotel. It reminded me of the sort of quintessential American family resort often portrayed in classic Hollywood movies. The hotel has a grand history: In 1944, the United States hosted forty-four countries at the Bretton Woods conference, which established a new global economic architecture, along with the International Monetary Fund and the World Bank. The luxurious interior, with its high chandeliered ceilings, artfully crafted moldings, and grand white wooden columns exuded tradition and comfort.

After settling in, I joined the other guests for a welcome reception at the Conservatory, a rotund hall topped with a grand cupola. I already knew almost everyone, and it felt more like a gathering of friends. The combined brainpower was focused on the fact that financial regulations and policy interventions had not yet caught up to our globalized financial system. The schedule was filled with interesting discussions and world-class speakers. Rob Johnson, the executive director of INET, who had been chief economist of the U.S. Senate Banking Committee and had worked at Soros Fund Management, gave the welcoming speech. The discussions were thoroughly academic and to the financial layperson would probably have seemed hopelessly abstract. Harvard Professor Ken Rogoff and George Soros spoke about the emerging economic and political order, while Columbia University Professor Jeffrey Sachs and Carmen Reinhart of the Peterson Institute discussed postcrisis macroeconomic management. Former U.K. prime minister Gordon Brown, whom I had previously thought to be rather dry, enthralled the audience with an insightful and passionately delivered lunch keynote on global financial issues.

The schedule was packed with sessions beginning in the early morning and stretching into the evening. Dinners started late, and many guests congregated in the bar thereafter. At dinner, one of my favorite speakers, Lord Adair Turner—at the time the head of the U.K. Financial Services Authority—reflected on the economics of happiness. Charles Dallara, head of the IIF, and Nobel laureate Joe Stiglitz illuminated the emerging financial system in Asia. The increasing wealth gap was a prevalent topic throughout the meeting. Other highlights included a discussion with George Soros and former Fed chairman Paul Volcker, and a dinner discussion with former U.S. treasury secretary Larry Summers. It was fascinating to meet these historic, larger-than-life figures, obtain insight into their thinking, and subsequently discuss their views with them in person. Between sessions, people broke away for informal talks in front of crackling fireplaces or in the cozy bar. The event's framework mirrored Davos's: Guests were "locked up" in a faraway, hard-to-reach location and therefore by default forced to engage with each other, creating the perfect environment for executive networking.

* * *

This chapter explained why the superhubs' networks equal their net worth, and how they employ relational capital to achieve the highest return on relationships. There are evolutionary and psychological reasons for the indispensability and irreplaceability of personal interaction in forming profound and robust relationships. Furthermore, executives' mindsets are programmed to connect, and they use their emotional intelligence, charm, and charisma to proactively build networks. Superhubs understand that networking is a vital part of the financial world, view it as creating mutually beneficial opportunities, and invest considerable time and money to expand and strengthen their links. As we'll see in Chapter 7, however, most of the executive networking practiced by superhubs occurs within the exclusive confines of members-only conferences and other private events that exclude all but the elite.

CHAPTER 7

Members Only

The Exclusive Networking Platforms of the Global Super-Elite

A DINNER OF CONSEQUENCE: ATTACK ON THE EURO

When the euro crisis was unfolding in 2010, I orchestrated a hedge fund dinner on behalf of Roubini Global Economics, featuring renowned economist Nouriel Roubini, with whom I worked at the time. We regularly held these events with industry heavyweights such as George Soros, Louis Bacon of Moore Capital, Steve Schwarzman of Blackstone, Michael Novogratz of Fortress Investments, Dan Loeb of Third Point, Eric Mindich of Eton Park Capital Management, and many more. The guests, around fifteen in number, would mingle at a cocktail reception and then enjoy a sit-down dinner, during which Roubini would give his macroeconomic outlook, followed by a stimulating exchange of thoughts. These types of events are customary in the financial world, and I was well versed in organizing them.

I had been involved in hosting biweekly idea luncheons at my former workplace, the broker-dealer Scarsdale Equities. These luncheons have been a tradition dating back to the 1960s.[1] Twice a week, we received a dozen guests in the glorious Rainbow Room on top of the landmark Rockefeller Plaza where our offices were located. The magnificent rotund, high-ceilinged room on the sixty-fifth floor offered panoramic views of

Manhattan's skyline and beyond. Its crystal chandeliers and mirrored decorations reflected the sunlight and drenched the festive tables and golden
chairs in a warm light. The Cipriani family ran the restaurant and catered
the richest and most delicious buffet in the city. Even for spoiled, wealthy
Wall Streeters, this was a treat, and many famous investors endured the
midday commute to discuss investments with peers in the sky. Afterward,
we circulated notes on the discussions amongst our clients.

Now organizing the Roubini dinner, I scrolled through my Rolodex. At
the top of my list was George Soros, who had attended many of my events
in the past. This time, however, to my surprise he scoffed at the suggestion
and rejected my invitation rather fiercely. As it turned out, a *Wall Street
Journal* report about a recent idea dinner, sponsored by the little-known
brokerage firm Monness Crespi Hardt & Co. for about eighteen hedge fund
managers, had triggered a PR disaster with unexpected legal consequences
for its guests.[2] According to the paper, the conversation had focused on the
euro's demise. The reporter suggested that this conversation resulted in
bearish bets on the euro, adding pressure on the European Union to stem
the Greek debt crisis. An unrelated quote from George Soros, who hadn't
even attended, warning that the euro might break apart, and the mention
of hedge fund legend and Lehman bear David Einhorn's presence, seemed
to corroborate the sinister purpose. The inevitable conclusion: A pack of
hedge fund predators colluded to attack the euro and Greece.

The story played right into the public's negative perception of hedge
funds as capitalizing on the misery of others and prompted an inquiry
by the Department of Justice's antitrust division. Some of the hedge fund
managers received notices to save any trading records involving market
bets on the euro for investigation into potential patterns of collusion. In
addition, the European Commission announced that, in light of the Greek
crisis, it would investigate trades in sovereign credit-default swaps, because
hedge funds weren't supposed to profit from the woes of the region's ailing
nations. It would be hard, though, if not impossible, for a few managers to
cause a country's bankruptcy by themselves, because the euro accounts
for over $1 trillion of daily trading in global currency markets.[3] In addi-
tion, an informative, conceptual exchange of opinions regarding currency
trades is hardly illegal.

Eventually, it turned out that the event had been misreported. Contrary to initial claims, the dinner had not taken place in secrecy, but at a public restaurant. The taped conversation—which had lasted 145 minutes and included twenty-three themes—had only focused on the euro for three and a half minutes and only involved three managers. When I asked Soros about the incident, he dryly responded, "Trust me, if I had a great trading idea, the last thing I would want to do is to share it." But considering the undue media attention, vilification, and potential legal ramifications, Soros had temporarily lost his appetite. The dinners eventually picked up again, but managers became even more guarded in their discussions.

Conspiracy Theories: An Explanation for Attempted Explanations

Given the highly exclusive nature of superhub networking platforms—members-only events, conferences, private parties, and charities—it's unsurprising that the financial system often finds itself at the center of conspiracy theories. Generally, these theories emerge because people dislike randomness and uncertainty. When threatening events like the financial crisis occur, they feel a lack of control. It is human nature to devise meaningful patterns to explain the uncertain, unexplainable, and uncontrollable, because it is unsettling to think that our existence is determined by randomness without any discernible purpose. Therefore, in an attempt to create order in this world, we try to match specific events with specific causes. When occurrences are too complex to be understood, we tend to weave narratives and assign blame to a perceived higher power—often exploitative financial masterminds colluding at the expense of the rest of society. This kind of thinking is influenced by confirmation bias, which means seeking support for an existing belief, or hindsight bias, the subsequent fabrication of explanations for something that already took place.

Conspiracy theories are dangerous because at best they dumb down the population and at worst they prevent finding real solutions; such theories deflect the relevant facts and, therefore, avoid a proper analysis. That is not to say that there may never be an occasional—at least attempted—conspiracy, but they are more often the exception than the rule.

WHY NETWORKS NEED
PLATFORMS: CONNECTIVITY

Networks need platforms to form, expand, and strengthen. The financial elite follow a yearly migration pattern, flocking to invitation-only conclaves such as the World Economic Forum in Davos, the International Monetary Fund, the Bilderberg Group, the Aspen Institute, the Allen & Company Sun Valley Conference, and many more. This tribal super circuit has evolved over time, and its members ritualistically attend these "ceremonies" to see and be seen, affirm their status, and receive acknowledgment. Reinforcing a sense of community, these meetings provide a safe cocoon for interaction, yet are unstructured enough to leave room for serendipity, which many powerful executives credit with at least part of their success.[4]

When it comes to power platforms, the magic word is "access"; they have high barriers to entry, and only superhubs get admitted. People must have the requisite degree of status, reputation, and power to be invited. Access can also hinge on associations with certain institutions, groups, and networks. For instance, if a CEO of a multinational corporation loses his position and fails to obtain a comparable one, chances are the WEF will not invite him to Davos anymore. In general, these meetings revolve around exchanging thoughts, sharing experiences, and cultivating relationships. Keynote speeches, panels, cocktail parties, and gala dinners reinforce the bonds of people who naturally gravitate toward each other. Thus, these power-cluster events create the connective tissue of socially cohesive circles of influence. Only superhubs have the "operating manual" on how to gain access and navigate these mechanisms.

THE ANNUAL POWER CIRCUIT:
DISPATCH FROM DAVOS

The World Economic Forum (WEF) in Davos is one of the most famous and effective of these platforms. Kicking off the meeting season in January, it unites the leaders of the financial industry along with those of corporations, governments, and academia. As the participants all belong to various multidimensional interdisciplinary networks—of people, businesses, institutions, and information—the cross-fertilization and disruption of "silo-thinking" is particularly effective. The magic formula of Davos's success is that the village is small, inconvenient to travel to, and hard to navigate. These drawbacks are actually the event's greatest asset as participants are literally forced to network.

Due to the myriad of international media present, the WEF is highly transparent to the public, and individual sessions can now even be viewed live on the Internet. Parts of the discerning public often regard Davos with suspicion because there are only a limited number of tickets available and the application process is extremely competitive. Access cannot be "bought" because criteria other than financial prowess—such as charitable work, academic achievements, or technological innovation—also determine admission considerations. Representatives from not-for-profit sectors as well as young leaders with extraordinary achievements are admitted gratuitously. However, the majority of participants must pay the steep fees, which—unsurprisingly—does not lessen demand. Fees for the most basic yearly WEF membership start at CHF 60,000. For strategic partners, the fees amount to CHF 600,000 and almost all large financial institutions opt for this top membership level. Add to that private jet travel, chauffeured cars, and other ancillary costs, such as hosting parties and dinners, and the tally easily exceeds $1 million.

Strategic partners have substantial influence on the agenda and privileged access to the WEF's most valuable asset: other high-profile attendees, particularly senior policy makers. Most sessions and events are open to all WEF attendees, but the Informal Gatherings of World Economic Leaders (IGWEL), are restricted to the highest-caliber attendees, such as prime ministers; foreign and finance ministers; central bank governors; corporate CEOs; elite academics; and senior policy makers such as the heads of the IMF, European Central Bank, WTO, and OECD. The attendees are well positioned to make the most out of the WEF. As superhubs, they optimize their relationship-building efficiency with the support of highly qualified staff members and generous budgets. Financiers meet their peers to compare notes on the industry and discuss mutual interests such as deregulation, a topic that they can raise directly with regulators and policy makers in attendance. Nowhere else is there a greater density of current and potential clients all congregating in one spot. It is a bankers' and fund managers' paradise. Top investors like George Soros, who need not seek out or cater to clients, capitalize on the opportunity to take the pulse of the market by speaking with heads of state, central bankers, corporate CEOs, and top global leaders in their respective fields.

The hierarchy among participants is visibly displayed on the color-coded badges. Royalty, such as Prince Haakon of Norway, King Abdullah of Jordan, and King Philippe of Belgium, and heads of state, such as Chancellor Merkel and President Putin, range at the top of the pecking order. One member of the WEF foundation board mentioned to me with an eye roll that in their meetings, everyone must rise when Queen Rania enters the room. Dignitaries usually fly in by helicopter and block the roads with their motorcades, but some of them, like Prince Haakon or Prince Andrew, are quite approachable. Tech giants such as Eric Schmidt and Sergey Brin of Google are also considered VVIP because of their "coolness factor." Another visually demonstrative status marker is the WEF car pass, available only to the most financially potent attendees. Limousines carrying the highly coveted license have access to all parts of town, including the Congress Centre. Their lucky passengers are chauffeured right into the garage underneath the conference facility. Even in the rarefied world of Davos, some attendees are more equal than others. Although the environment lends itself to mixing between disciplines and industries, homogeneity often prevails and media, tech, and finance people cluster around one another.

The parties, which are among the most efficient places to network, are also subject to a hierarchical order. The most popular one is the Google party, which boasts several hundred people but without exception only admits registered guests. I have witnessed the CEO of a major U.S. multinational corporation denied access because he was not on the list. He threw a major fit ("Do you know who I am??") and has had a standing invitation ever since. In 2014, instead of the traditional big bash, Google hosted a smaller gathering at the new Intercontinental Hotel with Grammy

Award winner Mary J. Blige. The superexclusive event featured tycoons such as Michael Dell, Richard Branson, and Bank of America CEO Brian Moynihan. The competing McKinsey party, the next-hottest ticket, was still bursting at the seams. The bank, CNBC/*Financial Times*, *Forbes*, and Burda DLD Nightcap receptions range on a similar level. It really comes down to personal preference, although events with no particular barrier to entry are less exclusive. After years of firsthand experience, I must say that most of the parties are overhyped and fairly similar. Especially at the WEF, the same people circulate everywhere, so if you remain at the geographic nucleus, everyone will pass by eventually.

The most exclusive events are the private dinners and ultrasmall parties, although they have the drawback of sticking you with a limited number of people for an inordinate amount of time—time that could perhaps be better spent networking with dozens of people at a reception. The advantage of a dinner is, of course, that people connect more deeply over shared meals and engage in longer conversations that surpass the small talk. Whenever I receive an interesting invitation, I usually accept. At the dinner hosted by Hong Kong tycoon Victor Chu, my tablemates were a Bahraini crown prince and the CEO of BASF. The smallest parties do not have a list at the door, only heavy security, such as the gathering of Elizabeth Murdoch and Matthew Freud at their rustic chalet on top of the Magic Mountain behind the Schatzalp Hotel. The extra effort of taking a cable car up the mountain followed by a ten-minute walk through heavy snow was rewarded with conversations with interesting people such as actress Charlize Theron, whom I would otherwise not have met.

Another encounter that could only be had in Davos took place with Vladimir Putin. A few years ago, the Russian president sent out heavy, cream-colored invitations printed with raised gold ink and decorated with the coat of arms of the Government of the Russian Federation, requesting the pleasure of one's company at an after-dinner reception. I did not have any business in Russia but had not met Putin before, so I attended out of sheer curiosity. The event was a study in status, hierarchy, networks, and the gravitational forces that a superhub possesses. It took place at the banquet hall of the Arabella Sheraton Hotel Seehof. Entering the hotel was like immediately setting foot in Russia. People looked and dressed differently and made no effort to speak English. Usually, the most sophisticated security is "invisible," but here grim-faced bodyguards, who looked like KGB agents right out of central casting, visually relayed very convincingly that it was better not to mess with them. Famed but controversial conductor Valery Gergiev, a close friend of Putin, conducted a small Russian orchestra to great applause. Russian music, Russian caviar, and Russian vodka were all in abundance—but there was only one Putin. As I had never seen before at a cocktail party, guests formed a giant circle around the president, like a membrane encasing its cell, slowly moving with him as he circulated the room. Such a large group, of mostly blue chip CEOs, bowing to the autocratic leader of a country with questionable policies was a curious sight.

I had little patience for this collective fawning and set my foot in Putin's path: "Now it's the lady's turn!" I said. Then I switched to German, which I knew he spoke, to throw him off guard so as to gain extra time to think about what to say next. But rather unexpectedly, he turned the tables on me, immediately responding in nativelike German without blinking an eye. I made a teasing remark on the Russian energy supply for Germany, which at the time was at dispute, but looking into his bare blue eyes, I sensed that we did not necessarily share the same sense of humor. I briefly froze and then swiftly pulled forward a CEO standing slightly behind me and said, "Oh, Dr. Kleinfeld also wanted to speak with you." And with that, *do svidaniya*, I hightailed my way out of there.

Even during the height of the Ukraine crisis in 2015, the resilient Russians, who had been largely shunned by the Western community politically as well as economically, showed up at Davos, seemingly unfazed by the turmoil. Many of their bigwig CEOs were in attendance, as were eight Russian billionaires, and they unabashedly hosted lavish parties just as they had in previous years. Admittedly, the mood was somewhat subdued, and Western CEOs uniformly characterized the situation as awkward. The all-inclusive emperor of networks, Klaus Schwab, true to form, made it a point to specifically and explicitly welcome his Russian friends.

THE GLOBAL FINANCIAL POWER CENTER: THE INTERNATIONAL MONETARY FUND

The International Monetary Fund . . . yawn. Sounds boring, right? Well, it had been a rather bureaucratic and unexciting institution until the financial crisis, which proved to be a turning point—and not just because of its colorful new leader, Dominique Strauss-Kahn. In 1944, 44 countries came together in Bretton Woods, New Hampshire, and set up the IMF and World Bank to establish and monitor a new currency regime. By the time the financial crisis rolled around in 2008, the IMF had grown to 188 member countries.

It has established itself as a platform for international policy makers. Due to its status on the political metalevel, representatively diverse setup, formal yet flexible decision-making process, and combined brainpower, the IMF is uniquely qualified to take a leadership role in coordinating and helping to implement rescue measures. Generally, its meetings are attended by central bank governors, finance ministers, bank CEOs, rating agency executives, executives of policy bodies, and other international institutions, think tanks, and academics.

Washington, D.C.: The Financial Shadow Capital

The IMF hosts two main meetings per year: the Spring Meeting with about 4,000 participants that mostly revolves around policy and the Annual Meetings in the fall with 12,000 attendees. The latter includes private sector representatives, such as bankers and fund managers. In addition, many other institutions organize "shadow conferences." While not officially affiliated with the IMF, they host client conferences thereby taking advantage of the fact that so many important financial sector representatives congregate in one place by holding parallel client conferences. The IMF's 2,500 employees from 150 countries are housed in two huge, nondescript concrete buildings in Washington D.C., near the quaint Georgetown neighborhood.

I attended the IMF meetings for the first time in October 2008, three weeks after the Lehman debacle and at the height of the financial crisis. Over the course of three days, I participated in several meetings at the IMF, the International Institute of Finance, the Group of Thirty, and various other think tanks. I knew very few people and only recognized the most senior ones from the media, such as Dominique Strauss-Kahn, Jean-Claude Trichet, and a few big bank CEOs like Joe Ackermann of Deutsche Bank. Throughout the weekend, I met a couple hundred people, and it was impossible to remember all of them. Often I was unfamiliar with the institutions they worked for and had no concept of how different entities were interlinked. It has taken me several years to become sufficiently acquainted with these vast IMF-related networks, learn the names of their members, and grasp the myriad institutional interconnections. It is like assembling a complicated puzzle consisting of countless unfamiliar pieces—the organizations, the individuals comprising them, and their respective networks—and fitting them together takes time to figure out.

The financial system is complex and can only really be fully understood, if at all, in its entirety. Because it is impossible for laypeople to know all the parts of this network, it is hard for them to get a true grasp on it. It also makes it difficult to explain because the theory is so abstract and dry. The resulting opaqueness of the system has provided ample fodder for conspiracy theories. However, in following the behind-the-scenes discussions of policy makers, I was disabused of any notion that they were using their superior knowledge to execute a master plan. In the wake of the financial system's collapse, I was perplexed at how little perspective and control over the system they had. Quite to the contrary, they seemed disconcertingly panicked and overwhelmed.

IMF Meetings in Istanbul: Dancing on the Titanic

The IMF and related meetings can be dull and the mood somber, but they are often hosted in magnificent locations with no expenses spared.

For two years in a row, the meetings take place in Washington, D.C., before rotating to an international location. Remote locations entail cumbersome and time-consuming travel, and in that respect, these meetings are inefficient. But this inefficiency provides them with the ultimate efficiency: Because participants invest so much effort into joining these gatherings, they tend to focus more seriously on them. People share experiences that bind them—whether it's a tediously long plane ride or getting lost in an unknown city. Over time, these bonds grow stronger and, in many cases, mere business relationships evolve into friendships.

In October 2009, when the crisis was in full force and many banks' survival was in question, the meetings occurred in Istanbul. In spite of the dire economic situation, financial institutions had taken up pricey head-quarters at the most exclusive hotels, including the magnificent Çırağan Palace located on the scenic shores of the Bosporus. Built in the 1800s as an Ottoman palace, it looks like something out of *The Arabian Nights*. Its grand architecture and baroque interior design feature marble columns, intricate marquetry, and heavy gold furniture. The world's financial elite arrived on the adjacent helicopter landing pad and gathered in elegant sun-drenched meeting rooms and on beautiful, panoramic terraces. It was surreal to see the same players from all over the globe regularly reappearing in formation at the same time in different parts of the world.

Many attendees discussed whether such expenses were appropriate in view of the fragile financial system and the fact that many of the splurging banks might need taxpayer support. However, reality had not quite caught up with many bankers, who still seemed frozen in the past. Bookings had been made far in advance, there was only a limited number of choices regarding accommodations, and bankers felt pressured to impress their clients and maintain appearances. All the banks were in the same predicament, and it was inconceivable for any of them to lead by example and open up shop in a low-rent location. Besides, any worries of an impending collapse of the system and possibly of one's own institution were much easier to bear in splendid surroundings with champagne and caviar.

The meetings wove together top politicians, central bank governors, bank CEOs, and fund managers. Prime Minister Erdogan (now president) keynoted at the gala of the International Institute of Finance in the grand ballroom of the Çırağan Palace. The event was so formal, festive, and glamorous that it felt more like a society ball than a dinner of bankers. Turkish Central Bank Governor Durmuş Yılmaz and Deputy Prime

Minister and Minister of State Ali Babacan circulated nonstop between events, meetings, and receptions all over town. One of the most breathtaking receptions was hosted by Commerzbank at the truly spectacular Esma Sultan Palace. The antique three-story waterfront mansion had been tastefully restored, its ambiance further enhanced with elaborate lighting. Everyone who was anyone was in attendance, even though the palace was located in an old, narrow part of the city that required a time-consuming commute. Commerzbank pulled out all the stops and spoiled its guests with haute cuisine and fine wines.

The Deutsche Bank reception featured the highest concentration of prestigious guests, which was at least partially due to CEO Joe Ackermann's clout. Among the guests were Turkish businessman Kahraman Sadıkoğlu, who invited Ackermann; Caio Koch-Weser, vice chairman of Deutsche Bank; Axel Weber, at the time president of the Bundesbank; their wives; and a few other guests—including lucky me—onto Ataturk's yacht, the *Savarona*. We received a private tour of one of the largest yachts in the world, which Sadıkoğlu had paid to restore, and discussed the state of finance while the men smoked cigars and one of the guests played the piano.

I was exhausted, but it was impossible to escape the gathering as the only way to reach the shore was by way of a dinghy. So another long evening concluded at three o'clock in the morning, but often such unique private gatherings forge tighter personal bonds. Eventually the overstimulation of these conferences causes mental exhaustion. I usually have what I call a "conference curve." On the first day, I am a bit shy and still busy absorbing impressions. On the second and third days, I surge to top form. And on the fourth day, I generally start to feel fatigue.

POWER SUMMIT: THE
BILDERBERG CONFERENCE

Perhaps the most exclusive gathering of the world elite is the Bilderberg conference. It was founded in 1954 to foster transatlantic dialogue and named after its first meeting place, the Hotel De Bilderberg in the Netherlands. The three-day event is strictly by invitation only, and about 150 of the world's most powerful people attend, among them many participants of the financial sector. Heads of state mingle with diplomats, generals, CEOs of blue chip companies, policy makers, aristocrats, thought leaders, and journalists. Past attendees include central bankers such as Mario Draghi and Ben Bernanke; finance ministers George Osborne, Jeroen Dijsselbloem, Hank Paulson, Tim Geithner, Larry Summers, and Robert Rubin; bank executives such as Lloyd Blankfein and Robert Zoellick of Goldman Sachs, Paul Achleitner of Deutsche Bank, and Ana Botín of Banco Santander; and big investors such as Philipp Hildebrand of Black-Rock, Peter Thiel of Thiel Capital, Ken Griffin of Citadel, Roger Altman of Evercore, and Henry Kravis and General David Petraeus of KKR.

The program remains undisclosed, and discussions are subject to the Chatham House Rule,[5] according to which participants may use the information received, but are prohibited from revealing the speaker's identity and affiliation, or that of any other participant for that matter. Attendees may neither bring partners nor personal assistants, and security detail is kept at a distance. Since participants do not attend the private meetings in their official capacity, they are able to interact more informally, affording them the luxury to brainstorm and speak freely. Constantly in the public eye, they usually must be vigilant of what they say, because their every utterance is scrutinized and can move markets. At Bilderberg, they can interact with their peers in a relaxed atmosphere and get a better sense of geoeconomic issues, impending developments, and business opportunities. I have never attended but know many people who have. Participants take the confidentiality surprisingly seriously, although most of them do drop hints here and there, adding pieces to the puzzle. The consensus seems to be that the Bilderberg meetings are far less exciting than commonly supposed, as nothing politically actionable and implementable is decided.

Yet secrecy evokes suspicion, and some outsiders believe Bilderberg to be a global corporate-controlled shadow government, bent on engineering the fate of humanity. While this is a bit far-fetched considering the varying participants and interests, the direct interaction of such powerful people behind closed doors without any involvement of civil society does pose a problem, because they are privy to the most valuable opportunities and can align their interests without any accountability. However, the most

dangerous collusions typically happen in plain sight, especially in the form
of lobbying. After all, even if they had nefarious intentions, there is no
need for Bilderberg participants to travel to faraway locations when they
could communicate in private over the phone. Since they all know each
other, they can have the same meetings and conversations in their favorite
three-star restaurants, on their yachts, and on weekend retreats, without
global media scrutiny. Possibly the greatest attraction for participants is
the public manifestation of their elite status.

STEALTH POWER: FAMILY
OFFICE GATHERINGS

The grounds of the Swiss Re Centre in Rüschlikon, Switzerland, are nothing short of spectacular. They comprise an expansive compound with
beautifully designed gardens overlooking Lake Zürich and the Alps. The
modernist conference center's clean architecture is the perfect backdrop
for its eclectic interior design and vast art collection. Across the garden,
an allée of lime trees leads up to the neobaroque Bodmer mansion, which
was built by a Swiss industrialist in the 1920s.

Such was the scene of one of the family office gatherings that I regularly attended. Bodyguards clad in black pants and turtlenecks protected
the family principals and their top executives, who represented a net worth
of about $150 billion under one roof. Throughout my career, I had only
dealt with institutional investors, but after starting my own company, I
stumbled into the private wealth space. Because I knew many ultra-high-
net-worth individuals globally, the family office of an IT billionaire asked
me to assist in building a global nonprofit platform for family offices,
where they could meet to exchange views and cooperate without the
involvement of financial intermediaries, such as bankers or other service
providers like attorneys and tax advisers. Such gatherings are among the
most exclusive and private, because these families and their representatives only open their ranks if you are one of them.

Family offices are the investment management companies of wealthy
families. Banks, financial firms, and multifamily offices typically manage

the assets of families worth up to $500 million. For families worth more than $500 million in liquid assets, having their own investment firms is expedient, because it affords them control, privacy, and cost efficiencies. The concept of a family office has evolved over a long time. Business tycoon John D. Rockefeller set up his family office in the nineteenth century. Often families have come into great wealth by building enormously successful companies, sometimes over the span of several generations. Among them are old industrial dynasties, nouveau industrialists, or tech billionaires. Some families consist of fewer than a dozen members, while others encompass hundreds. The priority of family offices is wealth preservation.

According to a saying, a fortune lasts for three generations: The first one makes it, the second one lives on it, and the third one squanders it. Most family principals are not financial titans in the classic sense because they have not made their money in the financial services industry. However, the wealth accumulated from building large, successful companies gives them enormous economic power. With their investments, they actively influence the international economic and financial landscape. In 2016 there were 1,810 billionaires in the world—with an aggregate net worth of $6.5 trillion—540 of which are in the U.S., among them financiers such as George Soros, Stanley Druckenmiller, Steve Cohen, Steve Schwarzman, and Leon Black.[6] Many of them have their own family offices. Family office principals, who typically are hardworking and well grounded, above all treasure privacy. They institute high barriers to entry, often employing gatekeepers to filter and vet requests, because their riches make them perpetual targets for people who want something from them.

As important job creators, taxpayers, and philanthropic supporters, family offices are powerful and influential forces in their communities. Whenever we invited public officials to a family office gathering, they would happily attend.

A family office platform facilitates networking so that families can benefit from each other's experiences, coinvest, and leverage buying power. A Saudi Arabian family in the oil business might share insights on commodity prices, while a German industrialist provides intelligence on potential acquisition targets in the highly coveted German Mittelstand companies. A British billionaire can invite other families to participate in his socially responsible infrastructure investments, while an Indian entrepreneur might look for coinvestors in the telecom sector. The point is to obtain original information directly from the source rather than secondary, diluted information from a third party with incongruent interests. Family offices are another example of how people with similar characteristics flock to each other and maximize their power. They have better access to opportunities and the means to capitalize on them, which self-perpetuates their network power.

FEEDING OFF POWER: POWER LUNCHES

In addition to structured events such as Davos and the IMF meetings, most superhubs regularly maintain their personal networks at power-player restaurants, one of which until mid-2016 had been the überexclusive Four Seasons restaurant in New York. It was located in the Seagram Building on Park Avenue in Midtown Manhattan, a building widely regarded as a modernist architectural masterpiece. The restaurant consisted of two dining rooms—the Pool Room and the Grill Room—which were connected by a corridor featuring the largest Picasso canvas in the United States, a stage curtain from the 1919 French production of the ballet *Le Tricorne*. The magnificent Pool Room was centered around a white Carrara marble pool and framed by large seasonal plants: palm trees in the summer, Japanese maples in the fall, birches in the winter, and blossoming cherry trees in spring. Both rooms were decorated with bronze-colored aluminum mesh chain curtains, which absorbed the subtle lighting as soaring twenty-foot-high ceilings gave the prolific modernist artworks adequate breathing room.

For lunch there was only one option: the Grill Room. In contrast to many other restaurants in New York City, where carrying on a conversation is a challenge due to the high decibel level, the dignified Grill Room's spaciousness seemed to absorb noise and ensure discreetness. The Four Seasons' history and character were palpable, and it commanded a loyal following among the world's elite. Henry Kissinger was a regular for decades, as were Steve Schwarzman, Pete Peterson, Larry Fink, and

Paul Volcker, among many others. Virtually every tycoon mentioned in this book passed through its doors. For me, every luncheon was a memorable experience—not only because I always got Kissinger's table in his absence—but because the surreal power concentration always seemed to trigger something meaningful to happen: an unexpected encounter, an introduction, an invitation, an opportunity, the beginning of a dialogue, or the resuscitation of a dormant connection.

Unfortunately, the Four Seasons eventually became the stage of its own demise. The historic and pedigreed restaurant saw its final act, its Picasso curtain removed and the lights turned off. The Seagram Building's German-born owner and New York social scene staple, Aby Rosen, put the gun to Four Seasons tenant Julian Niccolini's head to either pay a significantly higher lease or move out. As if this wasn't bad enough, the culinary temple then became the scene of an unappetizing scandal in which Niccolini was accused of sexual assault. In a deal with prosecutors, he pleaded guilty to misdemeanor assault to resolve the allegation.[7] Rosen will establish a new, more modern place at the old locale, and Niccolini will open his new Four Seasons on Park Avenue a few blocks down, with many of his loyal patrons likely in tow. It may be the end of the Four Seasons as we now know it, but it certainly won't be the end of the power lunch.

POWER WORKOUT: NETWORKING, WORKING, AND WORKING OUT

Executives don't just network over meals. They also belong to highly exclusive fitness clubs, such as Sitaras Fitness, where they can easily conduct business during a workout. From the outside, Sitaras Fitness is inconspicuous, without any nameplate to give away its presence. Yet dark limousines regularly pull up to the exclusive high-rise in Midtown Manhattan across from the futuristic Bloomberg Tower. As chauffeurs open the doors, investment legends such as George Soros, Jack Welch, James D. Robinson III, Paul Volcker, and numerous others emerge, clad in workout gear. Sitaras may have the highest concentration of financial top executives of any gym in the city. So exclusive is its clientele that it made the *New York Times*, the *Financial Times*, and various other international media.[8,9] Especially in

America, where athleticism is directly correlated with presumed vitality, dynamism, and a sharp mind, there is no alternative to working out—no matter how busy, athletically challenged, or age-advanced the executive. Fitness is a status symbol.

Founded by John Sitaras, a trainer and former bodybuilder, the private club accepts new members only by referral and after thorough background checks. Sitaras has perfected the art of the gym with his proprietary analysis program and individualized, personally administered exercise routines. Warm and personable, he has a natural gift of connecting with powerful personalities. With vision and unfailing instinct, he built relationships with a top clientele that doubles as his investors and advisers. In New York's ultracompetitive environment, Sitaras differentiates himself by catering to a niche market that comprises some of the most demanding and difficult characters on the street. The superhubs enjoy the privacy and luxury, but most of all the privilege of each other's company without being judged or bothered. In a city of more than 8 million people and a myriad of choices, these captains of industry are pulled into a force field of homogeneity where they feel comfortable and relaxed. As an ancillary benefit, they can casually discuss business and make deals while settling into the comfortable lounge chairs on the terrace, a lush oasis in the midst of the Midtown concrete desert. Word has it that major deals have originated there.

Although I am one of only a few women at Sitaras, just as on Wall Street, I feel comfortable there because of its private atmosphere and spacious duplex facilities. Of course, doing leg presses while Paul Volcker stretches next to you can be slightly awkward, but it makes for good banter next time you are seated next to each other at a formal dinner. For people who are on duty 24/7, there is no separation between networking, working, and working out.

"SUPERHUB-NOBBING": PRIVATE PARTIES

George Soros's Spanish Renaissance–style estate, El Mirador is located off the billionaire rows on Old Town Road in Southampton. The legendary investor spends the months of July and August there, with occasional trips to the city if need be. To some people, such mansions are visual manifestations of their success, others simply enjoy their beauty and luxury, but almost all use their homes as networking platforms where they entertain guests. The same applies to George Soros, who has built unbelievably intricate networks around the world. Every weekend he hosts a scheduled set of guests at El Mirador, usually an eclectic mix, which makes his social gatherings so interesting. If a group is too homogeneous, the conversation might lack stimulation, but if people are too different, it might lack a spark. The best combination is a mix of people who are already acquainted with a few new people. If temperaments complement one another, the conversation usually flows: Talkers are placed next to listeners, introverts mixed with extroverts, and funny people with more serious ones. Soros always puts together the right mix and also enjoys personally designing the seating chart. Artists, intellectuals, and financiers exchange views, argue, and joke in spirited conversations.

Guests are accommodated in comfortable quarters inside the main house or in the guesthouse complex, which is located in the beautiful garden amidst old trees, colorful flowerbeds, a pool, and a tennis court. The property is a three-minute walk from the beach, which Soros frequents after his tennis matches. The schedule is informal without a protocol, and guests are at liberty to spend their time as they please with the staff at their disposal. They can enjoy breakfast at their convenience and lunch in the vast gardens. The only formal events are the dinners. The evenings typically begin with cocktails on the front porch, which is a good time to mingle and engage with new acquaintances. After about an hour when the sun begins to set, the guests move on to the formal dining room, where stimulating discussions ensue. Soros's guests are often dear friends and leaders in their respective fields, and all have something interesting to contribute. The exchange of dialogue with groups of highly diverse people is one way in which Soros stays on top of issues. Sometimes he tosses out ideas for discussion and receives feedback he might not have previously considered.

For the rest of the year and absent traveling, Soros spends his weekends in the country at his stately yet homey Bedford estate, which sits on a hilltop nestled in sweeping lush gardens with breathtaking views of the surrounding countryside. The house has a slew of guestrooms, each designed according to a different theme. He enjoys the company of serious thinkers, more often than not people with intellectual rather than material wealth. Because Soros is a superhub, over the years his friends have become one another's friends. The diversity of people close to him reflects his diverse networks all over the world. Hosting private parties on their estates provides superhubs with yet another perfect networking platform to expand and strengthen their top positions.

THE HIGHER PURPOSE OF NETWORKING: THE CHARITY CIRCUIT

The financial elite have many opportunities to come together and network, but few events are a bigger draw than charities. Throughout the year, financiers rub elbows at various charity events all over the world. The most significant philanthropic galas—hosted by and for the elite—still take place in New York. Due to comparatively low taxes and a relatively weak social system, Americans traditionally have a more generous giving culture. Anglo-Saxon financiers are ideally positioned to optimize the efficiency of philanthropy by applying their financial and business savvy, a strategy that Matthew Bishop and Michael Green have coined "philanthrocapitalism."[10] For the wealthy, it is a social must to commit and give to a cause. This was how Bill Gates reeled in Warren Buffett and a few dozen other billionaires to join him in the "Giving Pledge" and donate at least half of their fortune to charitable causes. Many of them sit on the same boards of hospitals, museums, opera houses, ballet companies, and educational institutions, where they use their friendships and connections to attract donors and raise top dollars. The galas they host combine serious causes with lighthearted entertainment—replete with star wattage, glamour, and media exposure.

Since support is expected to be reciprocated, charitable contributions have skyrocketed. Despite falling significantly during the financial crisis, they have since recovered. Critics object that the engagement of billionaires in highly publicized charities is a self-celebratory endeavor. While it is true that philanthropy enhances their image, status, and probably happiness, self-serving motives cannot detract from charity's effects, and in the end the benefits far outweigh any drawbacks.

Helicopters, motorcades, and sirens are the hallmarks of the annual Clinton Global Initiative gathering in New York, which the *Economist* dubbed the "Philanthropy Oscars."[11] During the third week in September the city is bustling with energy and feels like the center of the universe. The event coincides with the United Nations General Assembly, for which representatives of 193 member states concurrently descend upon the city—including numerous heads of state, who typically stay in luxurious Midtown hotels. New York goes into virtual lockdown, with many streets blocked off for dignitaries and their police protection. Countless high-profile organizers take advantage of the presence of world leaders, CEOs, philanthropists, and Nobel Prize laureates and host shadow events.

The Clinton Global Initiative established itself a decade ago with much fanfare and, due to President Clinton's convening power, quickly rose to unprecedented success in terms of the caliber of donors and the money raised. He is a superhub extraordinaire, because of his and Hillary's positions and simply because he is so unbelievably popular that the world elite fawn over him. The mood is celebratory, and attendees network at informal events such as cocktail parties and private dinners.

Another fund-raiser that demonstrates how skillfully Wall Street uses superhub networks to optimize fund-raising is Mike Milken's charity event for prostate cancer in the Hamptons. The now-reformed philanthropist was diagnosed with stage III prostate cancer after his release from prison, where he had been serving time for securities fraud. He fought the disease with the same tenacity and commitment with which he once conquered the bond market, made a full recovery, and to this day has remained cancer-free. Dedicated to numerous philanthropic causes, he mobilized his enormous network of financiers and influencers. Every year, he organizes a fabulous party at the favorite summer spot of the wealthy: the Hamptons, where all his billionaire friends like Leon Black, Steve Schwarzman, John Paulson, and Richard LeFrak make sizeable donations, and receive public recognition.

* * *

In Chapter 7, we visited the exclusive, international, invitation-only platforms of the financial elite and got a better sense of what life in the executive suite is like. While prestigious meetings and events seem glamorous to those of us on the outside looking in, the reality is that these tycoons are always working. To maintain their network positions and increase their power, they must regularly travel to cultivate existing relationships and develop new ones. Being a superhub requires sacrifices and comes at a cost to one's physical and mental health, family, and quality of life. Chapter 8 will explore some of the negative aspects of belonging to the members-only financial elite.

CHAPTER 8

Opportunity Costs

The Downside of the Upside

MISSING OUT ON MEMORABLE MOMENTS

Paris is one of my favorite places, so I was delighted to receive an invitation to my friend Peixin Dallara's birthday party in the city of lights. Peixin and her husband, Charles, are classic "work friends." I had met Charles at one of my first IMF meetings and later been introduced to Peixin, a private equity professional, and over the years we have become friends. Charles had for two decades been head of the International Institute of Finance (IIF), yet another unexciting-sounding organization that is in fact incredibly powerful and important. The IIF is a global association of banks and other financial institutions that closely engages with policy makers to advocate for favorable policies. It also provides a platform for bank executives to meet with one another as well as with government officials and corporate CEOs. Charles was predestined for the job: A former high-ranking treasury and IMF official, he was immensely well connected across the entire spectrum of the financial industry and particularly so in the political arena. Likeable and articulate, he was well-connected across constituencies.

Together with Joe Ackermann, then CEO of Deutsche Bank, and Bill Rhodes, at the time senior vice chairman at Citigroup, Charles grew the IIF into the most powerful bank lobbying organization in the world.

Over the years, it has become an integral part of the financial landscape and is represented at many internationally important meetings. As an advocate, he mostly worked behind the scenes, but things changed dramatically during the European sovereign debt crisis, when he represented the banks in the biggest sovereign debt restructuring in history.[1] So much was at stake, including the potential breakup of the eurozone, and he was thrown into the center of the negotiations and the limelight that came with it.

At the time of Peixin's birthday, Charles was stuck in endlessly tedious talks in Athens as chief negotiator for the banks, discussing which creditors would bear what losses in order to prevent an imminent default of Greece. Private creditors had to agree to some participation along with the eurogroup; otherwise a bailout would not have been politically feasible. Charles had always been a passionately committed workaholic, but now Peixin acknowledged, with a sigh, that he was literally on the road nonstop. Such was the case on the weekend of her long-awaited fabulous birthday party. It was planned to take place at the legendary Ritz Hotel at the historic Place Vendôme, a stone's throw away from the Élysée Palace and the Louvre. The Ritz's majestic marble walls had borne witness to numerous historic events and hosted royalty, heads of state, billionaires, and captains of industry. With its gilded furniture, heavy draperies, and elaborate artwork, the hotel's Parisian elegance and old-world flair were reminiscent of times long past.

The night before the big bash, I met with Peixin at the beautiful hotel bar. As Charles had been consumed by the European debt crisis in the months preceding, he and his family had made many personal sacrifices that could not be replaced with money. She had always been understanding of Charles's workload, but now she expressed concern. He had been scheduled to fly in that afternoon, but with impeccable timing, just that day the negotiations reached a dramatic high point, forcing him to stay in Athens. He had spared no effort or expense to thoughtfully organize his wife's special celebration, and friends were flying in from all over the world. Yet below the surface of this sweeping glamour and luxury lurked potential disappointment and misery if the most important person in Peixin's life—her husband—was unable to attend. Although Peixin had already mentally prepared herself for the possibility, it was inconceivable that Charles would fail to make it. In the end, he flew in last-minute on Saturday afternoon, although he continued the negotiations via phone nonstop from their suite and it was not entirely clear if he'd have time to attend the dinner. Eventually he did, and if he was completely stressed, he did not let it show. Both Peixin and Charles graciously hosted their friends, of which many were financial superhubs. Referring to the incident, the press reported that "Charles Dallara left Greece for a long-standing engagement in Paris" and "negotiations will continue over the phone."[2] It was a wonderful evening and the Greece situation was shortly thereafter brought to a successful, if temporary, conclusion.

This story illustrates how being a superhub can take a toll on family. While in this particular situation, Charles was thankfully able to attend his wife's important birthday celebration, the uncertainty still caused significant stress. And there are many more times when a superhub is not so lucky and misses out on meaningful moments with family and friends. For a superhub, work is always the priority, and this can have serious ramifications on their physical and emotional well-being.

STRESS TEST: WHEN BEING A SUPERHUB IS NOT SO SUPER

As glamorous as it appears from the outside, being a superhub comes at a price. Top finance executives live in a rarefied and insular world rich in prestige, privileges, and pecuniary rewards. However, those rewards require sacrifices and trade-offs, and the negative risks are dizzyingly high. The tough culture behind the sparkly facade of financial firms manifests itself in phrases popular in the financial world such as, "You are only as good as your last deal," "What have you done for me lately?" and "You eat what you kill." Recruiters give promising young professionals the star treatment and seduce them with prestigious and high-salaried job offers. Initially, the stimulating environment is invigorating, and the strong culture and camaraderie provide a sense of community, purpose, and importance. However, the unpredictability of staying on call 24/7—without any control or ability to set boundaries—eventually takes a toll. The world of finance is a way of life, an all-or-nothing culture where either you're in or you're out; either you play the game or you sit on the sidelines. In strict hierarchical structures with military-style discipline, everyone must pay their dues, often at the expense of personal lives and relationships.

Many executives, being workaholics and travelholics, take refuge in pills and stimulants to compensate for perpetual sleep deprivation. One private equity billionaire, who constantly circles the globe in his private jet, told me that he couldn't survive without sleeping pills. The financial crisis only exacerbated these pressures. Ten percent of Wall Street jobs were cut, yet the workload essentially remains the same. Meanwhile, the zeitgeist has changed, and previously customary business practices are now considered unethical or illegal. Competition for clients and deals has become ever more cutthroat, while increased regulatory scrutiny and new bureaucratic compliance rules add a tedious and burdensome layer to the workload. Many people do not last long past the age of forty, and many break into the profession only to make as much money as possible before getting out as soon as possible. The average duration of an investment banker's job is seven to nine years.[3]

I have personally witnessed the glorification of being overworked and underslept, the celebration of exhaustion and deification of those who could boast the most all-nighters. In this testosterone-dominated, "my bonus is bigger than yours" culture, the ability to live on virtually no sleep is equated with being a high performer. When bankers say "nine to five," they don't typically mean five in the afternoon, but five o'clock the next morning. One of the most annoying features of this environment is "face time": staying at work even if there is nothing to do, simply for the sake of demonstrating your undying loyalty to the organization. Due to competitive pressures, no one wants to be the first one to leave, so everyone stays late trying to look busy. Then there is the "magic roundabout": A town car takes you home and waits with engine running while you shower and change, only to take you directly back to work.

This lifestyle may be cool and fun when you are young, but as you get older and more senior, it takes a physical and psychological toll. Executives who mastered the obstacle course on their way to the top are either equipped with personalities conducive to this environment or toughened up along the way. In this highly Darwinian profession, executives must always be at the top of their game to generate profits and fend off competitors. As they say, *it's lonely at the top*. There are only a handful of top executive jobs—and legions of ambitious executives who want them.

Married to Their Jobs: Work-Family Life Imbalance

The downside not only applys to the executives but also extends to their families. Superhubs are largely absent. When in town, they typically work late hours and entertain clients; the rest of the time they travel, and when they come home they are exhausted, especially if they don't have "travel talent" and cannot sleep on planes. Global interconnections across time zones, combined with modern communication devices, require round-the-clock availability, and I have heard countless stories of interrupted vacations, weekends spent on conference calls, and missed family celebrations. Yet, the divorce rate among superhubs is decidedly lower than among the general population. Warren Buffett remained married to his first wife for more than fifty years, Ray Dalio has been married for forty years, and Jamie Dimon has been with his wife for more than thirty years. This could be due to making the best out of the little time available, having fewer opportunities to argue, or tacit arrangements.

Moreover, the enormous costs of a divorce and the subsequent loss of privacy are definite deterrents. During former General Electric CEO Jack Welch's second divorce, his continued receipt of generous company benefits surfaced, which led to an SEC inquiry. As a result, Welch voluntarily gave up his $2.5 million yearly pension. The low divorce rate makes shareholders happy, as divorce can have a negative impact on performance. Depending on the financial arrangements, a CEO might lose a portion of his ownership stake in the company, thereby lessening his influence. In addition, a divorce can be an enormous distraction, negatively impacting the CEO's productivity, concentration, and energy level. It can also influence his attitude toward risk.[4]

Not only spouses are affected by a superhub's prominence but also—perhaps even worse—the children. For Catherine, the daughter of longtime CEO of Deutsche Bank Josef Ackermann, it had dramatic consequences. The terrorist group RAF had assassinated her father's predecessor, Alfred Herrhausen, with a car bomb, and one of her contemporaries—the young scion of the Metzler banking dynasty, Jakob von Metzler—had been kidnapped and killed. She also was present when her father received a letter bomb from Italian anarchists. As a result of growing up in fear of such threats, isolated and with bodyguards as her constant companions, she developed severe panic attacks, which she kept secret from her father for a long time. By her own account, he was there for her when she needed him, but during her adolescence he had largely been absent.[5]

Media Madness: Living Under a Microscope

Constant media scrutiny can also take a toll, especially when the stakes are so high. At a time where virtually every move is documented, the private lives of executives have become quasi-transparent. Nothing is off-limits, and family is often dragged in. Mathias Döpfner, CEO of Axel Springer and publisher of *Bild*, the sixth-best-selling daily tabloid worldwide, tidily summed up the laws of tabloidism when he stated that "whoever takes the elevator up with *Bild* will also take the elevator down with it."[6] The same applies to U.S. tabloids. No sooner had Lloyd Blankfein, CEO of Goldman Sachs, admonished his troops to avoid undue displays of wealth than the *New York Post*—a tabloid that everyone disses yet devours—ran a story about his wife allegedly throwing a fit at a charity event in the Hamptons. Supposedly, she had caused a huge scene, screaming that she would not wait in line with people who had paid less money than she had. Exaggerated or not, the report was presumably utterly embarrassing for the parties concerned.[7] In an era of full transparency, effective self-censoring is indispensable, a fact that Mr. Blankfein seemed to have experienced only three months later: Asked by the *Times of London* about bankers' high bonuses and remuneration, he stated that he was simply a banker "doing God's work."[8] Although he later claimed to have been joking, the blowback was significant.

When Jamie Dimon's 2014 Christmas card leaked, it caused a slew of negative media feedback. It pictured him and his family playing tennis inside their luxurious Fifth Avenue apartment. The shoot's creative director likely found this presentation dynamic and original, but the nonchalant and somewhat nonsensical presentation of opulence coupled with furniture-unfriendly tennis was portrayed by the press as decadent and inappropriate.

Sometimes relatives launch themselves into the public spotlight, much to the chagrin of superhubs. After Bob Diamond, CEO of Barclays, was ousted over the Libor scandal and heavily criticized, Diamond's feisty daughter showed her support by tweeting "George Osborne and Ed Miliband you can go ahead and #HMD," an abbreviation that refers to a certain male body part.[9] Actually, anything that the "Lucky Sperm Club"— a term coined by Warren Buffett—does seems to be of interest to the public. Popular media is always keen to report on the fabulous lives of Wall Street's hottest offspring. Having a famous parent certainly has its perks, but it also means operating under a magnifying glass. When Jamie Dimon's daughter, a journalist, devoted an article to the delicate topic of the lengths women take to hide "doing their business" at work, it made headlines.[10]

Super-Sick: Paying the Ultimate Price

The qualities that drive superhubs to the top—such as high motivation and resilience—can also be their downfall. Top executives are perfectionists who deem themselves irreplaceable and fear that showing vulnerability will be interpreted as weakness. In a competitive environment wrought with distrust and suspicion, they must keep up appearances. Hence, even during personal crises, they typically remain highly functional and hide their feelings of fear, anguish, and exhaustion. If enough stress builds up, it can morph into depression—or worse.

Especially during and in the aftermath of the financial crisis, many chief executives suffered from burnout, which in most cases was buried and treated with a regimen of prescription drugs, including antidepressants. The CEO of Lloyds, António Horta Osório, was the only high-profile case of a top executive admitting to exhaustion. After not even a year on the job, for which he received an annual compensation package of GBP 8.3 million and a sign-on bonus of shares worth GBP 4 million, he took immediate sick leave due to stress-related fatigue. Shortly before, Osório had mentioned during an interview that he had been working 24/7, and word on the street was that he had been struggling with the media scrutiny adding to the pressures. A couple of months later he returned to his job.

Many top financial professionals have been diagnosed with serious illnesses like cancer. Paul Calello, the CEO of Credit Suisse's investment bank and a genuinely nice guy, was diagnosed with cancer in 2009 in the midst of the financial crisis. He was forty-eight years old, athletic, married , and a father of four. Calello went from executive suite to cancer ward, where he made friends who would be gone a couple of days later. It was brutal. He mentioned that he thought the stress of the financial crisis might have triggered the disease.

Top financiers tend to equate professional with personal failure, and in the most extreme cases, they see no other way out of the psychological quicksand than ending their lives. The number of suicides of top bankers in the aftermath of the financial crisis has been staggering. Statistically, a banker has a 39 percent higher likelihood of killing himself than the workforce as a whole.[11]

The suicide of Pierre Wauthier, CFO of Zürich Insurance Group became a media spectacle, because in his suicide note, he held Joe Ackermann—then chairman of Zürich insurance—directly and personally responsible. He accused Ackermann of putting him under extreme pressure with his tough management style. Ackermann categorically rejected those claims, but nevertheless resigned the next day. The unfortunate incident remained somewhat puzzling, as there had been no warning signs. An official investigation by an outside law firm cleared Ackermann, finding no indication that the finance chief was subjected to undue or inappropriate pressure.

Who knows how many swashbuckling and seemingly invincible top executives are secretly suffering in misery? Of course they could break free from their self-imposed incarceration at any time, but more often than not they are unable to escape from the prison of their personalities.

Although they would likely have a wealth of opportunities upon leaving their posts, for many, the potential loss of status, recognition, and power is even more unbearable than the strains of the most arduous position. It's a highly addictive status game, and CEOs in golden handcuffs are entirely consumed by their efforts to stay at the top.

Clash of the Titans: Close Combat and Coups d'État

CEOs need to be great judges of character to sort out trustworthy confidantes, because virtually everyone they deal with is self-interested. There are many examples of coups d'état at the highest levels of large financial institutions.

The CEO of Citigroup, Vikram Pandit, was so ruthlessly ousted in a boardroom coup that it shocked Wall Street and dominated the international headlines. It all had begun so promisingly. Pandit, who immigrated to the U.S. from India when he was in his teens, was unanimously considered a genius and innovative thinker. He was an introvert, cerebral and quiet, but when he did speak, it was usually profound. Although he impressed those he knew with his sharp intellect, in social situations he was awkward and uncomfortable. Many mistook his shyness for arrogance, and were intimidated by his killer smarts. Extremely risk-averse, he tended to carefully weigh all options before making any decisions.

Years earlier at Morgan Stanley, Pandit himself participated in a coup d'état when he—along with a group of senior executives—tried to overthrow CEO Philip Purcell. Purcell survived the power struggle, however, and Pandit was shown the door. Eventually, he joined other ex–Morgan Stanley executives and formed a hedge fund: Old Lane Partners. In their quest to raise assets, they knocked on Citigroup's door, where Pandit had an entrée through former U.S. treasury secretary Robert Rubin, who was a great admirer of Pandit's intellect. With then-CEO Chuck Prince's approval, Citigroup invested $100 million into Pandit's hedge fund. But Rubin had other designs for Pandit: He hoped to install him as Citi's next CEO.

In 2007, Citi bought Old Lane Partners for $800 million in a transaction that was considered the biggest "sign-on bonus" in the history of Wall

Street. Unfortunately, the fund faltered shortly thereafter and was wound down not even a year after Citigroup's purchase. Then the subprime crisis erupted with a bang, and Chuck Prince had to resign amid billions in losses. Rubin lobbied for Pandit to become Prince's successor and, despite initial board resistance, eventually prevailed. On the plus side of his track record at Citi, Pandit repaid $45 billion in bailout monies, rebuilt capital, wound down poorly performing departments, and recalibrated the company's business lines. But he inherited a mess and had a hard time from the outset. Under his watch, the bank failed a stress test and had to take a $4.7 billion write-down on its Morgan Stanley Smith Barney stake; meanwhile, the government rejected his proposal to buy back shares and increase its dividend to shareholders.

When Citi humiliatingly lost out on the much-needed acquisition of deposit-rich Wachovia to Wells Fargo, the media attributed the failure to secure the deal to Pandit. Over time he had alienated many long-serving Citi executives; some loyalists were promoted, while other staff were pushed aside. Michael O'Neill, chairman of the board, who had previously vied for the CEO position himself and lost out to Pandit, raised concerns over Pandit's reign with the rest of the board. One after another, they were receptive, until Pandit had no sympathizers left.

Meanwhile, the victim was completely clueless. After publishing a positive earnings report, Pandit was in good spirits and unsuspecting when he was called for a meeting. That's when O'Neill dropped the bomb: He told Pandit that the board had lost confidence in him and gave him a choice of three different press releases announcing his ouster. Pandit could either resign now, at the end of the year, or choose to be fired without cause. The blindsided Pandit chose the most face-saving option under the circumstances—to resign. After his departure from Citi, he dabbled in consultancy and venture capitalism. He eventually teamed up with *Freakonomics* author Steven Levitt to head a consulting firm, TGG, where he uses his large network of CEO contacts to build a client base.[12]

In another industry coup d'état, Jamie Dimon, CEO of JPMorgan, who had been fired by Sandy Weill years earlier, paid it forward to Bill Winters. Winters, a senior executive who coheaded the investment bank together with Steve Black, was considered a likely successor to Dimon. He was credited with helping the bank avoid many risky investments in the run-up to the crisis, but his criticism of the role of banks during this time was said to have evoked Dimon's disapproval. Wall Street speculated that Dimon saw a rival in the popular and successful Winters and ousted him before he became too powerful.

Winters, who had spent a quarter of a century at JPMorgan and had no plans of leaving, was shocked. The announcement was made just prior to the Annual Meetings of the IMF, which that year took place in Istanbul. I did not really know Winters, but I had seen him around. He had always been friendly, and many of his colleagues thought highly of him and were stunned to hear the news of what sounded like a ruthless firing. I was taken aback even more when I encountered Winters in the receiving line at the JPMorgan cocktail reception at the Feriye Lokantası restaurant on the Çırağan Cad. Shaking hands, I expressed regret at the news of his dismissal. Disarmingly honest, he admitted straightforwardly that he was still shaken and did not really know what to say. I thought that his attendance showed great backbone.

The question of succession is a delicate one because it forces CEOs to confront their own expiration date. More dictatorial CEOs with big egos often fail to breed successors, and boards typically remain loyal to them. Investing time in planning out an orderly succession is logical; otherwise boards are forced to hire outside CEOs, who generally do not perform as well. A departing CEO also causes substantial transition costs, as he will receive a pay package and the new CEO a sign-on bonus. In addition, transitions bring with them disruptive and costly turnover, since new executives tend to surround themselves with loyalists, and those loyal to the old CEOs generally leave the firm and follow him.

Triumph and Defeat: A Turbulent Career

For a decade, Joe Ackermann headed Deutsche Bank, and under his leadership, "Deutsche"—as it is referred to on Wall Street—became one of the world's leading banks. The CEO of Deutsche Bank has historically had extraordinary standing and gravitas in Germany, since the public views the institution as a reflection of Germany itself and its CEO as its fiduciary. Throughout his tenure, however, Ackermann remained controversial.

Ackermann had always been a power broker who successfully placed himself in the center of relevant networks and crucial events. Wherever the financial elite congregated, he was sure to be in their midst. He spent so much time in the air that he became one of NetJets' top ten fliers in Europe. Due to his superhub position at the core of financial, economic and political networks, he achieved his greatest power at the pinnacle of the financial crisis. As Chancellor Merkel's confidante and finance minister Peer Steinbrück's adviser, his status morphed from that of mere banker to quasi-statesman. By virtue of his chairmanship of the International Institute of Finance, he became the unofficial ambassador of financial institutions globally. As such he played an important and constructive role in the negotiations regarding the Greek crisis. An extraordinary number of influential positions cemented his status as a superhub: In addition to his position at Deutsche Bank, he was a member of the supervisory board of Siemens AG, a nonexecutive member of the board of directors at Royal Dutch Shell, a foundation board member of the WEF, a member of both the Bilderberg Steering Committee and the Trilateral Committee, visiting finance professor at the London School of Economics, and honorary professor at the Goethe University Frankfurt. He thrived in the limelight and was in his element at the top of the financial power structure.

Yet in addition to incredible highs, his career was also marked by unexpected lows. The German public met him with skepticism, because his words and actions were sometimes perceived as tone-deaf. Particularly controversial were his aggressive 25 percent return-on-equity target, which he upheld throughout the crisis, and his enormous pay packages, which at times made him the highest-paid CEO in Germany.

In 2004, Ackermann, in his capacity as a member of the supervisory board of Mannesmann AG, was indicted along with five other executives for alleged breach of trust for approving bonuses in the amount of $74 million to Mannesmann executives after Vodafone Group's acquisition of the company. The trial lasted three years, during which Ackermann remained Deutsche Bank CEO despite the logistical challenges and a potential ten-year prison term hanging over his head. In the end, he was acquitted.

In addition, he was also charged with allegedly making false statements related to a civil court case brought by the heirs of Leo Kirch. The deceased media tycoon had sued Deutsche Bank, blaming its former CEO, Rolf Breuer, for driving his conglomerate into bankruptcy after Breuer publicly questioned its creditworthiness. The trial was marred by an unseemly spying scandal involving surveillance of two board members and a critical shareholder suspected of leaking information. Other dubious methods included a twenty-three-year-old Brazilian honey trap, a microphone concealed in a flower bouquet, and the infiltration of an alluring female spy into the opposing party's law firm. Such surreal lapses of judgment seemed grotesque in the dusty German corporate world and were at no time attributed to Ackermann himself, but were largely ascribed to outside detective firm contractors. After twelve years, Deutsche Bank settled the original case with Kirch's heirs for €775 million plus interest and other costs. Of the accusation of making false statements in the civil court case Ackermann was fully acquitted.[13]

He also displayed a talent for committing public relation gaffees. A snapshot taken during the Mannesmann trial—which captured him grinning and flashing the victory sign—was interpreted as the epitome of elitist arrogance and caused a media storm so severe that he publicly apologized. An infamous remark in connection with his authorization of outsized bonuses, ("This is the only country where those who succeed in achieving a good price for a company are dragged before court for it,") led to yet another backlash followed by yet another public apology.[14] His announcement of an 87 percent profit increase combined with the concurrent layoff of 6,500 employees wasn't exactly met with enthusiasm, either.

A couple other incidents involved—of all people—Chancellor Angela Merkel. While he had helped conceptualize Merkel's bailout program, Ackermann was said to have stated that he would be ashamed to take government help, a remark that earned him a public rebuke from the German government. He further alienated the chancellor when he publicly mentioned that she had hosted his sixtieth birthday party at the chancellery with thirty guests of his choice. That preferential treatment at taxpayer expense placed Merkel in hot water, and a court ordered the chancellery to disclose details. Sometime thereafter, Ackermann characterized his relationship with the Chancellor as cordial and professional, but he conceded that the financial crisis had made the relationship between banks and governments more challenging.

Despite the various ups and downs, Ackermann had always managed to gain the upper hand and prevail, but toward the end of his tenure things didn't seem to quite go his way anymore, which prompted critics to argue that he had missed the right time to abdicate. Because neither he nor Deutsche Bank's board had groomed a successor, he agreed to stay on for a few more months following the end of his term. Thereafter, he let it be known that he was available for the position of chairman of the supervisory board, but shareholders, the political establishment in Berlin, and other critics pushed back, fearing a dangerous concentration of power and possible interference with the work of his successors. When the lack of support became evident, Ackermann withdrew his bid.

Shortly thereafter, he accepted the offer to become chairman of the board of directors of Zürich Insurance, where he planned on utilizing his international network and his experience with Switzerland as a financial center. A few months into his tenure the company's CFO, Pierre Wauthier, committed suicide and implicated Ackermann in his note, as discussed earlier in this chapter. Although an official inquiry completely exonerated Ackermann, a certain unquantifiable stigma—however unjustified—remained. A couple of weeks following Ackermann's resignation, he also resigned from the supervisory board of Siemens.

Subsequently, Ackermann joined the board of private equity firm EQT Partners, as well as the board of Renova Group, which is primarily owned by the billionaire oligarch Viktor Vekselberg, Russia's second-richest man. Shortly thereafter, Ackermann was elected chairman of the Bank of Cyprus, of which Vekselberg was a significant shareholder. Another large investor in the bank, financier Wilbur Ross, emphasized the reasoning for this choice: "[Ackermann] has a huge Rolodex. You can imagine he knows practically everybody in Europe, everybody in Eastern Europe, and huge numbers of people in the U.S. and elsewhere."[15] Ackermann's choice of joining Renova raised some eyebrows, and one economist characterized his involvement with the Bank of Cyprus as "not exactly a career-enhancing move, from a G7 economy to $22 billion Cyprus. . . . They used to call Cyprus the graveyard for diplomats because of the Cyprus problem. Maybe it is now the graveyard for bankers."[16]

Regardless, few will have sympathy for this multimillionaire, who is still highly regarded. But superhubs measure their self-worth with a different yardstick, as their values and sensitivity are calibrated differently. Since public recognition, status and success are of utmost importance to them, public defeats impact the very core of their existence.

*   *   *

In this chapter, we have looked beyond the façade and shone a light on the personal sacrifices that superhubs must make. For top executives, work is not a job but a lifestyle, one with enormous demands and pressures. Financial superhubs are married to their jobs at the expense of their families and the massive workload, competitive pressure, and public scrutiny have subjected numerous superhubs to burnout, serious illness, and even suicide. This reputation fuels the perception that women are ill-equipped to succeed in such a cutthroat, family-unfriendly work environment. However, the lack of women at the top rather results from their systematic exclusion from the old boys' network, as we'll see in the next chapter.

CHAPTER 9

"Womenomics": The Missing Link

THE GENDER GAP: WOMEN MISSING IN ACTION

You may wonder why so far I have written almost exclusively about men. The reason is that, regrettably, women are largely absent from the top levels of finance, as homophily dominates and heterophily, or diversity, only exists at rudimentary levels.

I regularly hold speeches at industry conferences, and whenever I enter the stage and stand behind the podium, I see before me a sea of gray—gray suits typically paired with gray hair and glasses. The lack of women is palpable. The small female minority mostly consists of support staff: secretaries, assistants, and the like, huddled off to the side. Male attendees frequently assume that I am someone's assistant or a translator. In fact, I'm often asked, "Who are you here with?" "Who's your husband?" or, at more-social events, with curiosity that overcomes politeness, "Do you . . . work?" They automatically assume that I can't possibly be a peer but instead must be an accessory. When I mention that I am an attorney, 99 percent of the time I receive the dubious compliment, "But you don't look like an attorney," typically followed by a joke like "I wish my attorney looked like that." Upon disclosing that I have my own firm, the usual response is, "Oh. Marketing or public relations?"—two disciplines traditionally viewed as female domains.

THE ACCESS GAP: EXCLUSIVE
MEANS EXCLUDING

As a woman in the homogeneous, testosterone-infused world of finance, occasional insults must be borne with stoicism and advances fended off diplomatically, so as not to bruise the perpetrator's ego for fear of being perceived as difficult, suffering retaliation, or other negative ramifications. Women are underrepresented in the U.S. elite in general, but nowhere more so than in the financial industry. As of 2013, only 6 out of the 150 largest financial firms in the world are led by women, 5 percent of CEOs of Fortune 500 companies are women, and only one woman heads a major U.S. financial institution, namely Abigail Johnson, who in 2014 became CEO of Fidelity Investments after her father's retirement. The same applies to Europe, where, as of this writing, only one woman leads a large financial institution: Ana Patricia Botín, who upon her father's death in 2014 became his successor and chair of Banco Santander.[1] In addition, women only run 2 percent of mutual fund assets in the U.S., and for every female hedge fund manager, there are eighty males.

A decade ago, the New York Times stated that "Wall Street is still dominated by the white men who fill the bulk of the most powerful and highest-paying jobs in the industry,"[2] and not much has changed since. As studies have shown, success on Wall Street is not attainable through hard work and outperformance alone, considering that women who make it on average are smarter and better educated than their male counterparts. Despite women holding around half of all professional-level jobs, only 16 percent of senior positions are held by them, and they occupy merely 5 percent of executive positions in the largest U.S. firms.[3] The financial industry makes use of only half of our collective human capital. What impact does this fact have on the resilience of the overall system? Would the crisis have panned out differently if there had been a Lehman Sisters as opposed to Lehman Brothers?

The cost of discrimination against minorities in business amounts to $64 billion a year in the U.S. alone.[4] That women are capable of excelling in senior positions is a relatively recent realization,[5] and the business case for women seems obvious: For globally operating financial institutions, diversity is more important than ever, and the inclusion of women makes for a better representation to the customer base. They have different experiences and, thus, add more perspectives to the problem-solving process. For instance, companies' boards benefit from including a greater number of women, as their more holistic perspective of the company's wider context is an important asset in terms of assessing risks as well as capitalizing on opportunities.[6] Several MIT studies also demonstrate that women are much better at "mind-reading"—recognizing nonverbal clues—than their male counterparts. These skills, not just diversity, are ultimately what makes certain groups outperform others.[7]

In 2015, the *Financial Times* described female money managers as a critically endangered species. Although "funds majority-owned by women had outpaced the hedge fund industry as a whole in the preceding six-and-a-half years" and "female hedge fund managers outperformed men over 2013 as a whole,"[8] the number of female portfolio managers had steadily declined.[9] So despite research showing that greater diversity leads to lower risk-taking, more long-term thinking, less biased decision making, and greater return on capital, there are even fewer women in senior executive positions across the financial sector now than before the crisis. Even if they make it to senior levels, women typically get stuck in their late forties and early fifties because even in senior positions they are rarely plugged into the power and information channels to the same extent that men are. If they do make it to the board, they often are "token" women and isolated when compared to men.[10]

Even in the innovative venture capitalist industry, women are marginalized. It is less formal than other more established fields of finance, but the lack of tradition and rules does not make it any easier for women. Many have described the environment as hostile and unwelcoming, and it is difficult for them to fight against a male establishment that is successful precisely because it thrives on risk and disruption, does not follow rules, and is constantly on the lookout for the next boundary to push. Not only is it hard for women to break into the clubby environment, but those who have succeeded are "leaving the industry in droves."[11] As of 2014, only 13 percent of venture-backed companies had at least one female cofounder, and only 4 percent of leading venture capitalists are women, although a study found that female-run startups produce a 31 percent higher return on investment than startups run by men.[12] In general, white men hire white men.

This "progressive" sector is just as conservative and sexist as the rest of the financial industry, as numerous lawsuits have unearthed; especially when fund-raising, women often face misogynistic and inappropriate behavior. Tech billionaires, the history-making "industrialists" of our time, are exclusively male. In the venture capital industry, deep relationships are of utmost importance to source deals and form productive working relationships with entrepreneurs, who mostly happen to be male.

The main reason why so few women make it to the very top of finance is because they are largely excluded from the old boys' network. The superhubs in control prefer surrounding themselves with those whom they most identify with and feel comfortable around: other men. They develop tight inner circles of trust; which increases efficiency in big and impersonal institutions, as homogeneity and conformity increase comfort levels, facilitate communication, and reduce uncertainty. During the crisis, Sheila Bair, the chairwoman of the Federal Deposit Insurance Corporation (FDIC), experienced blatant exclusion from the boys' network. Consequently, she wondered whether it was "gross incompetence or unbelievable disrespect . . . or just the all-boys network wanting to make the decisions among themselves, as many commentators have speculated. Maybe the boys did not want Sheila Bair playing in their sandbox."[13]

The higher the rank, the more homogeneous the groupings become— and an all-male senior management team has few incentives to advocate women's cases. Exclusion from such networks—and the valuable informal connections formed within them—is a distinct disadvantage, and men's entrenchment in these structures gives them more social capital and bargaining power. Attempts to start women-centric networks so far have been of limited effectiveness, because too few women are part of the top-rank establishment, and lateral networking is necessarily limited in scope.[14] One woman expanding such a network is Sallie Krawcheck, who has been one of the most successful women on Wall Street as CEO of Sanford C. Bernstein, CFO of Citigroup, CEO of Citi Wealth Management, and lastly as head of global wealth and investment management at

Bank of America. The financial crisis cost Krawcheck her last two jobs, and after being let go from Bank of America she purchased the women's network 85 Broads, which had been founded by a female Goldman Sachs partner as a platform for female senior executives. In 2014, Krawcheck gave it the clever moniker Ellevate and launched the Pax Ellevate Global Women's Index Fund, which invests in companies highly rated in terms of advancing female leadership. The verdict on the Ellevate network's effectiveness is still out, but it is a promising start.

THE NETWORKING GAP: SCHMOOZE OR LOSE

The comparative weakness of female networks also results from women's dispositions. Studies show that women are more reluctant than men to use their peer-to-peer networks because they feel uncomfortable using connections opportunistically. Also, some argue that since women have had top job opportunities only for a few decades, they lack role models and are still learning practices that men have long internalized.[15] Often women are hired for their soft skills to attract new clients, sell financial services, and maintain client relationships. Despite excelling in these roles, they have largely been unable to break into the male-dominated high ranks of finance.

Although assumed to be better at fostering relationships, women have yet to change long-standing patterns of network behavior that have existed for centuries. Frequently, they are promoted to project diversity, lending predominately male boards a superficial "alibi," especially if their institutions cater to a diverse clientele. Moreover, it has been argued that women are hired to create "buffer zones" between management and the labor force or public, especially for positions in human resources or public relations.[16,17] This inertia is at least partly due to the fact that women are still constrained by ancient social values and norms originally based on physical strength, which was essential for many preindustrial professions. In today's world, many of these norms are outdated, but organizations reflexively perpetuate traditional practices that seek to preserve their structures. As a survival technique, many women simply try to fit in and be "one of the boys."

THE ASSESSMENT GAP: PERFORMANCE
VERSUS POTENTIAL

It appears that even mediocre men have an easier time rising up the ranks. Perhaps that is because, as a 2012 McKinsey study reveals, women are judged on performance while men are judged on potential.[18] The *Harvard Business Review* aptly notes that "we live in an era of self-celebration . . . where fame is equated with success, and being self-referential has become the norm. . . . [Bluster] and the alpha instinct are often mistaken for ability and effectiveness."[19] Women are typically more modest, and even when their performance is better, they lose out because masculine behavioral norms do not apply to them. Ambition in the current social context is not considered an asset for females, as it implies aggression, which is reserved for men.[20] Accordingly, when women act more competitively, they are negatively perceived as lacking warmth. The culture of money—where money yields ever more money coupled with power—skews social dynamics even more and often rewards ruthlessness. As a consequence, powerful women tend to work harder in an effort to stress their merits over the presumption that they get ahead by capitalizing on their feminine charms.

In addition, studies show that men engage in visible workplace behaviors, while women are more private and sacrifice themselves in doing the majority of "office housework"—time-consuming administrative tasks that don't get any credit.[21] Moreover, there is a tendency to expect help from a woman, whereas a man's help is rewarded. I have experienced this marginalization firsthand and attended meetings in which women were interrupted or ignored; when a man said the exact same thing ten minutes later, he was applauded. Women's fear that talking too much reflects badly on them is well founded. While powerful men who talk at disproportionate length are judged positively, women who do so are perceived as less competent by both men and other women.[22]

Male employees also tend to have more direct and better relationships with their bosses. And if a man takes credit for a woman's work, higher-ups will often naturally believe him, especially if the work product is excellent. Then there is the phenomenon of "mansplaining"—when a man condescendingly explains something to a woman that she is much more knowledgeable about. That happens to me frequently, and although being talked down to is humiliating, there really is not much one can do without appearing snappish. A charming example of "mansplaining" is Jamie Dimon's comment on Elizabeth Warren's expertise: "I don't know if she fully understands the global banking system," notwithstanding the fact that the senator is a former Harvard bankruptcy law professor, the architect of the Consumer Financial Protection Bureau, and chair of the government panel that oversaw the Troubled Asset Relief Program during the crisis.[23]

THE WAGE GAP: SELLING WOMEN SHORT

The difference in attitude and perception is also one of the main reasons for the persistent pay gap. This discrepancy is less prevalent on the highest executive levels. But on the way up, women, although often better educated and more accomplished, on average are still paid 20 percent less than their male counterparts. Part of the reason for the wage gap is the "ask gap." Whereas men have been conditioned to promote themselves, women are reluctant to negotiate; when they do, they often get penalized, making them even less likely to try again. The enduring societal stereotype is still that women should be kind, considerate, and caring. When they violate that norm by speaking out for themselves, they are perceived as aggressive. Sheryl Sandberg has appealed to women's personal responsibility to "lean in," and while she certainly has a point, public policy and institutions must also fundamentally change before the system can be remedied.

The ask gap is deeply ingrained, even on the CEO level: Satya Nadella, CEO of Microsoft, said in 2014 that women who do not ask for raises create "good karma" for themselves.[24] Those are the women he would trust and to whom he would give more responsibility. In other words, if you ask for a raise, you are not to be trusted. As shocking as this statement may be, Nadella only verbalized what many executives probably still believe but know better politically than to say in public. It does not help that women often hold self-limiting behaviors and beliefs. Since they are treated differently and have a harder time rising through the ranks, they often suffer from poor confidence. When successful, many feel they just got lucky or—worse—like imposters, while men tend to ascribe their successes to their exceptional ability.[25]

THE FAILURE GAP: DEMOTING PROMOTIONS

There is only one area where women are favored: When the financial industry tanks and the workforce must be reduced, it is "ladies first."[26] However, while women are often the first ones to receive the axe in a downturn, the cases in which they are actually promoted are usually a curse in disguise and a setup for failure. Michelle Ryan, an associate professor of psychology at Exeter University, coined the term "glass cliff" to describe the phenomenon of women being promoted in times of crisis. Dangerous leadership positions in dangerous times are no-win propositions.[27] Christine Lagarde has firsthand experience in sorting out messes: She became the first female chairman of Baker & McKenzie, the world's largest law firm, when it was a "complete mess," and she was chosen to take the helm at the IMF after her predecessor Dominique Strauss-Kahn resigned amidst a sordid sex scandal. She agrees that "women often end up in charge to sort things out when everything goes wrong."[28]

Activist male investors like Kyle Bass and Nelson Peltz have joined something of a trend in attacking women-led companies. Research demonstrates that female CEOs are perceived as less capable than their male counterparts and that the IPOs of women-led companies are considered less attractive investments. The subconscious bias may be that women are softer targets and less likely to fight back.[29]

THE MENTORING GAP: MISSING
OUT ON MENTORING

Men also have the benefit of being mentored by other men in positions of power. They schmooze with their bosses during golf outings, sports events, and nights out. Ina Drew, former chief investment officer at JPMorgan and one of the banking sector's highest-ranking and longest-serving women, explained that the paucity of female executives results in part from a lack of corporate mentorship: "If women remain unfulfilled by their positions without the potential for growth and discouraged by male aggression, the discrepancies will persist."[30]

Credit is due to Sheryl Sandberg for breaking the taboo: professional mentoring develops according to the rules of homophily. Men often gravitate toward sponsoring younger men to whom they relate more naturally.[31] In contrast, they shy away from mentoring women for fear of gossip. An executive can go for a beer at a sports bar with his male subordinate after work, but doing the same with a young woman might have the appearance of a date.[32] A few years ago at a formal event, I was seated at the head table next to a well-known CEO of a global financial firm. As the evening progressed and he had ingested a few glasses of wine, he blurted out, "My God, you are so smart, but if I hired you, everyone would think we had an affair." I was terribly embarrassed for him and kept the anecdote to myself.

THE SEXISM GAP: THE WOLVES OF WALL STREET ON THE PROWL

Next to career and pay discrimination, sexual discrimination based on appearance is still more prevalent than one would think. Women do not just act differently; they look different. In contrast to men, they must give their appearance much more consideration. While a certain level of attractiveness is expedient, they should not be too alluring. Hence, they must wear their hair conservatively and apply moderate makeup. Clothes cannot be too formfitting, low-cut, or short. As a deterrent, some women resort to wearing baggy clothes, glasses, and wedding bands even though they are not married. I was once asked by a human resource professional if I could not be persuaded to color my hair a darker color. "You would have so much of an easier time," she sighed. In a male-managed, male dominated, and homogeneous culture, drawing too much attention creates resistance. Women are continuously judged on their looks, whereas men are not.

Stricter internal policies have only made discrimination subtler and even harder to fight. According to a survey by the *Financial Times*, one in two female fund management staff has been subjected to regular harassment or sexist behavior in the office.[33] Fifty-four percent of women say they have encountered "inappropriate" conduct in the workplace. Speaking up is generally taboo, and one risks being shamed with character attacks and branded a tattletale and a liability. Also, being viewed as a victim is a total career-killer. Once a woman admits to sexual harassment, it can be hard to shed the "victim" image, which undermines power, promotes a perception of weakness, and makes it virtually impossible to obtain high-level leadership positions.[34]

Most recently, Goldman Sachs has been in the news with a suit that alleges a pattern of discrimination against female associates. It accuses the bank of a macho culture in which the marginalization of women was endorsed and males received preferential and disproportionate promotions and pay.[35] Many financial institutions settle lawsuits with multimillion-dollar payouts to avoid publicity-ridden trials that would uncover other injustices, such as lower compensation for the same type, amount, and success of work.[36] At the time of the book's completion the lawsuit was still ongoing.

Blythe Masters, one of Wall Street's top female executives, ended her twenty-seven-year career at JPMorgan after the bank reported the sale of the global commodities unit she had led to record revenues of close to $3 billion. She was previously the CEO of JPMorgan's investment bank, and when the crisis erupted in 2007 she became the subject of public abuse, presumably at least partially because she stood out as being capable as well as noticeably attractive and feminine.[37] The realities of the contemporary workplace are sobering and frustrating for a generation of women raised to believe that if they had an excellent education they'd have a merit-based career.

THE RESILIENCE GAP: MALE MIGHT AND FEMALE FEEBLENESS

More-conservative financiers opine that the lack of women in senior ranks is because their priorities shift once they bear children. Legendary hedge fund manager Paul Tudor Jones was forced to publicly apologize after stating that women can't compete after having children or going through divorce: "You will never see as many great women investors or traders as men. Period. End of story. . . . As soon as that baby's lips touch that girl's bosom, forget it."[38] Jones has a penchant for such expressions of evocative machismo, as when he said at a conference that we desperately need a "macro doctor to prescribe central bank Viagra."[39]

Others argue that women are just not made—physically or psychologically—to withstand the pressure-cooker environment at the executive level. Some indeed choose to leave this confrontational, competitive world for good in view of the low odds of rising to the top. They instead join smaller firms, change career fields, or start their own firms, where they are judged by market forces rather than male superiors.[40]

In the recent past, proponents like Sheryl Sandberg have publicly come to the forefront to convince women to claim the positions they are qualified to earn. However, similar statements have yet to be made by women renowned in the world of finance. On the contrary, women fall prey to the "superhuman paradox," where they do it all but are far from having it all. Many senior, accomplished power women who dare speak up, such as Anne-Marie Slaughter of Princeton University and Indra Nooyi, CEO of Pepsi, believe that women can "pretend to have it all," but that it is nearly impossible for women to balance work and family without help.[41] In finance, the work-life balance is particularly challenging due to the long hours, lack of control over one's time, and heavy travel. According to researchers at Harvard, women are judged more harshly than men for leaving work earlier than others. Colleagues likely assume that they are off to pick up kids, whereas men who leave early are presumed to have client meetings. Regardless of whether women are in effect more engaged in child care and household-related tasks, it is still widely assumed that they are tied to the home, which is why more travel-related assignments typically go to men. The preferential assignment of opportunities may help explain why women receive fewer promotions than their male counterparts.[42]

Unforgettable still is the depressing and unusually vocal reckoning of Erin Callan,[43] Lehman Brothers' CFO at the time of the bank's failure. She described in the *New York Times* how her boundaries slipped away until work was all that was left, an experience she does not wish on anyone.[44] Word on the street was that Dick Fuld, the CEO, had promoted her to the position of chief financial officer because she had no prior experience in this field and would, thus, be more easily influenced. In fact, she later recalled how she was made to be the "fall-girl" by both Fuld and Gregory.[45] A *Wall Street Journal* profile displaying her taste for expensive designer clothes and use of a personal shopper from Bergdorf Goodman,[46] combined with glamour shots, did not help her image as the CFO of a major bank, especially one that was about to go bust.

CLOSING THE GENDER GAP:
SUPERHUB CHRISTINE LAGARDE

Christine Lagarde, the head of the IMF, is one of the very few women who has defied the odds, proven her longevity, and risen to the top of international finance. On a mild September evening in New York, black chauffeured limousines lined up in front of the magnificent Plaza Hotel at Central Park, dropping off international policy, business, and finance leaders. Foreign dignitaries, CEOs of global companies, and international VIPs clad in evening gowns and tuxedos made their way amid heavy security to the opulent Grand Ballroom to attend the Atlantic Council's Global Citizen Award dinner. Dedicated to strengthening transatlantic relationships, the Atlantic Council hosts an annual award show that honors leaders tackling contemporary challenges. Fred Kempe, the president and CEO of the council, described the attendees as the "ultimate community of influence." One of the awardees on this festive occasion was Christine Lagarde. Tall, slim, and dressed in an elegant red evening gown, she circulated amongst the high-profile guests with ease. After being introduced by Klaus Schwab, founder and chairman of the WEF, she dazzled the audience with a captivating speech. The next day, she was back in Washington to preside over the Annual Meetings of the IMF.

Lagarde's exceptional career path has been an unlikely one, considering her beginnings. She was born in 1956 into a bourgeois French family and grew up in Normandy. Her father, a university professor, passed away when she was seventeen years old, leaving her mother, a teacher, to raise her along with her three younger brothers. Lagarde excelled in school and joined the national synchronized swim team, which she now says—with a wink—taught her to "hold her breath" and "work well in organized teams." After spending a year in the United States on a scholarship, she returned to Paris to attend law school. She applied twice to the École *nationale d'administration*, the elite school for top bureaucrats, but was rejected each time. When she interviewed for her first job with the most reputable law firm in France, she was told that—while they would gladly accept her—she would never be made partner simply because she was a woman.[47] She proceeded to join Baker & McKenzie, the world's largest global law firm; spent several years working in the United States; and, in 1999, became the firm's first female chair. Subsequently, she joined the French government, first as trade minister and then as agriculture minister. Just in time for the financial crisis, she became France's first female finance minister under President Nicolas Sarkozy, which also made her the first female Finance Minister of the G7 countries. After IMF head Dominique Strauss-Kahn's ignoble sex scandal, the prestigious position was awarded to Lagarde, who thoroughly impressed the twenty-four biggest member countries in a series of intense and grueling interviews for the job.

Lagarde has defied the laws of homophily, as she could hardly have been more different from the men dominating the professional environment around her. All of the IMF board members are male, as are most central bank governors and finance ministers. She succeeded despite lacking a prominent family background or the requisite elite French schooling. The nationalistic French perceived her as quasi-American, because of her years spent in the United States, her command of the English language, and Anglo-Saxon attitude. Lagarde is charismatic and oozes old-world elegance. She is always "on"—consistently gracious regardless of the circumstances, animated in podium discussions, and full of energy that is seemingly unimpaired by stress and jet lag. Perhaps even more extraordinary than her skill set are her personality, appearance, and demeanor, which so distinctly set her apart from the men in her orbit.

She climbed the career ladder while maintaining her femininity, glamour, and charm. In contrast to many women who prefer to assimilate and blend in, she sets herself apart in a rather dull environment, which takes great self-confidence and courage. Her style and sophistication have made countless headlines and landed her a coveted place on the *Vanity Fair* best-dressed list and a profile in *Vogue*. Pulitzer Prize–winning author Liaquat Ahamed, in his book *On Tour with the IMF*, characterizes her as "intriguing" and "charming," and the *Financial Times*'s Gillian Tett praises her chicness and her elegantly coordinated wardrobe. Even the respectable *Guardian* went so far as to ask, "Is this the world's sexiest woman?" *Forbes* surmises that "she uses her style to assert her individuality and dominance amid a seas of suits" and to help "convey her confidence and authority." Fashion blogs call her a style icon, and others laud her as proof that women can be both stylish and competent at the same time. However, her costly Chanel outfits, pricey Hermès bags, and expensive jewelry have also prompted critics to accuse her of flaunting her wealth and status in an environment beset with economic problems, poverty, and austerity.[48]

To this day, even in her top senior position, Lagarde still must put up with male condescension and patronizing remarks. When she rightly pointed out that European banks were in urgent need of capital, Christian Noyer, the governor of the French Central bank, responded, "Quite frankly, I do not understand what she said."[49] Translation: She does not know what she is talking about. Former French finance minister Laurent Fabius mused on her chances of landing the IMF job: "She'll make it. She is an elegant woman."[50] Translation: She is not qualified. When Lagarde is confronted with such snubs and insults, she usually grinds her teeth and brushes them off with a humorous remark. I cannot count how many times male economists and bankers have felt compelled to opine that—while she is doubtlessly an accomplished woman—she is unsuitable for the job since, as a lawyer, she does not have a full grasp of economic issues. I beg to differ. By all accounts, she has a spotless track record and is well respected inside and outside of the IMF. In 2016, she was reelected by consensus as the only candidate for Managing Director of the IMF for a second five-year term.

Lagarde often laments the lack of women in finance in an effort to bring awareness to the issue, which has earned her criticism from within the IMF for supposedly distracting from more pressing problems. She has argued that "Gender-dominated environments are not good, particularly in the financial sector, where there are too few women. Men have a tendency to . . . show how hairy-chested they are, compared with the man who's sitting next to them. I honestly think that there should never be too much testosterone in one room."[51] She has also warned that women cannot have it all and that those who try should brace themselves for failure. She has conceded that juggling her career with her family life has been challenging. The divorced mother of two sons is now in a long-term relationship with a Corsican businessman.[52]

Lagarde's oscillations between the private and public sector have exponentially expanded her worldwide network. It is unclear what her next career step will be after her IMF term ends, but it is not entirely impossible that she may become the first female French president. I wish I could infer some lessons from Madame Lagarde's steep ascent other than get the best education, have grit, and stay true to yourself, but many other women have done the same and not achieved her level of success. She is indeed uniquely qualified and possesses a high degree of both social intelligence and resilience, but I also think that in her case all the stars were aligned. Once she found an upward trajectory, she had the ability and good fortune to maintain that positive momentum. Generally, I must say that I am not too optimistic that things will significantly change for the better in the near future. This is a pity, as there is ample proof of the objective business benefits produced by more diversity of gender, backgrounds, experiences, thought, and opinions. By disrupting male groupthink and counteracting excessive risk-taking, female advancement will make the system as a whole more balanced and stable.

*   *   *

This chapter explored the reasons for the lack of women at the highest levels of finance. While also discussing the gender, wage, and opportunity gaps, we specifically focused on the "network gap": the fact that women are largely excluded from men's networks, have no sufficient networks of their own, and lack mentors. Christine Lagarde has proven a rare exception to the norm, perhaps because her experiences in both the public and private sectors significantly increased her network links. In Chapter 10, we will more closely examine the tight interconnections between the financial, corporate, and political sectors, which provide superhubs with enormous power.

CHAPTER 10

Revolving Superhubs

Creating Network Monopolies

PSYCHOLOGICAL KIDNAPPING

Financial networks interact with other networks, thereby reinforcing their structures. Two sectors inextricably intertwined by personal connections are finance and politics—a relationship that perpetuates itself through such means as the "revolving door," lobbying, and campaign financing. CEOs of financial institutions have financial power, while politicians have regulatory power. So long as financial firms provide funding for politicians, their interests are aligned. These interconnections raise various issues that we shall explore in some depth.

The symbiosis between the financial and political spheres poses a serious risk of "relational capture." The term reflects the fact that humans instinctively try to foster positive work environments through cooperation and conciliation. In essence, relational capture is a more amenable version of Stockholm Syndrome: After a certain amount of interaction, people become attached and, eventually, beholden to one another. Although leaders from the public and private sectors are supposed to keep an appropriate distance, each has something that the other wants—and political and regulatory influence is often exchanged for job positions and campaign contributions. Research has shown that within a short time of interaction, "relational capture" sets in. Mere "relational capture" evolves into "cognitive capture," when regulators work so closely with the regulated that they start to see issues through their lens. Cognitive capture can culminate in "regulatory capture," where regulators become dominated by the very financial sector that they are required to regulate.[1]

Another issue is undue concentration of power, which is accelerated by systemic forces that are difficult to break. The reality is that markets promote efficiency, which in turn rewards scale, which in turn leads to a concentration of economic—and therefore political—power.[2]

The Clintons perfectly exemplify this symbiotic relationship between the public and the financial sector. Since Hillary Clinton recognized during her tenure at the State Department that the U.S.'s global leadership was inextricably linked with its economic strength, she made economic considerations an integral part of foreign policy and created the Office of the Chief Economist. Financial firms have made large campaign contributions to both Hillary and Bill, paid them millions of dollars in speaking fees, and heavily donated to the Clinton Global Initiative.

This intermingling of government and private matters has led to frequent accusations of conflicts of interest. Personal and professional lives of public and private sector figures regularly overlap on the social circuit and at various professional events like conferences and fund-raisers all over the world. While the financial sector hedges its bets with contributions to both sides of the aisle, political animals like Hillary Clinton must carefully walk a tightrope to appeal to the populace while placating her benefactors at the banks. Issues such as financial regulation are an especially double-edged sword for politicians.

THE REVOLVING DOOR

The "revolving door" refers to a professional dynamic in which employees move between the public and private sectors, thereby weaving a tight web of connections. As Bill Moyers so aptly put it, there's a "revolving door between government service and big money in the private sector spinning so fast it becomes an irresistible force hurling politics and high finance together."[3] Such crisscrossing between sectors raises conflict-of-interest issues, but it is also a powerful way to build one's position as a superhub. Relationships across the private and public sectors facilitate the spread of information and influence ways of thinking in both directions. Public officials may attribute more credence to private sector opinions on certain issues; moreover, they may try to stack the odds in their favor of later getting a lucrative job in the financial industry. While public service is generally well compensated, it does not compare to the earnings potential typically found in the private sector. For instance, in 2013 Ben Bernanke earned a yearly salary of about $200,000 as chairman of the Federal Reserve. Shortly after leaving the Fed, he made a minimum of $250,000 for a two-hour speaking engagement on the conference circuit.[4]

The list of top financial industry executives and senior public servants who move back and forth between sectors, sometimes several times, is virtually endless. To name only a few examples: Former U.S. treasury secretary Tim Geithner joined private equity firm Warburg Pincus; former U.S. Treasury Secretary Larry Summers was a highly paid adviser to Wall Street firms before heading President Obama's National Economic Council and thereafter returned to Wall Street in various advisory roles; and Hank Paulson was co-CEO of Goldman Sachs before becoming U.S. treasury secretary under the George W. Bush administration. Peter Orszag, Bill Clinton's economic adviser and director of the Congressional Budget Office under Obama, landed top jobs at Citigroup and Lazard after leaving the public sector. David Lipton, who had served as undersecretary of the treasury during the Clinton administration, later held a senior position in global risk management at Citi before becoming special assistant to President Obama. For the past few years, Lipton has been deputy managing director of the IMF. Following his tenure as commerce secretary under President Bill Clinton, William Daley became head of global government relations at JPMorgan, before returning to the White House as Obama's chief of staff. In 2016, Mervyn King, the former governor of the Bank of England and outspoken bank critic, surprised many when he became senior advisor to Citigroup.[5]

The Oscillating Megahub: Robert Rubin

Any account of revolving doors would be incomplete without the mention of Robert Rubin. But where to start? With his positions at Goldman Sachs? With him becoming treasury secretary in the Clinton administration?

Or how about his subsequent role as board director and senior adviser at Citigroup during the crisis, or President Obama's unofficial "head of human resources," or cochairman of the Council of Foreign Relations? The number of prominent positions Rubin has held in the private and the public sectors is almost without precedent. He is the human embodiment of a superhub, located in the center of a densely woven, high-caliber web that covers all the bases: finance, politics, business, and academics.

Omnipresent and omnipotent, Rubin has had immense overt power as well as subtler influence. He outwardly seems like the antithesis of the stereotypical financier, yet he is the epitome of one. Rubin is low-key, with the benevolent air of a cerebral, slightly absentminded professor. He has full gray hair, and his wiry figure and alert eyes give him a youthful appearance. His demeanor is understated and unpretentious, and his reputation is one of decency and trustworthiness. In a world dominated by loud and flashy characters, Rubin exudes serenity and tranquillity. He is known for retaining self-control at all times and his ability to remain detached from the events around him.

After earning an undergraduate degree from Harvard, Rubin attended London Business School and thereafter graduated from Yale Law School. He began his career at the prestigious law firm Cleary Gottlieb, where he had his first brush with arbitrage traders, who contacted him to elicit information on deals. After a couple of years, he moved on to Goldman Sachs, where he started out as a risk arbitrage trader. Arbitrageurs exploit price differences in the markets by legally obtaining information, typically through close relationships with people who likely have it, such as lawyers, accountants, and other finance professionals. Rubin had a knack for making connections and thrived on Goldman's platinum network and access to information. With his intellectual and sociable personality, he was practically predestined for arbitrage. His sound and quick decision-making ability earned Goldman and himself a fortune. Soon he rose to the top position of cochairman.

In 1993, Rubin made a quantum leap to the public sector when he became the director of the National Economic Council, a position President Clinton had created specifically for him. Charged with designing and implementing economic policies, his influence was substantial because

Clinton was not an economics expert and relied heavily on his advice. Two years later, the former Goldman Sachs luminary became the seventieth secretary of the treasury. He is widely credited with "Rubinomics," a policy that achieved a balanced budget by way of tax increases and spending cuts. Clinton praised him as the most admired U.S. treasury secretary since Alexander Hamilton. But Rubin had also presided over the repeal of the Glass-Steagall Act, which separated investment and commercial banking activities and is now considered to have been one of the main causes of the crisis.

After Rubin left the White House, Sandy Weill, the architect of the Citi conglomerate, worried about losing Rubin to a competitor and made him an offer that was very concrete in terms of remuneration—$15 million a year—but vague when it came to obligations. Rubin's job came down to drafting strategies, which gave him authority but no operating responsibilities. In addition, he essentially acted as brand ambassador and point of contact for high-level clients who enjoyed interacting with a former U.S. treasury secretary, and as "chief lobbyist officer" due to his excellent Washington contacts. A person of such standing can open any door, obtain invaluable information, and effectively represent the bank's interests vis-à-vis clients and regulators.

To some extent, the intangible benefits of stature and access are hard to measure, but they certainly make a difference. For instance, Rubin introduced the highly profitable Mexican Banamex Bank acquisition opportunity to Citi through a Goldman connection. In addition, he also provided guidance during the financial crisis, served as a sounding board for senior executives, and supported efforts to stabilize the bank via his direct line to ex-Goldmanite and treasury secretary Hank Paulson and other Washington contacts. Unfortunately for Citi, Rubin's hiring did not prevent the bank from almost imploding and requiring a $45 billion taxpayer-financed rescue package. The optics were less than ideal, especially in view of the fact that his last official act before joining Citi had been to help repeal Glass-Steagall. The existence of Citi as a combination of a commercial and investment bank would not have been possible had Glass-Steagall been upheld. Regardless, the debacle did not leave a lasting dent, neither on his reputation, nor on his career prospects.

Rubin's next endeavor took him back to the public sector. He had long been a backer of the Democratic Party and supported Obama's election. It did not come as much of a surprise when Obama chose Rubin to work on the transitional economic advisory board and filled most key positions with Rubinites. Among them were his protégé Timothy Geithner, who became treasury secretary; his friend Larry Summers, who served as director of the National Economic Council; his acolytes Peter Orszag, who served as director of the Congressional Budget Office, and Gene Sperling, who became counselor to Tim Geithner. Sheila Bair, the former chairwoman of the FDIC, recalled that Obama's coronation of Tim Geithner felt like a punch in the gut. She "did not understand how someone who had campaigned on a 'change' agenda could appoint someone who had been so involved in contributing to the financial mess that had gotten Obama elected." The only explanation she could think of was that Rubin had pushed him to do so, and she called the other economic appointments a "veritable hit parade of individuals who had served in Bob Rubin's Treasury."[6]

Rubin has since fashioned himself as a public intellectual, and he holds the positions of cochairman of the Council on Foreign Relations and cofounder of the Hamilton Project at the Brookings Institution, which focuses on growth policies. Rubin's great wealth, power, and networks lead us to wonder: What is the magic formula that allowed him to navigate the highest realms of the system with such seemingly effortless ease? He has substance, competence, and credibility—characteristics shared by countless other people in finance. But what sets him apart? First, it is noteworthy that he developed an intellectual construct (mentioned in Chapter 4), which he outlines in his best-selling book *In an Uncertain World: Tough Choices from Wall Street to Washington*. Second, Rubin has been excellent at building relationships. He placed himself at central network intersections like Goldman Sachs, the White House, and the Harvard Corporation, among many others. In an interview, he said that one reason for returning to Citibank was to be more at the center of things.[7] With every move, he raised his reputation and status and increased his "transactional capital," by exchanging valuable favors and information with other superhubs. By cross-capitalizing on his various positions, he optimized his network exponentially. In the same interview, he also stated that working at Citi would keep him current and better equip him to handle public policy.

Rubin's personality was ideally suited to becoming a superhub because he ranges among the most emotionally intelligent financiers. His introspective and self-aware nature allowed him to evolve from a coarse trader into a worldly executive and statesman. In contrast to overtly aggressive colleagues, his self-effacing and understated demeanor was disarming and reassuring. He freely lent his ideas to others and generously gave credit when it was due. Throughout his life, Rubin has been committed to building an inclusive society and economy that benefits all. According to Clinton, Rubin quite frequently acted against his own interests when drafting policies.[7] He has also been actively involved in philanthropy on behalf of the underprivileged. Was he merely selfishly selfless to advance his career? And how do his altruistic pursuits square with his high remuneration at the time of Citi's life-threatening losses and public bailout? Is the dichotomy between self-interest and altruism a paradox or perfectly logical?

Up to what point are self and public interest aligned, and where do they diverge? And finally, at what point does self-interest veer into wrongdoing? We can at least assume that someone who has worked so ambitiously and successfully in finance all his life cares about money, and Rubin has referred to himself as a "reasonably commercial person."[8]

To his critics, Rubin's public and private crisscrossing signifies everything that's wrong with the revolving door. Defenders argue that transferring knowledge across sectors benefits each respective institution, but that does not negate the fact that the individuals involved disproportionately profit from the arrangement. Rubin is also extraordinarily gifted in his reputation management. He has made relatively few enemies, maintained excellent relations with the media, and suffered only a limited number of PR crises.[9]

Like most top executives, Rubin has tirelessly expanded his relationship footprint. He placed his acolytes in key positions of power, ensuring the flow of information, access, and "political capital," all reinforcing his own position. With support from the Brookings Institution, Rubin started a new network, the Hamilton Project, where influential people congregated around him as a hub. At the Council of Foreign Relations, he sits atop many different converging networks in terms of industries, geographies, and mission. While at Goldman Sachs, he gave a number of younger employees seed money when they left the firm to start their own funds. Today, some of these managers preside over the biggest and most successful hedge funds in the world (Dan Och of Och-Ziff, Eric Mindich of Eton Park, Frank Brosens of Taconic Capital, and Richard Perry of Perry Capital),[10] and Rubin can count on their loyalty. Billionaires, sheiks, CEOs, and the like—Rubin's capital network is capable of mobilizing financial forces of almost unfathomable dimensions. Such access is particulary useful when it comes to enlisting political forces.

Open Doors: Tony Blair

The former British prime minister Tony Blair has taken the concept of the revolving door to a whole new level. He has been a fixture at the JPMorgan cocktail party in Davos for the last few years. The charismatic and dynamic politician-turned-entrepreneur-turned-financier stood in the receiving line for three full hours, tirelessly shaking hands with hundreds of JPMorgan's top clients, including private equity kings, hedge fund titans, billionaires, and oligarchs. He enthusiastically focused his full attention on every single guest and patiently smiled for a myriad of pictures. The luster of his premiership was still glistening, his status palpable, and his network power larger than ever.

After leaving public office, he set up a business consultancy, Tony Blair Associates, where he used his stellar international connections to advise governments, broker negotiations, open doors, and act as matchmaker between cash-rich investors and governments. As chairman of the JPMorgan Advisory Council, he has made himself available for corporate events and high-level client meetings, rendering advice on international matters for a reported $3 million a year. He was also on retainer for Petro Saudi, an oil company related to the Saudi royal family, for $66,000 a month plus an additional 2 percent of any deal resulting from his efforts, as well as to Zürich Insurance for $750,000 a year.

Moreover, he has advised Abu Dhabi's sovereign wealth fund, Kazakhstan's President Nursultan Nazarbayev, and Paul Kagame, the president of Rwanda. He has had business dealings with China, Kuwait, Azerbaijan, Mongolia, Sierra Leone, Liberia, Mozambique, and East Timor. For a three-hour engagement, facilitating the $66 billion merger negotiations between Glencore, Xstrata, and the Qatari ruling family, he received $1 million. He is also a highly sought-after speaker and on average charges $200,000 per speaking engagement. As one paper put it, he logs enough frequent flyer miles in one year to make it to the moon.

In addition to providing consultancy services, his firm has also obtained a Financial Services Authority (FSA) license, which authorizes it to advise clients and invest money on their behalf. Bloomberg estimates that from 2007 to 2013, his business generated at least $90 million. That number is likely an incomplete reflection of his actual earnings, as many of his activities do not have to be disclosed.[11] Until early 2015, he headed the "Diplomatic Quartet," an organization that tries to foster peace in the Middle East. Peace has yet to come, but for Blair the position had the convenient side effect of cementing his status and giving him a calling card for the Arab elites.

Blair has stated that he uses the significant cash flow from his business to finance his philanthropic efforts, which mainly focus on promoting religious tolerance and open, rule-based economies. Because of the seemingly opaque and complex structure of Blair's companies and foundations, he has been widely criticized by the media and a disaffected British public. Some decry the alleged conflict of interest resulting from his overlapping for-profit and nonprofit activities and his engagement with autocratic regimes with spotty human rights records. In response to such accusations, Blair has countered that he engages with these regimes to promote political reform, arguing that incremental improvement is better than no progress at all.[12] Fringe countries benefit from the respectability Blair confers on them and the connections he provides. In turn, they are attractive clients with deep pockets and enormous growth potential, which converts into deal-making opportunities.

Despite his massive earnings, Blair seems less driven by money than by public recognition and a desire to retain a seat at the table. Being driven and restless, he—by his own account—has worked very, very hard in building a platinum Rolodex following his departure from office.[13]

CROSS-CONNECTIONS: COOPERATING
CONSTRUCTIVELY IN TIMES OF CRISES

The depth and reach of the international policy makers' and financial superhubs' tight-knit networks became particularly clear during the financial crisis. When the financial system was close to collapsing, they convened to coordinate unprecedented emergency responses. While the legitimacy, fairness, and effectiveness of their efforts can validly be questioned, it is by now relatively undisputed that the global financial system would have most likely imploded with incalculable consequences if leaders had not taken unconventional measures.[14]

Most of what had been going on behind the scenes was kept secret at the time in order to avoid a market panic and run on the banks. However, in the years following the Lehman debacle, many officials who had been actively involved in the crisis response, later wrote books in which they lifted the lid on what really happened. Among those who recounted their firsthand experience were Ben Bernanke, Hank Paulson, Timothy Geithner, and Sheila Bair. All their reports have one theme in common: the crucial role that personal relationships played in solving problems too large for any individual to tackle alone. For instance, Hank Paulson, President Bush's "war general" during the crisis, repeatedly stressed the significance of deep relationships in his book *On the Brink*, an account that was mirrored in Andrew Ross Sorkin's book *Too Big to Fail*.[15]

While Paulson may come across as aloof and somewhat dry, he is actually the embodiment of a master networker. Prior to serving as secretary of the treasury, he was CEO of Goldman Sachs and forged relationships with leaders all over the world, particularly with the Chinese elite. His connections in China were said to have been better than even those of the U.S. administration and would later become an important asset during the financial crisis. After becoming treasury secretary, he sought to reinforce his relationship with Condoleezza Rice, then the secretary of state whom he had previously helped in her job search. On his second day at the treasury, he took her to lunch, where she shared that the best way to relate to President Bush was to spend time alone with him. At that time, Paulson did not know President Bush very well, but he already understood that gaining direct access to him would be crucial. In his opinion, any negotiations would be meaningless unless he was able to gain the president's trust.

Paulson continued to maintain close ties with the finance executives he knew from his time on Wall Street, and during the crisis he benefited from their cooperation and firsthand intelligence from the front. In addition, he made an effort to develop relationships with politicians on both sides of the aisle. Applying his Wall Street frame of mind, he viewed the 535 members of Congress as new "clients" and courted them with the same zeal he had employed in his commercial career.[16] He also developed a "special bond" with Ben Bernanke and maintained a "constructive relationship" with Sheila Bair, chairwoman of the Federal Deposit Insurance Corporation (FDIC) at the time.

Paulson's successful passage of the emergency rescue package known as TARP (Troubled Asset Relief Program) demonstrated his emotional intelligence and social skills. TARP could hardly have been more controversial, and it was, consequently, very difficult to convince Congress to back it. Just before the vote, he even bent down on one knee and begged Nancy Pelosi, then Speaker of the House of Representatives, not to block the deal, to which Ms. Pelosi replied wryly, "I did not know you were Catholic."[17] Throughout the crisis, Paulson, Geithner, and Bernanke formed a trifecta that essentially prevented the U.S.—and, by implication, the global financial system, from falling off a cliff.

LAUNCHING A PRESIDENT

The surest strategy for achieving access and influence within a network is to initiate its creation. If your new network combines money with politics, it will be all the more powerful. This is what happened when several Wall Street heavy hitters backed a little-known senator from Chicago named Barack Obama. George Soros, the multibillionaire hedge fund titan, contributed to Obama's rise by endorsing him and donating to his campaign. In May 2007, Soros hosted a fund-raiser at his lavish Fifth Avenue apartment and convinced another hedge fund legend, Paul Tudor Jones, shortly thereafter to throw a big fund-raising party at his gorgeous Connecticut waterfront mansion, where many of the attendees were wealthy Wall Streeters. Soros and Jones are admired and emulated opinion leaders in their industry, so their support sparked a large following and sent Obama's campaign on an upward trajectory. Financial contributions are important, but at least equally as powerful is access to the superhubs' networks. Once superhubs mobilize them, this in turn mobilizes various subnetworks, thereby tipping off a multiplier effect that results in exponentially higher funding.

Shows of support generally increase the likelihood of gaining access and influence to a given network, but they are certainly no guarantee as Wall Street came to learn. The financial sector supported Obama's second-term 2012 campaign to a much lesser extent after experiencing "buyer's remorse"; they felt that he had turned against them by embracing the hostile "fat cat" narrative. And while Obama acknowledged big donors like Warren Buffett, who has the image of a benevolent grandfather, by asking him to join his advisory circle, he has, for the most part, shunned George Soros, who is much more controversial. For the longest time, Obama's staff failed to respond to Soros's requests and only reluctantly arranged for a brief unofficial meeting. Soros, who had always appreciated Hillary Clinton's accessibility during her time as First Lady, felt disrespected.[18]

The CEOs of the largest financial institutions also maintain close ties to the president, and many of them share the same alma mater. Jamie Dimon, Lloyd Blankfein, Michael Corbat, and President Obama are all Harvard University graduates. Big bank CEOs also have direct access to the president simply because they steer systemically important institutions holding trillions of dollars in deposits. According to official statistics, they visited and had calls with President Obama, Timothy Geithner, and other top officials many times during the crisis.[19] In Germany, similar statistics reveal that top bankers frequently interacted with Chancellor Merkel and her staff.[20]

"LEGALIZED CORRUPTION": THE BEST
DEMOCRACY MONEY CAN BUY

Another way to further one's access and interest is through the retention of lobbyists on both sides of the aisle. In our modern economy of influence, reciprocal relationships are a tradable currency.[21] Former senior officials leverage their preexisting relationships to provide executives in the financial sector with access to public figures.[22] According to a study by the National Bureau of Economic Research, the main role of lobbyists is to maintain connections with politicians. Those relationships in turn determine the subject matter they work on, and when the politicians move to another position, the lobbyists follow them. Expertise on issues is good, but the premium is much larger for lobbyists with deep connections to the political establishment.[23] In line with these findings, a study by the University of Warwick quantified the value of personal connections by determining that the revenue of U.S. political lobbyists falls by 24 percent if their former employer leaves government office.[24] Wall Street lobbyists' influence even extends to writing legislation, and lawmakers who support those bills typically receive more contributions than those who do not.[25]

Purchasing Political Protection

If you feel that some firms are less scrutinized than others, it may not be your imagination. The discretion possessed by the SEC opens it up to the possibility of manipulation. A study from the London Business School illustrates that politically connected firms are on average less likely to be involved in an SEC enforcement action and face lower penalties if prosecuted. The study further substantiates statistically that the more a company spends on political donations, the more lenient the treatment. It follows that the SEC has focused not on the worst but on the least-connected offenders. Unsurprisingly, financial contributions are most efficient if made to high-ranking politicians from the majority party and those setting the SEC budget or sitting on oversight committees.[26]

Critics argue that buying influence in a democracy borders on legalized corruption and that the lucrative financial sector prevails at the expense of the common good. This argument makes sense for a variety of reasons. While it is completely legitimate to represent one's interests to the powers that be, there are few restrictions and checks and balances when it comes to purchasing favors in Washington. Former officials have been critical as well, among them Sheila Bair of the FDIC. In her book *Bull by the Horns*, she criticizes the "undue influence of the financial services lobby."[27] In her opinion, the relationship between Washington and Wall Street had become too cozy, and too many of the people involved in handling the crisis—at both the senior and staff levels—had been responsible for some of the regulatory errors and missteps that had brought us the crisis to begin with."[28]

But this argument also works in the reverse: Regulators with private-sector experience have a much better understanding of financial institutions' operations. Since these institutions are staffed with highly qualified, highly incentivized, and highly creative people—many of whom are world-class experts in circumventing legal provisions—this can come in handy. Case in point: Robert Khuzami, who has traversed between the public and private sectors several times. After working as general counsel for Deutsche Bank, including during the years of the financial crisis, he joined the SEC, arguing that his experience in the private sector would improve his enforcement results. When he left the SEC in 2013, he accepted a $5 million offer from the law firm Kirkland & Ellis and complied with a one-year "cooling off period" before joining his new employer.[29]

RELATIONSHIP POWER: DIFFUSING THE EURO TIME BOMB

During the course of the financial crisis, the role of policy makers and politicians became crucial, and relationships were put to the test. Washington D.C., temporarily replaced New York City as the financial capital of the U.S.; in fact, many laid-off bankers moved south for jobs in the Capitol. Politicians all over the world were out of their element and lacked the financial acumen to manage the complex situation. In addition, politicians were first and foremost committed to their own constituents, while preserving the international financial system required cross-border measures. Therefore, they were forced to compromise in a highly uncertain situation where the value of their concessions was impossible to calculate. The euro's design defect had contributed to the fundamental fragility of the financial, economic, and political system, which made cooperative goodwill even more important.

In the spring of 2010, Greece became increasingly more cash-strapped while violent social unrest erupted on the streets. As a result, international financial markets started to panic and became extremely volatile. Within just five days, one of the smallest economies in Europe had sparked a crisis that threatened to spread to Portugal and Spain, leading to fears of a currency breakup with incalculable consequences. A disorderly currency implosion, or only the fear thereof, triggering a run on the banks and a market crash was everyone's worst nightmare.

Following the traumatic collapse of Lehman Brothers in 2008, the U.S. administration was particularly worried about contagion in the global financial system spreading to U.S. shores. Therefore, it took the liberty of volunteering unsolicited advice and exerting gentle pressure on Europeans. From the perspective of their own more unified system and proactive mentality, they could not understand why the Europeans seemed so lethargic. Meanwhile, the Greek situation grew much worse very fast, and within days it became clear that—for the very first time—one of the eurozone states needed rescue. Heads of state such as Angela Merkel, Nicolas Sarkozy, and Silvio Berlusconi hurriedly assembled with finance ministers and central bank governors over the weekend to search for a solution, while the public was kept in the dark. A "time bomb" was ticking: On Monday morning, Asian markets would open, and if they crashed, they would likely take the global markets down with them. The leaders of Europe feared that the euro was in acute danger of unraveling.

With the cooperation of IMF chief Dominique Strauss-Kahn, central bank governors—under the guidance of Jean-Claude Trichet, the president of the European Central Bank; Mario Draghi, the Head of the Central Bank of Italy; and Fed chairman Ben Bernanke—took a leading role in coordinating measures. It was extremely difficult to align seventeen different eurozone countries and many other leading nations around the world within just a few days, as opposing ideologies and competing interests clashed. While their overarching mutual interest—the integrity of the financial system—provided a strong motivation to reach an agreement, there were many legal, political, and logistical hurdles to overcome. Nerves frayed, and contentious discussions ensued.

In the end, their cooperation was effective because so many of the policy makers knew and understood one another. Bernanke, Draghi, and Trichet had a close bond and could speak in shorthand. Strauss-Kahn was respected and had a good working relationship with virtually everyone, so his word carried weight. Many of the politicians had built relationships over the years, were familiar with one another's idiosyncrasies; and knew how to push the right buttons, build alliances, and negotiate to reach a mutually beneficial solution. Germany and France were close because Angela Merkel and Nicolas Sarkozy were close. Together, they corralled other leaders into their corner and reined in more-difficult characters such as Berlusconi. Eventually, they came to an agreement once vociferously opposed by the Germans: government funding by printing money. Bernanke provided a swap line, and Strauss-Kahn generously contributed money on behalf of the IMF, even though it exceeded his authority and necessitated retroactive approval by the IMF board.[30]

In the end, the eurozone created a rescue mechanism that amounted to a total of EUR 750 billion. The solution was hastily stitched together and had many flaws, but it prevented the system from breaking apart. Such complicated negotiations would have been exceedingly difficult and likely less constructive if the participants hadn't had—at least for the most part—close relationships.

SUPER-ENTITY: THE CAPITALIST NETWORK THAT RUNS THE WORLD

The key players in the financial sector are also closely intertwined with members of the corporate sector.[31] Global corporations are mega-power centers. In terms of economic entities, many of the world's largest corporations rank higher than countries when measured by returns and GDP and many of these corporations are financial firms. Only 737 shareholders retain at least 80 percent of the control over these corporations. A study from the Swiss Federal Institute of Technology reveals the network of their interwoven ownership structures. Researchers started out with a database comprising 37 million economic actors, which they narrowed down to 43,060 transnational companies. They then modeled the cross-holdings and discovered that a tightly knit group of 1,318 companies hold a large portion of the corporate control in the world. The inner core consists of 147 companies, which are the most powerful and essentially all own parts of one another.

Not surprisingly, most entities of this supercore are banks. Financial institutions dominate the top ten, with Barclays occupying first place, closely followed by AXA, State Street, JPMorgan, Vanguard, UBS, and Merrill Lynch.[32] This structure epitomizes the interlocking relationships between institutions and, therefore, the people who preside over them. Frequently, individuals are directly linked through board seats at different companies, a fact that creates information flows, aligned interests, and opportunities.[33] These network dynamics tend to promote corporatism, where major interest groups have great influence on the state.

* * *

In this chapter, we have seen that the revolving door, lobbying, and campaign contributions weave a tight and powerful web of interpersonal relationships between the financial sector and the political establishment. Personal linkages skew the system in the superhubs' favor, and while conflicts of interest can pose dangers, solid relationships can preserve the system in times of crisis. But what happens to those precious relationships during personal crises? How resilient are those networks if a superhub violates legal, ethical, and societal rules? Chapter 11 will explore superhubs who lose their links to the system and whether or not they can recover them.

CHAPTER 11

De-Linked

Expulsion and Comeback

BEING A SUPERHUB IS NO GUARANTEE for a privileged and everlasting network status. However, considering the multitude of links to other hubs, complete expulsion from the network is rare. Even after the abysmal crisis—which many financiers had a hand in causing—very few top financial executives disappeared from the map. One who suffered a total fall from grace, to a large extent due to his failure to maintain a resilient network of personal relationships, was Dick Fuld, the former CEO of Lehman Brothers. Most other top executives have found new positions either in the financial industry, related industries, or even entirely different fields. Their strong connections form a safety net that prevents them from irrevocably falling through the cracks. However, for those who violate the law, commit a serious betrayal of trust, or demonstrate a fundamental lack of integrity, a return is certainly much harder.

SENT INTO EXILE: DICK FULD

Having vast power over resources and people can be addictive and lead to distorted perception and irrationality. Overconfidence, intolerance of dissent, and excessive risk taking are often the result. One example is Lehman Brothers' Dick Fuld, whose hubris catalyzed the demise of a storied institution and his expulsion from the financial network.

Fuld began his career as a bond trader at Lehman Brothers, which was founded in 1850 and in 2008 was the fourth-largest investment bank in the U.S. He steadily rose through the ranks during the rough-and-tumble heydays of banking. At heart he remained a trader, which was perhaps why he never quite fit in with the more genteel bankers. Fuld embodied the testosterone-driven macho culture of Wall Street. Of imposing stature, he wore a perennial grim expression on his face. His intimidating glare left others in a state of constant fear, and people around him walked on eggshells, careful not to trigger any of his infamous outbursts.

Fond of military lingo, Fuld liked exaggeratedly brutal formulations. He once told John Thain of Goldman Sachs, whom he suspected of spreading rumors about Lehman, that when he discovered the culprit, he would reach down his throat and tear out his heart. Accordingly, he employed a martial management style: He expected obedience, did not tolerate opposition, and obliterated disloyal employees. Other executives quickly figured out that life was much easier if they did not challenge him. In line with this personality cult, they fittingly referred to Fuld as "King Richard" and "the Gorilla." In Lehman's alpha male universe, female executives were virtually nonexistent. Fuld not only neglected to build a network of goodwill within his organization but also failed to build strong relationships with his Wall Street peers and other strategically important executives. Never really a relationship person, he focused on the one and only area that directly affected his bottom line: clients and transactions.

The inefficient information flow resulting from the lack of a healthy network contributed significantly to Lehman's implosion. Unlike Robert Rubin or Hank Paulson, who were famous for relentlessly working their phones, Fuld preferred to isolate himself. He outsourced operational duties to a trusted executive, Joe Gregory, and also physically distanced himself from his subordinates in his palatial offices on the thirty-second floor, preferring to rather not mingle much with the rest of the bank. Because he failed to keep a finger on the pulse of Wall Street and Washington, he completely misjudged the mood of the markets. Instead of following up on red flags, Fuld motivated his troops with empty phrases about Lehman's unbeatable strength until the bitter end. Lehman was leveraged to the hilt with an extremely high exposure to subprime assets, and when trouble came, it needed a loyal network it did not have.

On September 10, 2008, Lehman announced a $3.9 billion loss for the third quarter, the worst result in its history. President Bush later wrote that there was no way the firm could survive the weekend and that the best solution was for the government to help find a buyer in the two days that remained. Fuld's liaison to the government was treasury secretary Hank Paulson. Fuld had always harbored resentment toward Goldman, which he had revealed at a private dinner with Paulson in the spring of 2008. As a Goldmanite who was highly trained in EQ, Paulson found Fuld to be arrogant with few redeeming qualities. Unfortunately for Fuld, Paulson was now in charge of the rescue. It is highly likely that the brittle relationship helped tip the scales against Lehman.

To his credit, Paulson did try hard to help find buyers for Lehman. Two possibilities circulated: Bank of America and Barclays. However, London regulators rejected Barclays's purchase of Lehman as a whole, and Bank of America decided to buy Merrill Lynch instead. Lehman was out of options. Fuld begged regulators to convert his investment bank to a bank holding company, in order to obtain access to federal funding. But, as the New York Times reported, Geithner turned him down and President Bush refused to take his call.[1] The view in Washington was that Fuld had brought the troubles upon himself and overplayed his hand. Lehman filed for bankruptcy on September 15, 2008.

In contrast, when AIG got into trouble, the government bailed it out with record amounts of money. Treasury secretaries Paulson and Geithner had Goldman CEO Lloyd Blankfein on speed dial, who was more than willing to act as their eyes and ears on Wall Street. Within a year, they spoke dozens of times, mostly during the AIG incident. Both parties had reason to worry: AIG had written billions in credit default swaps for Goldman, and if AIG folded, Goldman would incur a huge loss. Paulson and Geithner feared that billions more were at risk at other firms who were counterparties of AIG, which would likely render them insolvent and wreak havoc on Wall Street. Following their discussions, the New York Fed authorized a loan of up to $85 billion to AIG in return for a 79.9 percent equity interest. In total, the AIG subsidies amounted to $182 billion, of which Goldman Sachs as an AIG counterparty received $12.9 billion.

Following Lehman's collapse, Fuld stayed out of the public eye. He spent most of his time on his multimillion-dollar estate in Sun Valley, Idaho, which he put on the market with an asking price of $59.5 million. It was sold at auction in 2015 for a "record breaking" price of at least $20 million.[2] Not much is known about his firm, Matrix Advisors, and, now a pariah, he is seen only rarely at social occasions. In mid-2015, he reemerged for the first time to speak at a conference. Largely unrepentant, he placed most of the blame for the crisis and Lehman's failure on the U.S. government.

SHOCK-RESISTANT: LARRY SUMMERS'S NETWORK

During the Annual Meetings of the IMF, Nouriel Roubini and I had a meeting with Larry Summers, the director of the National Economic Council, at his office. It was a bright, sunny day as I made my way to the White House, which looked postcard-perfect set against deep-blue skies and the lush green lawn. In reality, it is much smaller than one would imagine. We checked in at the Northwest Gate for our appointment in the West Wing, which is located on 17th Street and Pennsylvania Avenue. Visitors must be announced at least twenty-four hours in advance for routine Secret Service background checks. I presented my passport, went through security screening, and received a temporary badge. After entering the West Wing, we took a seat in the waiting area, and I pretended to read a paper while observing the goings-on around me out of the corner of my eyes with great fascination. A general, whom I had just seen giving an interview on television the previous day, walked by and said hello. Some other generals and visitors headed for the Situation Room, and a staffer collected their cell phones in a basket for security reasons.

After a while, we were led through offices completely crammed with staffers and piles of papers. At the top of a narrow staircase, Summers awaited us. His spacious office was located just above the Oval Office and overlooked the Rose Garden. We settled into our seats across from his desk. Summers very much lived up to his public image: Outside of his office pallets of Diet Coke were stacked up against the wall, his shirt was untucked, and he put his feet on the coffee table in front of us. But he was a gracious host, in good spirits, and a lively conversation ensued. It was fascinating to gain unedited insight into his thinking.

Larry Summers, who is known to be a somewhat prickly intellectual genius, is atypical yet exemplary of the dynamics that rule the world of high-level networking: Despite courting controversy throughout his career, he occupies a central position that touches upon virtually all other networks. Ever restless and on the lookout for new challenges, pushing boundaries and climbing to new heights, Summers has had several exceedingly successful careers and held some of the most important positions in the U.S. government. His platinum resume was practically preordained in his DNA, as he is the son of two economists and the nephew of two Nobel laureates in economics, Paul Samuelson and Kenneth Arrow. His father taught at Yale University, and Samuelson had been an adviser to President Kennedy.

Meteoric Rise

Summers's stellar professional rise occurred with lightning speed. He was accepted into the Massachusetts Institute of Technology at age sixteen and received tenure at Harvard University at only twenty-eight years old. That same year, personal tragedy struck when he was diagnosed with late-stage Hodgkin's disease and endured nine grueling months of chemotherapy. He later said that this experience made him focus all the more on his body of work, since he felt it kept him distracted, social, and sane.

In 1988 he joined the presidential campaign of Massachusetts governor Michael Dukakis, where he met many high-profile political fixtures such as Gene Sperling, George Stephanopoulos, Laura D'Andrea Tyson, and Robert Rubin, who over time would become allies and close friends. Three years later, he landed the prestigious position of chief economist at the World Bank. After a two-year stint, he became secretary of the treasury for international affairs and was awarded the John Bates Clark medal for his achievement as the most accomplished economist under forty years of age. Short of the noble Prize, it is considered the most prestigious award.

In 1999, Summers became secretary of the treasury in the Clinton administration. After serving his term, he returned to Harvard to become its twenty-seventh President—an extremely prestigious position. Thereafter, he returned to the White House to serve as the director of the NEC under President Obama. Considering the seismic shifts the economy underwent during the greatest crisis since the Great Depression, this was an incredibly influential post.

Against All Odds

However, controversy frequently disrupted Summers's seemingly unstoppable rise. Most of this was the result of his own doing, as he often turned out to be his own worst enemy. Over the years he has alienated numerous people with what they perceived as arrogance. Often described as the smartest guy in the room, he can be intellectually domineering, dismissive, and prone to imperious outbursts of temperament. His autographing dollar bills, which already carried his signature from his days as treasury secretary, raised eyebrows. Idiosyncrasies such as his table manners, his penchant for falling asleep—including in meetings with the president and foreign heads of state—his avoiding eye contact, interrupting people and occasionally being less than polite, led some at Harvard to speculate that something might be off.

He has always been rough around the edges, but over the years he has made an effort to improve. He was helped early on by Robert Rubin, who took him under his wing during the Dukakis campaign and eventually helped pave his way to the White House. Summers, being aware of his shortcomings, tried to adopt some of Rubin's fortes, specifically his highly developed social skills. They made a curious team. Rubin was soft-spoken and sophisticated, whereas Summers was disheveled and confrontational. Yet, they complemented each other well. Rubin opened doors for Summers, who closely studied his mentor and began to evolve. Today, Summers often speaks in an exaggeratedly polite manner and seems to habitually wear a smile.

The Bull in Charge of the China Shop

Summers has a tendency to blow himself up in the most spectacular manner. The first implosion occurred in 1991, during his time as chief economist at the World Bank, in what has been dubbed "toxic memo gate." One of Summers's aides had written a memo, which Summers had signed, on exporting polluting industries and toxic waste to Africa, an argument that was interpreted to imply that human life was of lesser value there. Once the firestorm erupted, the aide claimed he had employed irony to provoke a critical dialogue. Unfortunately, that subtlety was lost on the discerning public, and when the *Economist* got wind of the memo, they featured it on their front cover with the headline "Let Them Eat Pollution."[3] Economists, environmentalists, and politicians were appalled by the incident, which seemed to reinforce the negative image of the World Bank. The aide offered to take responsibility, but Summers insisted on taking the blame.

In 2001, the next chapter in the Summers career drama ensued. While serving as president of Harvard University, Summers summoned Cornel West, a fellow professor at Harvard, in African American Studies, to his office. There, he criticized his colleague for missing too many classes, handing out too many favorable grades, and producing a "disgraceful" hip-hop CD. He called upon West to reinforce his authority by writing an academic book and suggested regular follow-up meetings. West was incensed. After much back and forth, and what seemed like a conciliatory meeting in which the two men shared their experiences with cancer, the situation finally escalated. West claimed that Summers had apologized, which Summers vigorously disputed. West exploded and characterized Summers as untrustworthy and lacking character, calling him the "Ariel Sharon of higher education." Thereafter, all hell broke loose, with West being accused of anti-Semitism and eventually leaving Harvard for MIT. No one came out looking good, particularly the president of Harvard University, whose conduct was considered at best undiplomatic and at worst undignified.[4]

Eventually the dust settled, only for Summers to create another out-
rage. At a conference, while discussing why fewer women succeed in science and math, he suggested that "there are issues of intrinsic aptitude,"
a remark which was widely interpreted to mean that women were less
likely to possess the intellectual capacity to complete high-level quantitative work.[5] This was a startling statement to have been made publicly
by the president of such an influential educational institution, especially
considering that the rate of female academics obtaining full professorships
had significantly declined under his presidency. A frenzy ensued among
professors, alumni, and the public. After first trying to defend his statement, Summers eventually apologized.[6] In the course of the controversy, it
emerged that other complaints had been made about him, and eventually
he had no other choice but to resign.

A short while thereafter, Obama won the presidency and looked for a
secretary of the treasury. Summers was interested in the coveted post, but
because of the previous high-profile controversies, the position went to
Timothy Geithner, the young former head of the New York Fed. Instead,
Summers was chosen to lead the Council of Economic Advisers—a distinguished and influential position to be sure, but not quite as much as
treasury secretary.

In 2014, a search ensued to find a successor for Fed Chairman Ben
Bernanke. Summers wanted the position badly, and although he had a
tight web of powerful supporters including President Obama, countless
others inside and outside the Beltway voiced opposition. Critics pointed
to the fact that Summers had driven the deregulation that resulted in
the repeal of parts of the Glass-Steagall Act, separating investment from
commercial banking and insurance activities. Since Summers had also
opposed regulation of complex derivatives, they argued, he had significantly contributed to the crisis. Some pointed out that he lacked relevant
monetary policy experience, especially when compared to his main competitor for the job, Janet Yellen, who at the time was the vice chair of the
Federal Reserve under Ben Bernanke. Others saw his commercial activities as evidence of overly tight connections with the financial industry.
Before joining the Council of Economic Advisers in 2009, his advisory
engagement with the hedge fund D. E. Shaw, for which he received $5.5

million in 2008 made headlines. He was also a board director at Taconic Capital, a hedge fund founded by Goldman Sachs alumni. In addition, he received $2.7 million for speaking engagements in 2008, including $135,000 for a single speech at Goldman Sachs.

Despite this criticism, Summers lobbied hard behind the scenes for the prestigious and powerful position of Fed chair. Renowned *New York Times* columnist Maureen Dowd characterized his proponents as the "boys club around President Obama, the bullying cool kids around Wall Street types like Rubin, a bunch of alpha males who prefer each other's company and flatter themselves that they are smart enough to know how smart Summers is."[7] When he realized that he would likely not be confirmed, he withdrew his name in a gracious letter to President Obama. Not landing the position was a disappointment, but Summers occupied himself with becoming more deeply entrenched with the financial sector. He joined the boards of the payment company Square and the financing company Lending Club; moreover, he became part-time special adviser to the venture capital firm Andreessen Horowitz. In subsequent interviews, he made sure to point out that in his new positions, he would focus on providing macroeconomic advice rather than merely functioning as a door opener.

Summers is an interesting case considering his unstoppable rise within the system and apparent immunity from expulsion. While his exceptional brilliance is undisputed, he has a penchant for committing faux pas and alienating people. Despite his flawed emotional intelligence, he realized that in order to reach the very top of finance—especially in Washington, where social skills are pivotal—he had no choice but to develop humility and become more conciliatory. His longtime mentor Bob Rubin, the embodiment of emotional intelligence, was particularly helpful in this transformation, by instruction and example. Even in the early stages of his career, Summers was smart enough to build sustainable alliances with more-senior superhubs, who not only helped him advance but also lent their support in crises. With every step up the ladder, Summers accumulated more network capital. As he became more powerful, other players in his network had a more vested interest in him retaining his position, because it indirectly strengthened theirs. When it came to the Fed chairmanship, likely the second most powerful position in the

United States after the presidency, Summers turned out to have alienated too many people and had insufficient social capital to obtain the necessary support. However, we have likely not yet heard the last of Larry Summers when it comes to public office. If history is any indicator, he will continue to build ever stronger alliances to one day become a hyperhub.

Why has Summers, despite his many missteps, proven so unassailable? For starters, in America, the land of second chances, his indiscretions for the most part weren't considered capital offenses. Rather, he was perceived as an overly intellectual professor with perhaps not the best social skills, who wasn't ill intentioned but merely prone to sticking his foot in his mouth. In addition, he successfully converted his image as a genius into a brand and over the years accumulated a great amount of social capital, which lent him protection. Despite his polarizing personality, most people—if only out of an abundance of caution—prefer to stay on good terms with him. Because of his many resilient links with other superhubs, his own superhub status is virtually guaranteed.

DEN OF THIEVES: MIKE MILKEN

When I lived in Germany, I read *Den of Thieves*, the tale of the 1980s "junk bond king," Mike Milken. It provided insight into the epicenter of finance, a world of fascinating personalities and exciting transactions. I so longed to be there. A decade later, when I worked with famed economist Nouriel Roubini, we traveled to the Global Conference of the Milken Institute in Los Angeles, where he had a speaking engagement. And there I met Mike Milken, the living legend I had read so much about. He was just as I had imagined: bald, with big, fixating eyes and an intense presence. We had a chance to speak behind the scenes, and absolutely everything he said sounded ingenious. Afterward, he invited us to a charity dinner at private equity honcho Leon Black's brother-in-law's house in the Santa Monica Mountains. The scene reeked of wealth and was like something right out of a Hollywood movie. The elegant white house and the beautifully manicured grounds were the epitome of beauty, and the grass, steel-blue sky, and flowers seemed perfectly color-coordinated. Brainiacs, doctors, researchers, and billionaire donors, connected by common cause, chatted animatedly. Milken was in his element, holding court and chatting with the guests. I had a fabulous time and could not help but think that this was exactly how I had imagined this parallel universe to be when reading about it so many years earlier, half the world away. The tale of junk bond king Mike Milken is one of triumph, tragedy, redemption, and comeback.

In the Gordon Gekko–ish 1980s, this ingenious financier revolutionized the financial system by opening up capital markets to companies which had previously not been considered creditworthy. He created a market and channeled billions of dollars into companies by issuing high-yield bonds, also dubbed junk bonds. So great was the boom he created that at some point it exceeded the financing of investment-grade companies.

Born into a middle-class family in California, by the mid-1980s Milken had become a billionaire. However, in 1986 this steep ascent came to a screeching halt when he became entangled in a federal insider trading investigation and eventually pled guilty to six breaches of securities law. He was convicted and received a ten-year prison sentence, of which he served twenty-two months, and was forced to pay $600 million in fines and restitution. In addition, the SEC barred him and his brother Lowell, with whom he had closely collaborated, from the securities industry for life. He went from hero to villain, his world shattered and reputation destroyed. For the public, he symbolized everything that was wrong with Wall Street and became the poster boy of greed.

Milken had been the superhub of superhubs, creating an unbelievable network all by himself. Then—suddenly—the links were cut. Excluded from the financial industry, he became an outcast, and even those still close to him feared social and reputational contagion. Shortly after his release from prison, he was diagnosed with terminal prostate cancer and given eighteen months to live. He fought the disease with the same resolve and determination that he had applied in his financial career and—to the surprise of his doctors—made a full recovery. He then began to turn his life around by raising and donating millions of dollars for cancer research. The most effective way to rehabilitate a damaged reputation is to engage in philanthropy and associate oneself with prestigious universities. Milken taught at UCLA and became a generous donor to medical research and education. He used his vast network and celebrity status to raise awareness in the media and optimize his fund-raising efforts.

In 1991 he founded the Milken Institute, which also hosts an annual global conference sometimes referred to as "Davos with palm trees," although it is more U.S. and finance-sector centric than the annual gathering of the WEF. The conference takes place at the Beverly Hills Hotel, where Milken in his previous life had hosted his legendary junk bond conference called the "Predators' Ball," which has been colorfully immortalized in the book by the same title.[8] Members of the financial elite, Washington power players, and world-renowned researchers attend the event. Billionaires Leon Black, Steve Schwarzman, Steven A. Cohen, Mort Zuckerman, and Richard LeFrak are regulars, as are former U.K. prime minister Tony Blair and Rwandan president Paul Kagame. It is one of the highest-caliber events in the world, and the attendance by global power players is an implicit endorsement and indicator that Milken's social standing has been largely restored.

Considering the gravity of Milken's offense, his rehabilitation is remarkable. It resulted from the deep and resilient relationships he had forged with people throughout his life and from his proactive approach to creating new networks that all revolved around him, automatically making him a superhub. He had created original networks in connection with his junk bond empire in the 1980s, and later with his medical research efforts, and various endeavors via his Milken Institute.

Milken possesses many essential qualities that contribute to his superhub status. Some people have great ideas but do not execute them. Others are good at executing ideas but cannot generate any original ones. Milken combines both: He is an ingenious idea generator as well as a perfect executor. Just like many other thought leaders, he created a philosophy that formed the basis of his thinking and doing. As discussed in Chapter 4, according to his formula, $P=EFT$ (DHC+ESC+ERA), prosperity is the sum of financial technology times the sum of human capital plus social capital plus real assets.

His extraordinary drive, grit, passion, and perfectionism made his reinvention possible. He applied such force and pressure that he wore down most resistance. But once tainted by scandal, especially one that entails violations of law, limitations and opposition will likely remain. At an intimate fund-raiser for Mitt Romney in Las Vegas, I teasingly said amongst a small circle of his friends that perhaps Milken should run for president. I was immediately cautioned by a friend of his never to say that in his presence, because as a convicted felon, he was ineligible to run for public office. He said that the stigma still weighed heavily on Milken.

COMPLETE NETWORK COLLAPSE: DOMINIQUE STRAUSS-KAHN

Unless you lived under a rock, you could not possibly have missed the spectacular implosion of Dominique Strauss-Kahn, the mighty former head of the International Monetary Fund. I first met him prescandal during one of the IMF Annual Meetings in Washington, D.C., where Nouriel Roubini and I had an appointment with him. Despite his crammed schedule, he squeezed us in, probably as a favor to Roubini. He received us in his spacious and bright office, which featured 1980s furniture and dark wooden floor-to-ceiling bookcases, and we settled into comfortable seats in front of his heavy desk. He seemed in good spirits and was charming and affable. At the time, Strauss-Kahn was highly respected. He was considered to have smart and balanced views. In addition, he had the gift of finding the right tone and a talent for building consensus, which was of particular importance when dealing with the multitude of conflicting interests in the European debt crisis. He was popular amongst his staff, and people in my circle seemed fond of him, which heightened the shock when the unfathomable headlines hit.

En route to a meeting with Chancellor Merkel, Strauss-Kahn was arrested for sexual assault in the first-class cabin on an Air France flight at JFK Airport and transferred to a decidedly less comfortable Rikers Island prison cell. The international media had a field day and reveled in his shame, as he was publicly paraded before the whole world in handcuffs. We were aware of his reputation as a ladies' man but had no idea of the extent of his extracurricular activities. Many people, including Nouriel Roubini, George Soros, and political scientist Edward Jay Epstein, surmised that he had been set up by political enemies. While his enemies were quick to seize the opportunity, a setup seemed far-fetched in view of the circumstances. A few days after the initial arrest, Strauss-Kahn resigned as head of the IMF and was eventually allowed to leave for France. The charges of sexually assaulting a hotel maid in New York were dropped several months later, but the shocking headlines did not subside. New allegations of rape surfaced in the so-called "Carlton affair," in which he was charged with aggravated pimping in connection with an alleged prostitution ring.

Up to the moment of his spectacular arrest in New York, Strauss-Kahn had been seen as France's next president, but now all hopes of a political comeback were crushed. In fact, he was deemed so politically and personally toxic that most of his former colleagues and friends—even his wife—distanced themselves from him. After suffering one of the steepest and most dramatic downfalls in history, virtually no remnants of his old life remained. He lost his reputation, his status, and his allies, and—expelled from the center of the network—he became an isolated node at the fringes. Regardless, Strauss-Kahn still craved recognition and respect and, in an effort to regain his status as a superhub—or at least a hub—tried to reinvent himself as a respected former quasi-statesman and financial adviser. Such comebacks can be pursued solely from the fringes, because under no circumstances do other superhubs want to be tainted by association with an outcast. Left with few alternatives, expelled superhubs typically try to work their way back toward the center via second- and third-tier advisory engagements with developing and emerging countries, or those facing great difficulties or with questionable regimes. Strauss-Kahn had to lower his standards as well as his price, but he was able to land advisory agreements with Greece, Sri Lanka, and South Sudan and became a member of the supervisory board of the $10 billion state-backed Russian Direct Investment Fund. In addition, he was booked for speeches at conferences in Beijing, Seoul, Marrakech, and Yalta, among others.

Eventually, he took his efforts up a notch by venturing into the money management world, where real riches are made. He teamed up with French-Israeli banker Thierry Leyne, whom he had not previously known and who was not a player on the international stage. Although Strauss-Kahn was cautioned by friends concerned about Leyne's questionable reputation, he went ahead and formed Leyne, Strauss-Kahn & Advisors. Together he and Leyne planned to raise $2 billion for a macro hedge fund focused on emerging markets by utilizing Strauss-Kahn's expertise and contacts. A fund that size was an ambitious endeavor by any measure, but especially so for an unknown money manager and an economist who had never managed any money. Strauss-Kahn went from emperor presiding on the IMF throne to knocking on doors, tin cup in hand. That transformation must have been particularly humiliating when they failed to raise much money. The potential prison sentence hanging over Strauss-Kahn's head in connection with the Carlton affair probably didn't infuse trust in the viability of his endeavor. At some point, Strauss-Kahn left the firm after, as he said, he became aware of excessive borrowing. Two days after his departure, Leyne, a father of four, whose wife had already committed suicide several years earlier, jumped to his death from a high-rise in Tel Aviv. At the time of this writing, it is unclear whether Strauss-Kahn would be implicated, if at all, and if he would be held liable for the firm's losses.

In the aftermath, Sri Lanka's new government terminated its advisory agreement with Strauss-Kahn, according to which he received $750,000 to help attract foreign investments. His failed comeback as a fund manager dealt another blow to his reputation. In 2016, he joined the supervisory board at Bank Credit-Dnepr, owned by Ukrainian billionaire Victor Pinchuk (net worth $1.4 billion), the son-in-law of former Ukrainian president Leonid Kuchma.[9] Had the initial scandal not triggered a litany of further allegations, he probably would have landed a senior advisory role at a top-tier investment bank. However, once thoroughly disgraced, he was left with few choices. While any official position at least for the time being seems inconceivable, the stigma surrounding him has somewhat subsided—though it will likely never fully disappear. The French establishment has slowly lowered its guard and begun opening up its ranks and including him again. Thus, while regaining his status as a superhub is highly unlikely, becoming a well-linked hub again seems feasible in the absence of further jaw-dropping scandals.

PONZI SCHEMES AND SEX SCANDALS:
BUDDY FLETCHER AND ELLEN PAO

Minorities in high finance are rare; rarest of all are minority couples in which both partners are superhubs. One of those power couples was Buddy Fletcher and Ellen Pao. In network terms, they started out as nodes at the fringes of the system before equipping themselves with the preconditions and qualities needed to move to the center of the financial network.

I met Fletcher at hedge fund manager Paul Tudor Jones's fund-raiser for Barack Obama in May 2007. In the previous month, I had met the future president at a small fund-raiser, and he could not have been more personable. Talking to Obama felt like chatting with an old buddy from law school, so I looked forward to lending him my support. The fund-raiser took place at Jones's magnificent oceanfront Monticello-style mansion in Greenwich, Connecticut. As we approached Jones's estate, security personnel hovered everywhere. Security barriers and black SUVs dominated the streets, and Secret Service agents outfitted with earpieces spoke into microphones attached to their sleeves. Dozens of chauffeured cars lined up for clearance to drive up the scenic oak-tree-lined driveway to the stately entrance. Jones's white column-adorned, 13,000-square-foot estate is majestic yet comfortable, and his teenage children running around with their cousins and friends gave the home an informal family feel.

Obama received more than 300 guests in the lush garden covered with elegant white tents. There, one of the most respected fund managers in the world introduced me to Buddy Fletcher, endorsing him as a success-ful investor and philanthropist. Buddy was friendly, and during our brief conversation I realized that I had just met his brother Todd Fletcher, a composer and writer, earlier that month at a dinner at U.S. ambassador William Timken's residence in Berlin. Buddy invited me to a luncheon with philanthropically minded investors he was hosting at the Harvard Club a few days later.

The following month, he he asked me to join his mother's birthday celebration with just a handful of relatives at the Yale Club, including his other brother, movie producer Geoffrey Fletcher. The gathering was somewhat formal and everyone was terribly nice, especially considering that I was a new friend. I was also asked to join a cocktail party at Buddy's historic offices located at 48 Wall Street. The prestigious building, an architectural landmark, formerly belonged to Bank of New York. Behind the elaborate stone façade were Buddy's impressive offices, featuring twelve-foot ceilings, original antique crown moldings, and an English-style conference room with mahogany desks, elegant leather chairs, and fine art decorating the walls.

I found Buddy Fletcher hard to figure out. It was more a gut feeling than conscious analysis, but somehow I felt that my various impressions did not quite match up. He struck me as somewhat pretentious and inauthentic, with a chip on his shoulder. Beneath his smooth exterior, a subtle aggression seemed to be lurking.

In the fall, I received a request from Buddy for a conference call, during which he outlined a supposedly unique opportunity to acquire a huge financial institution. He was secretive and only elaborated that he had privileged information and a way in. But he needed coinvestors, claiming the transaction was too large for his fund. He asked me to formally introduce him to George Soros and other investors of similar caliber. I get approached for such introductions all the time, with most people expecting this service as a gratuitous favor. Then I usually respond that I would be delighted to work together and quote my consultancy fee. In the case of Fletcher, I didn't know what to make of him or of the transaction. If I do not know enough to personally vouch for someone's integrity, I won't make the introduction, so I graciously declined. Fletcher, unable to find coinvestors, ultimately folded his acquisition plan. Eventually I learned that Fletcher had been trying to acquire Bear Stearns, the investment bank that would falter only a few months thereafter.

After that conference call, our contact fizzled out, and the last I heard from his brother Geoffrey was that Fletcher had met the woman of his dreams, embarked on a whirlwind romance, and set a wedding date. Then I forgot about him. Imagine my surprise when a few years later I spotted the following headline in *Fortune*: "A Tale of Money, Sex and Power: The Ellen Pao and Buddy Fletcher Affair"—about the unraveling of Fletcher and his wife, Ellen Pao. As it turned out, the superstar couple had imploded by way of sensational lawsuits, fraud, and bankruptcy. The extreme rags-to-riches-to-rags story of a minority Wall Street couple was captivating.

The primary influence on Buddy Fletcher's life had been his ambitious mother, Bettye. She had high hopes not only for herself but also for her three sons. They were expected to overachieve, and even at the birthday party, Bettye exuded the air of a powerful matriarch presiding over her sons' lives. She reveled in Fletcher's accomplishments, led his philanthropic endeavors, and held down the fort in his office.

Fletcher attended Harvard University, where he was very popular and even became president of a student club so exclusive it later rejected Mark Zuckerberg, the founder of Facebook. There, Fletcher was accused of misappropriating funds but later was cleared. After graduation Fletcher accepted a job as a trader at Bear Stearns before moving on to Kidder, Peabody & Co. When he felt that he was paid an unfairly low bonus, he quit his job there and sued for racial discrimination. The suit was settled for $1.3 million, though the arbitration panel dismissed the discrimination charge. A human resources manager revealed later that the real reason the firm refused to pay the bonus was because Buddy refused to disclose how he had generated his profits, a wrinkle in the story that would later gain significance.

Upon leaving Kidder, Fletcher set up his own firm. Despite the fact that he had started out with little capital and a limited track record, he seemed to prosper almost beyond belief, displaying a lavish lifestyle and the accoutrements of wealth. Of slightly pretentious demeanor, he always looked dapper in expensive custom-tailored suits and a bow tie. His opulent offices on the forty-eighth floor of the venerable General Motors Building, with sweeping views of Central Park, included a personal dining room with a private chef and full-time waitress. He later moved offices to a pricey, ultra-elegant townhouse on East 66th Street and eventually settled at the prestigious landmark building in the heart of Wall Street. An assortment of luxury limousines—including a Mercedes, a Bentley, and a Jaguar—was at his disposal to be chauffeured in style. He owned not one but several apartments in the über-exclusive Dakota building on the Upper West Side adjacent to Central Park. The building is a historic landmark that has counted John Lennon, Lauren Bacall, Leonard Bernstein, and billionaire financier Wilbur Ross amongst its countless famous residents. He also bought several multimillion dollar homes in the Hamptons, and topped off his real estate holdings with a seventeen-room "castle" in Connecticut, including 1,100 acres of surrounding forestland.

Fletcher actively engaged in philanthropy early in his career and established a foundation in his name. The newly minted patron of the arts and sciences became a regular on the charity circuit and frequently hosted events at his glamorous Dakota apartment. In 2004, he pledged $50 million to support work on civil rights and $9 million to Harvard University. As is crucial for cementing a truly powerful network position, Fletcher also became involved in politics by giving to the Obama campaign. As a major donor, he was even invited to President Obama's inauguration and hosted a star-studded pre-gala cocktail party. Through his alignment with major Wall Street donors such as Paul Tudor Jones and George Soros, as well as many others, a whole new world of networking opportunities opened up to him. He developed an excellent reputation, and his social standing steadily increased. The press feted him as a rising superstar. Later, his employees described him as a person who was quite different from his public persona. They claimed that he terrorized them with his irascible temper and disappeared for prolonged lengths of time. Joseph DiMartino, chairman of the Dreyfus Family of Funds and former senior adviser to Fletcher Asset Management, soon quit after believing that Fletcher was not sufficiently focused on his day job.[10]

Fletcher's wife-to-be, Ellen Pao, had been an overachiever throughout her life. After graduating with an engineering degree from Princeton University, she went on to Harvard Law School and later to Harvard Business School. She began her career in Silicon Valley and eventually accepted a position at Kleiner Perkins Caufield & Byers. Kleiner Perkins is a highly respected venture capital firm with a mind-blowing track record of successful investments, including Amazon, Google, Netscape, and Genentech. There, Pao became head of staff for billionaire John Doerr, one of Kleiner Perkins's most successful partners. It was an enviable position at the intersection of tech and finance with invaluable exposure to top people and unique opportunities.

Then Fletcher's and Pao's lives fatefully intersected in the summer of 2007 at the Henry Crown Fellowship Program at the Aspen Institute, a leadership seminar for extraordinarily gifted professionals. A whirlwind courtship ensued, culminating in a wedding four months later and the birth of a baby girl a few months thereafter.[11] Perhaps most stunning was the fact that throughout his life Fletcher had been openly gay, for many years living with a male partner, and in 2005 accepted the Harvard Gay & Lesbian Caucus's annual Civil Rights Award. Now in his early forties, Fletcher had arrived: He was a multimillionaire, established fund manager, respected philanthropist, and top political donor with a direct line to President Obama; had an Ivy League educated and professionally accomplished wife, and a baby. Life was great. And then his house of cards collapsed.

The catalyst was a lawsuit that Fletcher himself had launched. When the board of the Dakota denied his application to buy his fifth apartment in the building in April 2010, he sued for racial discrimination. The board countered that discrimination had nothing to do with the rejection. Fletcher had previously been elected to the board, his mother was on the board at the time of his application, and he had close social ties to many residents in the building. The board contended that Fletcher's financial statements seemed inaccurate and that he could not afford the purchase. According to the board's president, Fletcher "has virtually no liquid assets . . . is highly leveraged, with significant debt, [and] his current level of annual interest expense far exceeds his annual income." He further noted that there was a "blurry distinction between Fletcher's personal accounts and business accounts" and that he regularly withdrew money from his stake in the fund in the millions of dollars.[12] The lawsuit set off a series of events that led to Fletcher's eventual demise.

After the controversy became public, the Wall Street Journal reported further irregularities. Thereafter, three Louisiana pension funds sued, trying to recover $145 million. Upon liquidation, the court-appointed liquidator stated that $125 million appeared to have vanished and that investors' monies were handled inappropriately, including the drawing of opaque and excessive fees at multiple levels and payment to Fletcher-affiliated entities without any benefit to investors and payment to Fletcher-affiliated entities. It also surfaced that Fletcher had financed his brother Geoffrey's movie *Violet & Daisy* with $7.7 million of public-pension-fund money, an investment that unfortunately yielded a multimillion-dollar unrealized loss.[13] According to the trustee's report, "In many ways, the fraud here has many of the characteristics of a Ponzi scheme, where, absent new investor money coming in, the overall structure would collapse."[14]

While building his impressive portfolio of prime real estate, cars, and relationships, Fletcher also continued to build an impressive portfolio of high-profile lawsuits. In addition to his racial discrimination suits against Kidder Peabody and the Dakota, he was sued by two of his Harvard friends-turned-employees, Michael Meade and Stephen Cass, who alleged sexual harassment after being fired for spurned advances. Eventually the suit was settled. A few years later, two caretakers at his Connecticut mansion also sued for sexual harassment and settled. By the same token, the donation Fletcher made to Harvard ended in a lawsuit. Instead of donating money as is customary, he had donated a contract to buy shares in a company called Calgene. However, Calgene stated that it had voided the contract prior to Fletcher passing it on. Harvard and Calgene eventually settled. Fletcher even managed to get his attorneys in trouble. The storied law firm of Skadden, Arps settled allegations that it had not adequately protected Fletcher's investors for $4.5 million.[15]

At the height of Fletcher's troubles, his wife, Ellen Pao, launched her own explosive lawsuit against Kleiner Perkins for gender discrimination, alleging that she suffered professional retaliation after spurning the sexual advances of a colleague, Ajit Nazre, and claiming systematic firmwide discrimination. The suit rocked Silicon Valley, which prides itself on its young, innovative, and merit-based culture. According to Pao, Nazre pressured her into a sexual relationship. When she broke it off, he—meanwhile promoted to senior partner—allegedly retaliated against her over the next five years by excluding her from meetings and curtailing access to business opportunities. In addition, she accused another partner of giving her a book containing "sexual drawings and strong sexual content." To top it off, she claimed that when she brought her grievances to the attention of senior management, they were ignored.

Pao sued for lost back pay and punitive damages that some experts estimated had the potential of reaching $100 million. Kleiner partners alleged that she had been an entitled misfit, who conveniently blamed her professional issues on colleagues rather than taking accountability for her shortcomings. The media speculated that the suit had been brought at a terribly opportune time, right when it became clear that her husband would likely lose his fortune and the family might run out of cash.[16] Curiously, the plain and reserved Pao had until then never stood out for anything other than academic and professional achievements. Suddenly, after five years of supposed suffering, she launched a sensational discrimination suit, just as her husband had done twice before. The media had a field day.

In network terms, the story of Buddy Fletcher and Ellen Pao is remarkable. They began as outsiders on the margins. As minorities—Fletcher African American and Pao an Asian woman—they seemed to do all the right things to propel them to the center of the network. Specifically, Fletcher appeared to do everything by the book to cultivate homophily with superhubs. By attending the right school, he stacked the odds in his favor, and becoming a successful trader at Kidder Peabody further increased his chances. However, suing one's employer is viewed as a betrayal which would typically catapult one back to the fringes. But Fletcher then made the right move by starting his own firm, which, if sufficiently successful, is one smart way to become a superhub.

And then he pulled out all the stops by acting as if money were no object. Abiding by the motto "fake it till you make it," he donated to charities so generously that it was sure to attract attention, and with those donations he became an increasingly bigger creditor of social capital. The old boys' network in finance has very few African American members, and knowing that he would never fully fit in, Fletcher carved out his own philanthropic niche by focusing on the nexus of race relations, Hollywood, the arts, and academia. He was not a warm and fluffy person per se, but he pursued people and dazzled them with invitations to glamorous salons and soirées. His Ponzi scheme extended not only to investments but also to his social status, and he projected a powerful image he had not yet earned. Pretending to be more than you are may work initially, but if appearances are not filled with substance, at some point the artificial edifice will crumble. He tried to signal to others that he was on their level with his car collection, impressive real estate holdings, and charitable endeavors, but he failed to pay his dues and, distracted with his extracurricular activities, did not complete the necessary groundwork. However, his scheme was so grand and bold that few people doubted it.

At the time of this writing, Fletcher owed more than $140 million in judgments and tax liens and $2.7 million in unpaid legal bills. He lost his racial discrimination suit against the Dakota, which sued him for unpaid maintenance, assessments, and legal fees for over $2.5 million. Three of his Dakota apartments were on court-ordered sale for an $10 million to $20 million to satisfy his creditors, who had won an order attaching $50 million of his assets. His Connecticut "castle" was on the market for $6 million. Fletcher has denied all wrongdoing.

After leaving Kleiner Perkins, Pao became interim CEO at the Internet platform Reddit, where she remained controversial and was eventually forced out by a revolt of Reddit users. A San Francisco jury ruled against her, and she lost her $16 million discrimination suit on all counts. In 2016, Pao landed a book deal with Random House to write a memoir called *Reset*, a "fearless first-person account exposing the toxic culture that pervades the tech industry."[17]

The future of the once so promising couple is uncertain. Even under the best of circumstances, Fletcher will likely be considered tainted, with superhub-network reentry denied.

OMNI-CONNECTED: MICHAEL KLEIN

Many senior executives completely identify with their jobs and define themselves through their positions of power. They cling to their careers, fearing that losing their jobs will result in a loss of prestige, social standing, and sense of self. However, once arrived in top ranks, the chance that a senior executive is completely dropped by the network is highly unlikely, as we've seen earlier. Through board interlinkages and other interconnections, most executives either resurface in the top ranks or leverage their priceless networks to establish themselves independently.

Much of Michael Klein's professional identity had been tied to Citigroup for almost two decades. As the chairman and co-chief executive-officer of markets and banking, he operated right below CEO Chuck Prince. Before a trip to the WEF in Davos, a senior executive of Citi in Germany told me that I absolutely had to meet Klein. When our paths crossed at the Citigroup reception, I was surprised. I had imagined someone so senior to be much older, not a youngish-looking man in his early forties. Not only was Klein an excellent, sharp, and creative banker, but he also possessed consummate networking skills. It's difficult to determine what mix of qualities precisely makes a person likeable and trustworthy. But whatever it is—that certain *je ne sais quoi*—Klein had it. He had a charming personality and self-effacing demeanor and if he had a big ego or was ruthlessly ambitious, he hid it well amongst the alpha males of his set.

At Citi, Klein was a superstar miracle rainmaker. He convinced Steve Schwarzman to take private equity giant Blackstone public, making its founder $8 billion and Citi a pretty penny in fees. The timing—just months before the financial crisis hit—was impeccable. When Citigroup almost tumbled due to its massive subprime losses, Klein activated his formidable connections and raised $7.5 billion on a short trip to the Abu Dhabi Investment Authority. He had been one of Sandy Weill's favorites and a likely prospect for the Citi CEO position; however, when Robert Rubin installed outsider Vikram Pandit as new CEO—who in turn brought in his own loyal followers—Klein was pushed to the side. His departure was a bitter one, albeit well compensated. He received a record payout of $42 million and proceeded to set up his own shop.

The talk at the time was that Klein's greatness had only been possible due to his affiliation with one of the world's largest banks. It would be an entirely different story for him to sit in a lonely office and make calls without having a premium brand behind him. But Klein exemplifies the fact that virtually everything can be taken away from you except your relationships. The ones he had built could not have been higher caliber, and his successful use of them as a solo agent was truly astounding.

He now reportedly employs a sizable team, although it's hard to say because he shuns the spotlight and stays under the radar. He is close to many government leaders in Washington as well as abroad and hedges his bets by donating to both political camps. His role as adviser to the United Nations World Food Programme provides him with further exposure to the international political establishment. He advised Prime Minister Gordon Brown on the U.K.'s bank rescue plan and the government of Dubai on its debt restructuring. Klein is so close to former prime minister Tony Blair that rumors of a formal professional cooperation won't subside. He has a tight relationship with many of the world's leading industrialists and wealthy Middle Eastern sheikhs such as Prince Al-Waleed of Saudi Arabia.

Citi agreed to cut short Klein's noncompete clause when the CEO of Dow Chemical, Andrew Liveris, asked him to advise on an acquisition. Barclays CEO Bob Diamond retained Klein to advise on the acquisition of Lehman Brothers' operations, a two-week engagement that earned him $10 million. Even more attention grabbing was his role as strategic adviser to the CEOs of Glencore and Xstrata, who needed someone to broker a mutually agreeable compromise for their $42 billion merger. Klein's success in organizing such large and important transactions is exceptional, but it shows the extremely high value of personal, trusted connections. Any of those parties could just as easily have gone to any of the premier investment banks like Goldman Sachs. But they chose an individual they knew and trusted, one who was respected and had standing in the international banking community. Klein is a perfect example of how a superhub can lose a coveted position and yet remain firmly entrenched within the high-level network precisely because of his multitude of connections.

* * *

We have seen that the networks of the financial elite are so tightly knit that people rarely fall through the cracks. By banding together and blocking reform, superhubs perpetuate the system to their benefit at the expense of everyone else. Based on network science, we will see in Chapter 12 how their collective actions have lead to a crisis of capitalism, revolt, and risk of system failure. We will examine how the system should be recalibrated in order to create a more inclusive society with a fairer economy that benefits all.

CHAPTER 12

Super-Crash:

"Executive Contagion"

THE CRASH OF A TITAN:
JOHN MERIWETHER

Few people can take credit for generating billions of dollars in losses and single-handedly bringing the financial system to the brink of collapse. John Meriwether of Long Term Capital Management (LTCM) is one of them. At a wine tasting at Chef Daniel Boulud's DBGB in the East Village, hosted by my friend Jim, a financier and avid wine collector, I met the now infamous Meriwether. I arrived later than most of the other guests, who had gathered in the center of the private wood-paneled room featuring an elegant table set with a myriad of different wine glasses, shiny silverware, and sharply folded napkins. In a tribute to Château Mouton Rothschild, the theme of the tasting was "Mouton Madness." An array of bottles had been carefully lined up on a side table, and the menu was designed to enhance the tasting experience.

As we mingled during the cocktail hour, I checked the place cards. To my delight, I saw that I would be seated by John Meriwether, *the* John Meriwether, who had made Wall Street history. In light of his colorful background, I expected a charismatic and swashbuckling personality who would mesmerize us with fascinating anecdotes; yet, contrary to my expectations, in walked a slight, unimposing, and shy man. He talked the entire evening about sports, despite my best efforts to move on to more compelling subjects. Intensely private, he was possibly trying to avoid talking about what everyone was most interested in: his notorious experience at LTCM.

As outlined in Roger Lowenstein's book *When the Genius Failed*, Meriwether began his career at Salomon Brothers, where he had made a name for himself as the head of the enormously profitable bond arbitrage group.[1] In the course of a trading scandal that implicated his subordinates, though not him, he resigned. Motivated by a desire to vindicate himself, he set out for bigger and better things and in 1994 created a hedge fund that invested on the basis of global economic trends. With his stellar reputation, two highly regarded Nobel laureates—Myron Scholes and Robert Merton—on his team, and wide-ranging contacts, he went on an aggressive global marketing tour, selling the fund as a low-risk market outperformer.

LTCM's investments were based on complex computer formulae that hardly anyone fully understood but which Meriwether and his team believed to be infallible. Investors flocked to the fund, eager to join the ride and associate themselves with a circle of managers uniformly considered to be simply ingenious. For the privilege of investing, they were willing to accept high minimum investment thresholds, unusually long lockup periods, large management fees, and very little disclosure of where and how their money was actually invested. The more money LTCM received, the more it attracted, and in short order it accumulated $126 billion in assets. In 1995 and 1996, the fund generated in excess of 40 percent return after fees. Such outsized returns were only possible with extremely high leverage, which magnified the returns. However, when the tide turned, the debt also magnified the losses.

LTCM hedged itself within a known range of volatility based on past data, but its financial models failed to consider close correlations between a variety of asset classes. When in 1998 Russia defaulted and sent markets tumbling, the value of LTCM's investments fell steeply. Within a couple of months, the fund lost over 50 percent of its value. Alarmed by its dramatic losses, the New York Fed intervened—although technically the fund was not within their purview—because many Wall Street counterparties, among them countless banks and investors such as pension funds, were intertwined with LTCM and in danger of failing. Consequently, the Fed feared that a disorderly unraveling of over $100 billion in derivative positions would cause the entire financial system to crash. William J. McDonough, the extraordinarily well-connected president of the New York Fed, had sufficient pull to congregate the superhubs of Wall Street, who within hours coughed up $3.6 billion for a 90 percent stake in the fund. Among the rescuers were government entities, such as the People's Bank of China, and Wall Street icons George Soros and Donald Marron, chairman of Paine Webber.[2]

Following the implosion of LTCM, Meriwether subsequently launched two other funds, and, despite his prior spectacular failure, investors were still willing to entrust their money to him. The first successor fund faltered in the throes of the financial crisis and had to be wound down. The next fund he started, he eventually converted into a family office.

The LTCM debacle foreshadowed the financial crisis that would engulf the entire global financial system a decade later. Meriwether, a bona fide superhub, held so much network power over people and capital that he nearly toppled the entire financial system. Reassured by his then-stellar reputation, investors lined up to give him their money even under unfavorable conditions, submitting themselves to an unproven and opaque investment approach. Other financial institutions generously loaned him enormous amounts of capital based on his pedigree while lacking the information necessary to control their risk exposure—therefore increasing the risk for the system as a whole. In accordance with power-laws, once this superhub started spinning, he attracted everyone and everything in his path like a tornado set for destruction.

THE BIG PICTURE: CAPITALISM IN CRISIS

The global financial crisis has laid bare a capitalism gone awry with dramatic consequences for us all. What happened? When I visited the U.S. for the first time over three decades ago, I was struck by how prosperous it seemed compared to Europe. American middle-class families appeared to have much higher living standards than Germans, with huge houses, numerous cars in their driveways, and apparently unconstrained financial means. Later in my career in structured finance, where highly leveraged assets like homes and companies are securitized and sold all over the world, I came to wonder how all of this was sustainable. Today we know that the engine behind excessive consumption has been financialization fueled with debt.

Debt and Financialization

Debt has been one of the key drivers of inequality. According to a McKinsey study, "global debt has grown by $57 trillion . . . outpacing world GDP growth" and "no major economy has decreased its debt-to-GDP ratio since 2007."[3] In the decades preceding the crisis, an increasingly greater share of GDP had been based on financial services, which in turn had been based on credit growth. However, financialization only contributes to growth up to a certain point before this trend reverses.[4] As finance takes up an increasingly larger share of GDP, investment in the real economy falls.[5] The author and former banker Satyajit Das notes that "[at] its peak, the finance industry generated 40 percent of corporate profits."[6] As a result finance decoupled from the economy, and while Wall Street got richer, everyone else got poorer, thereby increasing the wealth gap. Financialization has also contributed significantly to corporate ownership and control, which has expanded and strengthened elite networks even further.

What does the financial services industry actually do? Financial intermediaries primarily deal with each other by moving money around in complex transactions, to a large extent through securitization, in which assets are transformed into securities and resold countless times. By far the greatest part of the financial flows is recycled back and forth, with the main purpose to generate profits and outdo competitors. Only a fraction actually flows into the real economy to finance sustainable businesses and create jobs.

Wealth Gap and Inequality

Now the world is faced with extreme income, wealth, and opportunity gaps. In the U.S., only 50 percent of the population still belongs to the middle class, the lowest level since the 1970s.[7] Between 1979 and 2013, the wages of the top 1 percent grew by 138 percent; today they earn over 20 percent of the national income, and CEOs on average make 296 times what a typical worker earns.[8] In contrast, real wages of the bottom 99 percent have remained flat over the last four decades, while productivity has increased by 80 percent.[9] If wages and productivity had grown in lockstep, the minimum wage would currently be over $18 per hour.[10] So what Americans lacked in earnings, they compensated for with debt, with many of them becoming overindebted. While college graduates are 8 times likelier to live in the upper-income tiers—though often with a debt-albatross around their necks—those without a degree have virtually no chance of improving their station in life.[11] As a consequence, Americans have come to realize that the American dream has been just that, a dream, and their typically optimistic outlook has given way to gloom, with only 14 percent foreseeing a better life for their children.[12] The life expectancy of American whites has been falling as suicide rates are on the rise.[13] As evidenced by a recognized measure called the Gini coefficient, the level of inequality in many parts of the world is dismal.[14]

Globalization Winners versus Globalization Losers

To make matters worse, many governments, together with central banks and the financial sector, have resorted to using "accommodative monetary policies"—meaning expanding the overall money supply, or what is commonly referred to as "printing money"—to reduce debts and stimulate demand. In effect, this so-called financial repression acts as a tax on savers, transferring benefits from lenders to borrowers. Meanwhile, the 1 percent have benefited the most from these policies, pocketing 95 percent of income growth in the first three years after the crisis.[15] In addition, the 1 percent have the expertise and means to play the global system to their advantage, an example of which is the use of tax havens like the Cayman Islands. Leaks such as the Panama Papers offer only a minuscule glimpse into this parallel universe. According to estimates, about 8 percent of global wealth, or $7.5 trillion, is squirreled away in tax havens, $6 trillion of which has not been taxed.[16] This hidden wealth distorts the picture of inequality, which if factored in would likely be even greater.[17]

Approaching the Tipping Point

The situation is so egregious that even members of the establishment have begun going rogue. "Class traitors" such as George Soros, Nick Hanauer, and Paul Tudor Jones have warned of the potentially dramatic consequences of inequality and suggested measures to reduce it. Even Asher Edelman, the real-life Gordon Gekko on whom the movie *Wall Street*'s ruthlessly greedy protagonist was partly modeled, has turned dissident, arguing for the self-proclaimed democratic socialist Bernie Sanders as the best option for the U.S. economy.[18]

The economic discontent has led to unprecedented political polarization, pitting the "have-nots" against the "haves," the proletariat against the intellectual elite, and the young against the old. People are acutely aware of the democratic deficit resulting from the undue collusion of the financial, corporate, and political sectors, and many feel that the system has been hijacked and rigged by special interests. They have come to detest crony capitalism—in which gains are privatized and losses are borne by the public, while bankers continue to award themselves record-setting bonuses.

EU populist parties and "extremist" U.S. presidential candidates reflect the explosive anger of globalization's losers, who are now lobbying for radical change in greater numbers. Protectionism and isolationism are resurging, manifesting themselves in the opposition to trade agreements, and in separatist movements in the U.K. with regard to Europe, in Scotland with regard to the U.K., and in Catalonia with regard to Spain. Global inequality has also driven mass migration, which in turn polarizes politics even further. According to the WEF's *Global Risk Report*, we are currently seeing the highest level of protests since the 1980s, because through access to information on the Internet, people realize the extent of inequality and their own powerlessness.[19] Several years ago, former National Security Advisor Zbigniew Brzezinski warned of the impending "global political awakening." He, too, pointed to the fact that for the first time in history, humanity is politically informed yet mostly disempowered.[20] In line with these findings, the global communications firm Edelman reports that trust in the establishment is dramatically declining.[21]

WHEN AN IRRESISTIBLE FORCE MEETS AN IMMOVABLE OBJECT: BREXIT

In the summer of 2016, the people of the United Kingdom shocked the world when a majority voted to leave the European Union. What has been termed "Brexit" (Britain: Exit) is symptomatic of a global systemic crisis of society, democracy, and capitalism. The revolt against the establishment was primarily driven by renewed feelings of nationalism and a desire to reclaim control of the U.K.'s economy, culture, and communities. While globalization has had numerous positive effects such as lifting millions of people out of poverty, it has also increased the wealth gap and is widely perceived as little more than a pyramid scheme for the enrichment of the transnational elites. According to Oxfam, "The U.K. is the world's sixth largest economy, yet 1 in 5 of the U.K. population live below our official poverty line, meaning that they experience life as a daily struggle."[22] Thus, unsurprisingly, the proponents of Brexit were predominantly older and less educated individuals who felt marginalized in the Darwinist meritocracy, in which IQ and education are the primary metrics for success, and blue-collar jobs are increasingly replaced by machines and given to migrants. Feeling that their lives and sense of identity were disrupted, they came to resent the elite and the EU technocratic bureaucracy, which they regard as disloyal and exploitative.

At the time of this writing, barely a week after the vote, it is still unclear whether the U.K. will actually leave the European Union, and if so, when and how. However, the paralyzing political "anarchy" and uncertainty following the vote have already impaired the economy—halting vital transactions, putting spending on hold, and curtailing investment. Disruptions to the cross-border flow of trade, capital, and people and rising taxes coupled with austerity could possibly contribute to a self-reinforcing downturn. Ironically, those who most vociferously propagated the U.K.'s exit will likely suffer the most from its repercussions.

Brexit is emblematic of the chaos and the unintended consequences that ensue when a complex system is suddenly short-circuited. It may turn out to merely have been a corrective shock; however, perhaps more likely, it could instead be the harbinger of an incipient global revolt that will eventually change the existing world order.

THE NEXT CRISIS: SYSTEMIC FAILURE AND CONTAGION

Most experts agree that a new crisis is just a matter of time. The IMF has warned of a new financial crisis that could overwhelm the world's defenses.[23] Claudio Borio of the Bank for International Settlements suggests that we may be seeing the "signs of the gathering storm that has been building for a long time" and that central banks, which have kept the global financial system on life support, are running out of options.[24] Andrew Haldane, chief economist of the Bank of England, believes that recent events could form the latest leg of what he calls a three-part crisis trilogy,[25] and the former governor of the Bank of England, Mervyn King, writes in his book *The End of Alchemy* that without reforms another financial crisis "will come sooner rather than later."[26] Countless other economists all over the world, including Sheila Bair, former head of the FDIC, view the current system to be unstable.[27] In her opinion, "people need to understand that we are at risk of another financial crisis unless the general public more actively engages in countering the undue influence of the financial services lobby."[28]

The Culprit: The Superhubs or the System?

Systemic stability has mostly been analyzed on the basis of institutional interconnections rather than at the level of individuals. Yet it is human beings, not abstract entities, who make decisions on the institution's behalf and ultimately impact the system. However, in contrast to institutions, whose transactions and capital flows can be quantitatively calculated, human relationships are much harder to categorize, measure, and stress-test. Superhubs have a quasi-monopoly on top-level, globalized relationships, which provides them with enormous network power. The resulting hyperconnectivity—especially in its combination with capital acting as an amplifier—poses a risk to the public good of systemic stability.

One of the key questions to consider is whether the superhubs are to blame for the fragile state of our financial and economic system. Has the crisis been a failure of individuals, or the system itself? Have they held the system prisoner, or are they themselves prisoners of the system?

Many experts, like former governor of the Bank of England Mervyn King, believe that blaming individuals is no substitute for acknowledging the failure of a system.[29] It would be counterproductive to assume that if all the lever-pullers were punished, we would never experience a crisis again. Rather, he argues, "the crisis was a failure of the system, and the ideas that underpinned it, not of individual policymakers or bankers."[30] Similarly, Adair Turner, former head of the U.K. financial regulatory authority FSA, says that "if we think the crisis occurred because of individual 'bad apples' who corrupted the system . . . we will fail to make adequately radical reforms."[31] In the same vein, William Dudley, president of the Federal Reserve Bank of New York, thinks the focus should be less on searching for bad apples and more on improving the apple barrels.[32]

Yet, the picture may not be so clear-cut. As we've seen in Chapter 1, individual superhubs are neither in charge of, nor do they have control over the system, because finance is a complex self-organizing system, where the actions of autonomous individuals lead to collective activity. Although there is no "central command" directing events, the large-scale effects of all the individual players' independent actions determine the overall behavior of the system. Therefore, it is the interaction between both the system and the individuals that determines developments.

Disequilibrium: Superhubs Preventing the System from Correcting Itself

Interconnectedness is to some extent an inherent component of the financial system and indispensable for the exchange of goods and services. In order to optimally scale and capitalize on the system, top executives tend to build ever more interlinkages, thus making the system increasingly more complex. Up to a certain point, a high number of links tends to make the system more stable, because it creates greater balance between individual nodes and—specifically in finance—facilitates risk sharing.

However, too many connections are destabilizing because they enable failure to cascade through the system. In contrast, if a system has more nodes with fewer connections, the domino effect cannot spread much further than those affected nodes.[33] Lehman Brothers illustrated how the failure of one node can unexpectedly multiply and travel through the system with unprecedented speed. Man-made systems are generally more fragile than natural ones, and when complexity coincides with homogeneity, these system becomes robust yet paradoxically fragile, so when a crisis event strikes, superhubs become superspreaders of risk and disruption.[34]

Why does our system's default mode seem to be destined for failure? Because in every system—be it the ecology, epidemiology, or physics—network dynamics eventually lead to greater levels of homogeneity, interconnectedness, and complexity.[35] Generally, systems are adaptive and self-correcting; when they become too lopsided, autocorrecting feedback mechanisms kick in and stabilize the system. Systems with unchecked reinforcing loops, however, ultimately destroy themselves.[36] Through feedback loops and power-laws, superhubs and their networks have significantly contributed to skewing the system. Potentially corrective shocks like the financial crisis have failed to rebalance it because the overly influential superhub networks have blocked fundamental changes to protect their vested interests.

An example of this is the persistence of systemically important "too big to fail" banks, which still present a risk to taxpayers. Wall Street CEOs have put up a fabulous fight against measures threatening the size of their institutions, and, thus, their financial interests. Even Neel Kashkari, who as assistant secretary of the treasury was instrumental in orchestrating the bank bailouts, is now spearheading efforts to decrease the size of banks to minimize the risks for taxpayers.[37]

"Executive Contagion": Executives Becoming Super-Spreaders of Risk

The formation of hubs and superhubs follows the laws of nature, so that the same type of network topology will always form, be it among tradespeople in a city, students at a university, or movie stars on the global stage. Due to human beings' proclivity to surround themselves with people who are like them, top executives have similar mind-sets, influence and emulate one another, obtain the same information, and make like-minded decisions. Accordingly, their views, business models, and risk appetites closely resemble one another.[38]

The tendency to act in concert leads to "executive contagion" when collective behavior at the highest level spreads through the system and destabilizes it. The term "contagion" is derived from epidemiology and means transmission by contact. In finance, such contagion can be triggered by panics such as bank runs, in which so many savers concurrently withdraw their deposits that institutions become illiquid and eventually insolvent, as in Jimmy Stewart's *It's a Wonderful Life*. By the same token, loss of faith and panic can spread among executives as well. Such executive contagion starts at the top, spreads laterally, and cascades down the system—often with grave consequences. Executives govern powerful institutions, direct billions of dollars, and institute impactful policies. If one executive suffers a shock, his reaction can influence other executives to think, feel, and act in the same way, be it for perfectly rational reasons or unfounded assumptions. As a result of contagion, their individual actions multiply and create a domino effect that ripples through the system.

During the time of the impending AIG failure, an executive of a private bank told me in confidence that the C-suite had given orders to halt all trading with Goldman Sachs and that their decision had led executives at other institutions to do the same. Similarly, in the case of Lehman, financial executives made the decision to hoard liquidity, which led to a crisis that spread through markets and brought the entire global financial system to a screeching halt. Executives have control over their own actions, but they have no control over the contagion effect, and there are few if any circuit breakers.

As discussed in Chapter 10, checks and balances by supervisory authorities like the Federal Reserve or the SEC often fail due to "relational capture," which typically leads to "cognitive capture" and "regulatory capture." Most people are rarely only transactional but also have an inherent desire to create a collaborative and positive work environment by fostering good relations. After a certain amount of interaction, they typically begin to relate to one another and bond. At that point "cognitive capture" sets in, according to which they begin to view matters from each other's perspectives. This in turn leads to "regulatory capture," meaning that regulators become biased toward, or even dominated by, those they are supposed to regulate. The revolving door phenomenon further inclines people to be accommodative rather than confrontational.

Averting Collapse: Thinking Differently

Why is the system ever more fragile? Why have so few improvements been made after the dramatic global financial meltdown of 2008? Perhaps—as Einstein said—we don't need to think *more*, but think *differently*.

Traditionally, we have been trained to think analytically and deal with parts of problems separately. However, today's multidimensional, complex world is not linear, but is the result of dynamic, simultaneously interacting phenomena. Brexit, unpredictable monetary policies, mass migration and terrorism are but a few examples. We can attain a deeper understanding of these problems by employing a different approach called "systems thinking" and focusing more on the relationship of individual parts than on the parts themselves, which alone say nothing about the system's behavior.[39] According to organizational theorist Stephen Haines, "major change fails 75 percent of the time because of a piecemeal and analytical approach to a systems problem that tries to cure one problem at a time."[40] And in the opinion of world systems analyst Immanuel Wallerstein, part of the problem is that "we have studied . . . phenomena in separate boxes to which we have given special names—politics, economics, the social structure, culture—without seeing that these boxes are constructs more of our imagination than of reality."[41] The postcrisis banking regulation exemplifies the analytical, one-dimensional approach to problem solving. When looking at individual cases, progress seems to have been made; however, viewed in a wider context, stricter regulation has had the unintended consequence of relegating the riskier financial activities to the lightly regulated shadow banking system, where they have the potential to cause even greater harm. So instead of minimizing risks, bank regulation has created new ones.

In any case, urgent action is required because the forces of nature will inevitably eventually kick in to recalibrate the system. Whether such circuit breakers will trigger gradual, managed, and orderly change or sudden, uncontrollable chaos is uncertain. But the longer we wait, the more difficult it will be to effect constructive change. Experts agree that even remote minor events can trigger failure of complex systems. This has been termed the "butterfly effect" and characterized as "the notion that a butterfly stirring the air today in Peking can transform storm systems next month in New York," meaning that even slight disturbances may have dramatic consequences.[42] As Wallerstein explains, disorderly transitions are usually painful because they entail battles over pieces of the pie.[43] As paradigms shift, "structures and processes oscillate wildly," as manifested by volatile markets, fragile economies, and geopolitical conflicts. Some people advocate for letting the system collapse to allow a better one to emerge, but such a process would likely be arduous for all segments of society, and the rebuilding could take a very long time, as the Great Depression has shown.

Karl Marx argued that capitalism carries the seeds of its own destruction, and it indeed appears that impermeable elite networks have distorted the dynamics of the capitalist system and prevented adaptation. To paraphrase Winston Churchill, capitalism might be the worst economic system, except for all others. Socialism and communism have historically led to dramatic power vacuums and even smaller and tighter networks corrupting the system. Particularly in times of crisis and transition, elite groups form and absorb large parts of a country's wealth. Russia is a classic example. During the transition from communist U.S.S.R. to a market-based Russia, a handful of oligarchs-in-the-making with government connections and access to financing acquired state assets on the cheap and made billions. Estimates of President Putin's personal fortune range up to $200 billion.[44]

The Growth Premise: A Paradox?

Our society and economy are predicated on growth as the engine for jobs, prosperity, and social stability. However, since the crisis, the recovery has been stubbornly slow and weak, as the world lacks demand, struggles with a huge debt overhang, and the political establishment procrastinates crucial structural reforms. Globalization has run out of steam, and central banks are trying to overcompensate for governmental inertia. The lack of growth exacerbates inequality even more and threatens social stability. But growth also comes with often overlooked costs and unintended consequences, such as the depletion of natural resources, exploitation of others, misallocation of human capital, and distortion of political systems.

In his book *Throwing Rocks at the Google Bus: How Growth Became the Enemy of Prosperity*, Douglas Rushkoff argues that we are caught in a growth trap, where we have lost track of the purpose of the economy and made growth an end in itself, driving a jobless recovery and low-wage economy.[45] But what if we are unable to produce substantially stronger growth? What if growth is limited? The think tank Club of Rome argued in its 1972 research report *The Limits to Growth* that growth cannot continue indefinitely because resources like water, food, and energy are limited. More-recent research has only corroborated this theory, concluding that the drive for limitless economic growth could disrupt many local, regional and global systems and would end either through an uncontrolled collapse or human adaptation.[46]

Northwestern University economist Robert Gordon predicts significantly slower growth for the foreseeable future, because the most significant innovations that triggered disproportionate growth over the last 150 years—such as the internal combustion engine, running water, and electricity—were in his opinion unique and unrepeatable.[47]

Culture: The Value of Our Values

To a certain extent the drive for growth is expedient, as the economy is like a plane that must fly at a certain speed to stay airborne. Generally, it is human nature to be dissatisfied with the status quo and strive for more. While this desire is an essential driver of progress and growth, the mere self-interested drive to accumulate excessive wealth has a tendency to be socially destructive. In Alan Greenspan's opinion, humans haven't become any greedier than in generations past, but have more avenues to express greed.[48] The pope stated that "once capital becomes an idol and guides people's decisions, once greed for money presides over the entire socioeconomic system, it ruins society."[49] Indeed, if greed isn't mitigated by a strong set of personal values, it tends to impair judgment and lead to illegitimate behavior.

The superhubs and their elite networks thrive in our system because of the significant role that money and wealth play in our society. Like every system, our society organizes itself around rules. Those rules are reflected in our culture in the form of our commonly accepted values, norms, objectives, and modes of behavior. Therefore, our culture acts as the operating system of our society. In recent decades, Wall Street has celebrated the self-indulgent glamour and desirability of greed, wealth, and excess, just as society has glorified the financial world's unbridled capitalism, often on TV, in glossy magazines, in Hollywood blockbusters such as *Wall Street*, and best-selling novels like *Liar's Poker*. Wall Street's excessive compensation to some extent is also a manifestation of our society's values. Surgeons don't get paid bonuses if they save lives, and policemen make a fraction of bankers' salaries even though they put their own lives at risk for the benefit of others. This compensation gap implies that our society assigns greater value to making money than it does to preserving lives.

The scandals that have unfolded in the aftermath of the crisis have significantly tainted the financial world's reputation and prestige. In a 2009 speech, President Obama criticized the attitude on Wall Street "that valued wealth over work, selfishness over sacrifice, and greed over responsibility."[50] Meanwhile, Wall Street legitimized its push for ever greater profits as part of their fiduciary duty to investors. Shareholders and lawmakers allowed boards to get away with outsized growth targets and outrageous compensation even as performance dramatically declined.[51]

RECALIBRATING THE SYSTEM: REVOLUTION OR EVOLUTION?

Inequality and social corrosion are not force majeure but the result of self-imposed paradigms and behaviors. All of us have participated in our system as it has evolved, be it through a mortgage, a checking account, or a bank-sponsored civic event. This system is now on a trajectory towards failure if we only cure the symptoms and don't address the underlying causes of system deficiencies. There is no panacea to effect the requisite changes, and a discussion of the many measures necessary would exceed the scope of this book. Nevertheless, I will subsequently touch on some relevant considerations to the human angle on which this book focuses.

The Law and Ethics

Governor of the Bank of England Mark Carney, who promotes an ethical business culture, called the pre- and postcrisis years "the age of irresponsibility," where unethical behavior went unchecked and became the norm.[52] These behaviors, which have aggravated the increasing wealth gap and social stratification, have fundamentally shaken society's trust in our system. That is problematic, because trust serves as one the fundamental pillars of society and is a precondition for cooperation among its various segments.

Stricter laws, regulation, and supervision can provide valuable guidelines for human action. Yet, it is important to keep in mind that laws are limited in their effectiveness, as by their very nature they are subject to rule-beating behavior and attempted circumvention, which creates new distortions. Also, it is impossible to regulate all nuances of human relationships and to control every interaction of people who are close to one another.

We should also keep in mind that, as economist John Kay puts it, "too many safeguards may actually increase the risk of failure."[53] In a fast-changing, ever more complex world, rules must remain somewhat flexible and adaptable. Rigid norms may make the system even less stable; by the time they kick in, the system may already have changed, and outdated rules applied to a different set of facts may cause more harm than good. That is why in complex, nonlinear systems, oblique—indirect and gradual—actions based on constant reevaluation and adaptation may be more effective than stern and inflexible approaches.[54]

Legal norms should be underpinned with ethical standards to prevent harmful actions that may be legal, but which should be avoided with the right moral compass. The Group of Thirty also recognizes "grey zones, in which conduct is a matter of judgment, not necessarily the law," as a challenge.[55]

Since the regulation and supervision of ethical standards is difficult, personal and professional responsibility should be stressed, just as doctors must take an oath and lawyers must take regular ethics classes. Andreas Dombret, an executive board member of Bundesbank, suggests the stipulation of an ethics code. None of these measures by themselves will cure the problem, but they can contribute to establishing standards and raising awareness.

Corporate Culture: Psychological Detachment and Willful Blindness

Culture as the foundation for ethical behavior also plays an important role. The Group of Thirty in 2015 released a report titled *Banking Conduct and Culture*, which criticized poor cultural foundations, unhealthy cultural norms, and significant cultural failures. The report asserts that "restoring trust in banking is a public trust and economic imperative, as it is the bedrock of a safe and effective financial system."[56]

A study by economists at the University of Zürich suggests that the culture in the banking industry undermines honesty.[57] The lines between what's inappropriate, unethical, and illegal are also blurred by the fact that bankers have become increasingly more detached from their clients because of the complexity of their products and the corresponding greater division of labor. Financial engineers who created the computer models for collateralized debt obligations were, for the most part, unaware of the robo-signing of subprime mortgages that took place further down the production chain half a world away. The resulting moral inertia encouraged a "catch me if you can" culture in which everything not explicitly prohibited was allowed, and executives pushed the boundaries to see what they could get away with. Under performance pressure and incentivized by short-term rewards, people rationalized their actions by working within the rules and abdicating responsibility to a system that rarely held them accountable.

In fact, researchers found that bankers severely disassociate themselves from their work in order to cope with their demanding environments. In what has been coined "teflonic identity maneuvering," financial executives rationalize their detachment with their high remuneration.[58] Another study demonstrates that willful ignorance often serves as an excuse for selfish behavior. Most people are willing to sacrifice personal benefits if they are known to come at the expense of others, yet when given the choice, they often insulate themselves from negative information to protect their self-image and avoid harsh judgments by others.[59] In her book *Willful Blindness*, Margret Heffernan elaborates how competitive environments exacerbate mutually reinforcing conformity. In choosing to stick with the crowd, we steadily blind ourselves to individual values and doubts.[60]

And then there is, of course, the more explicit problem of an organizational culture that tolerates and encourages unethical or even illegal behavior. After the Volkswagen emissions scandal broke in 2015, managers described a culture of fear and a corporate mind-set that tolerated rule breaking. The carmaker is, in a sense, also a financial services company, as over 40 percent of VW's balance sheet consists of financial services.

CEOs and other top executives must be role models and lead by example. The Group of Thirty argues that values and conduct should be evident in tone from the top, and the voices of middle managers should be heard in an echo from the bottom.[61]

Ethical behavior also makes good business sense because losing public trust leads to adverse financial consequences such as higher borrowing costs and reduced lending. The Group of Thirty agrees and posits a value-driven culture and appropriate conduct as a competitive advantage.[62] Indeed, there is evidence that there is "return on character": Highly principled leaders with a strong character who do the right things achieve better business performance.[63]

Vice Chairman of the Federal Reserve Stanley Fischer warns that "regulators should not be tempted to think that Wall Street would one day be clean. . . . This is not a battle that can be won. . . . Even in the best barrels, there will always be bad apples, so we must keep up that fight."[64]

Incentives

Finance's quasi "monopoly power" has also contributed to a sense of entitlement, excessive compensation, and flawed incentives as its culture has focused on profit as the only metric of success. Any other consider-ations, such as ethics and the common good, have fallen by the wayside. By some estimates, financial sector employees were overpaid by as much as 50 percent relative to skill, often without creating genuine value, as the result of greater risk taking underwritten by the government.[65] In War-ren Buffett's opinion, Wall Street "makes a lot of money relative to the number of people involved, relative to the IQ and relative to the energy expended." In a rather unorthodox fashion, he argues that bosses and their spouses should lose everything if a bank is bailed out, because spouses would presumably "do better policing than the regulator."[66] This would be particularly expedient considering that fines lack deterrent power as they are not paid by individuals but by banks with other people's money. When Elizabeth Warren expressed her concern that JPMorgan might be breaking the law with regard to a certain provision, Jamie Dimon just smiled and replied, "So hit me with a fine. We can afford it."[67]

For change to gain momentum, all segments of society must par-ticipate: company boards, prominent business leaders, superhubs of all spheres, the media, and members of the community. And feedback from the public—such as recognition and shaming—can help because, as we have seen earlier, people tend to value social standing and respect more highly than monetary rewards.

A Sense of Purpose: Creating Value for Society

Subordinates in hierarchical institutions typically adapt to the rules set at the top, and people at the top adapt to the rules of the system while concurrently influencing them. In line with the system's overall purpose—growth—executives strive for growth, profits, and shareholder value at the expense of everything else, when companies should really benefit all stakeholders of the larger community beyond just shareholders. The purpose of the upper layers of the hierarchy is to serve the purposes of the lower layers, and WEF founder Klaus Schwab thinks that all compa-nies—as both economic and social entities—have a duty to consider the common good. Next to "hard power," firms also need the "soft power" of public trust and acceptance as a license to operate, which also creates long-term value for shareholders.[68]

Past crises have demonstrated that rather than focus on short-term gains, we should think longer-term and aim for a culture that attributes greater value to societal contributions. "Since in the long-term, no business can succeed in a society that fails," as the Archbishop of Westminster notes, finance should allow for a more inclusive capitalism, more equal access to opportunities, and a fairer distribution of wealth.[69] In Christine Lagarde's opinion, "the goal of the financial sector must be not only to maximize the wealth of its shareholders . . . but to enrich society by supporting economic activity and creating value and jobs—to ultimately improve the well-being of people."[70]

Boards must support CEOs in their efforts to govern with more social responsibility. Although boards have become more independent, their members are almost always part of tight-knit superhub networks, with roughly 85 percent still made up of white men.[71] Since research has shown the indispensability of diversity for a system's resilience, and since supervision in this incestuous milieu has not been terribly effective, a good first step would be to encourage drastic diversification in the upper ranks. Diverse systems are better equipped to adapt to suddenly changing environments than homogeneous ones. In addition, they create significantly better business results, as we've seen in Chapter 9. Therefore, institutions should be incentivized to recruit from a wider range of socioeconomic, educational, cultural, and ethnic backgrounds. The integration of women and other minorities with different viewpoints and strengths will help balance and fortify the system.

An "Evolving Revolution"

As mutually exacerbating clashes of classes and cultures continue to unfold worldwide, the risk of a sudden and uncontrolled systemic unraveling becomes ever more likely. Most experts within the IMF and the CIA failed to predict unexpected historic turning points—such as the 2008 financial crisis, the fall of the Soviet Union, and the Arab Spring—and how these events would unfold. Given the danger of other impending but unpredictable crises it is high time to act. To transform the system gradually— the preferable alternative—the biggest changes must be instituted at the top, yet the pressure on the top must come from the bottom. Hierarchies naturally oppose change in order to preserve their existence; accordingly superhubs are inclined to protect their vested interests and perpetuate the dynamics that propelled them to their positions. Larry Summers of all people acknowledged to noted Wall Street critic Elizabeth Warren that his choice was to either ben an insider or outsider: "Outsiders can say whatever they want. But people on the inside don't listen to them. Insiders, however, get lots of access and a chance to push their ideas. People—powerful people—listen to what they have to say. But insiders also understand one unbreakable rule: They don't criticize other insiders."[72]

In such monocultures, the winners are those who operate best in the system, and they exclude others who could potentially reform it from within.[73] Evolutionary patterns, learned behaviors, and resulting reflexive tendencies—which have so far ensured the players' survival—are difficult to change.

Particularly for this reason, politicians must apply pressure to the superhubs, because even though market forces shape inequality, government policies shape market forces.[74] Since we are all nodes, who drive the system with our individual actions and the resulting cause-and-effect feedback loops, we must all actively contribute to change. Hopefully, in a concerted effort we will succeed in changing the monopolistic structure of networks to create a more diverse, equitable, and sustainable system that benefits all.

* * *

The fundamental challenges threatening the integrity of our financial system, our economy, and society are too complex for this book to offer a master plan. But by connecting the dots and providing a 360-degree meta-level view, it aims to give the reader with a better understanding, heightened awareness, and factual basis for an informed, critical, and constructive discussion regarding our shared future.

Acknowledgments

SUPERHUBS DOESN'T JUST TELL the story of networks, it is also the result of my own personal networks. A project that started out as merely one more professional task, over time evolved into a labor of love. Ignorance was bliss, for I'm not sure I would have taken on the challenge had I known how it would gradually take over my life. This enriching, at times arduous and occasionally frustrating experience would not have been possible without of the support of the "superhubs" of my own life.

As such, I'd like to thank first and foremost my grandparents, who are in my thoughts forever, and my parents, who have always believed in my potential and supported me unconditionally.

I'm also grateful to my friends who have tolerated my disappearing into self-imposed "book prison" for months on end, with only occasional release from "solitary confinement." To all my companions: I couldn't have stayed the course while maintaining my sanity without your understanding, encouragement, and support. Many thanks also to those of you who read drafts of the script and provided feedback.

Furthermore, I am indebted to George Soros for including me in his community of family, friends and colleagues, and for teaching me that it's not so much what to think, but more importantly how to think.

I owe profound gratitude to Nouriel Roubini, who has been a generous mentor and steadfast supporter. Nouriel has always been a pleasure to work with, and has become a close friend. I was touched by his thoughtful foreword.

I'm particularly grateful to my agent, Kelly Falconer, who as a super-hub in the publishing world has placed $uperHubs with great expertise, enthusiasm and diligence.

I'd also like to thank Nicholas Brealey, who completely "got" the book's essence and commissioned it. In addition, I am thankful for my outstanding $uperHubs-Team at Hachette: My exceedingly supportive and capable editors Nick Davies and Alison Hankey, who put the book on the fast-track, my super-efficient production manager, Michelle Morgan, as well as the UK and US sales and PR teams, Ben Slight, Melissa Carl, Yassine Belkacemi, Louise Richardson and Tess Woods, who have done an excellent job of spreading the message. All of you have been an absolute pleasure to work with.

My editor, Lara Asher, who did a terrific job helping to improve the book's structure and clarity, also deserves great praise. Her competence and wonderful attitude were instrumental in pushing $uper-Hubs over the finish line.

At Penguin Random House, I'd like to thank Markus Dohle, who has provided valuable guidance throughout the book's evolution and Roger Scholl, who encouraged me to make it accessible to a wider audience by conveying its message through stories, rather than solely through academic theory. Having been a complete neophyte, their pointers at various stages were extremely valuable.

Moreover, I'd like to thank FinanzBuch Verlag's CEO Christian Jund, and my editor, Georg Hodolitsch, who without hesitation enthusiastically commissioned the German version of $uperHubs, and their great team, including Julian Nebel, who have helped make it a bestseller.

I'm also grateful to the leaders and the wonderful staff at institutions and think tanks, who have generously included me over the last years. In particular, I'd like to thank Klaus Schwab at the World Economic Forum; too many people to thank individually at the IMF, but specifically Christine Lagarde and David Vannier; Paul Volcker, Jacob A. Frenkel, Jean-Claude Trichet, Guillermo Ortiz, Geoffrey Bell and Stuart P.M. Mackintosh at the Group of Thirty; James C. Orr and Randy S. Rodgers at The Bretton Woods Committee; Frederick Kempe at the Altantic Council; Steven E. Sokol and Karen Furey at the American Council on

Germany; Rob Johnson and Chris Canavan at INET; Tim Adams, Abdessatar Ouanes at the International Institute of Finance and Charles Dallara, when he was still there; Liz Mohn, Aart De Geus at the Bertelsmann Foundation, and Annette Heuser when she was still there; Steffi Czerny, Dominik Wichmann, Alexandra Schiel, and Franziska Deecke at DLD Media, and Anthony Scaramucci and Victor Oviedo at SALT.

At n-tv I'd like to thank Hans Demmel, Sonja Schwetje, Uli Reitz and, my mentor at the time, Martin Kerscher, for giving me a platform and having been loyal supporters.

One of the greatest debts I owe to the brilliant scholars and other members of a large intellectual community, on whose works *$uperHubs* is based. Their research has been the inspiration, stimulation, motivation for and foundation of this book.

Last but not least, I'd like to thank the superhubs mentioned and those who have kindly provided their endorsements, many of whom have had a great influence on my life and certainly on this book.

About the Author

M s. NAVIDI is the CEO of BeyondGlobal, a management consulting firm, where she renders macroeconomic and strategic positioning advice. In addition, she also engages in strategic relationship management, connecting people, platforms, and organizations to advance their interests by leveraging her expertise and network.

Previously, Ms. Navidi worked closely with renowned economist Nouriel Roubini as Director of Research Strategies and Senior Relationship Manager at Roubini Global Economics. Prior to that, Ms. Navidi held positions as investment banker at Scarsdale Equities, general counsel at Muzinich & Co., and consultant at Deloitte. Ms. Navidi holds a law degree from the University of Cologne School of Law, Germany, and a Master of Laws Degree in Banking, Corporate, and Finance Law from Fordham University School of Law, USA. She is admitted to practice law in the Federal Republic of Germany as well as in the State of New York.

Ms. Navidi is an expert commentator on financial markets and has given over 600 interviews in international media outlets and keynoted at dozens of large industry events among Nobel Prize laureates, prime ministers, senior policy makers, and top investors. The German language version of her book $uperHubs has been a bestseller.

Notes

INTRODUCTION

1. Stefania Vitali, James B. Glattfelder, and Stefano Battiston, "The Network of Global Corporate Control," *PLoS ONE* 6(10) (2011): e25995, doi: 10.1371/journal.pone .0025995.

CHAPTER 1

1. Melanie Mitchell, *Complexity: A Guided Tour* (New York: Oxford University Press, 2009), Kindle location 3811.

2. Steven Johnson, *Emergence* (New York: Scribner, 2012), 39–40, 70, 78, Kindle edition.

3. For reference, see also: Nassim Nicholas Taleb, *The Black Swan: Second Edition: The Impact of the Highly Improbable Fragility* (New York: Random House, 2010), Kindle locations 4881–87, Kindle edition.

4. Steven H. Strogatz, *Sync: How Order Emerges from Chaos in the Universe, Nature, and Daily Life* (New York: Hachette, 2012), 231–232, Kindle edition.

5. "Homepage," Douglas Rushkoff, http://www.rushkoff.com.

6. Robin Greenwood and David Scharfstein, "The Growth of Modern Finance," *Journal of Economic Perspectives* 27(2) (Spring 2013): 3–28.

7. Oxfam International, "Richest 1% Will Own More Than All the Rest by 2016," press release, January 19, 2015, https://www.oxfamorg/en/pressroom/pressreleases/2015 -01-19/richest-1-will-own-more-all-rest-2016.

8. For reference, see also: Thomas Piketty, *Capital in the Twenty-First Century* (Boston: Harvard University Press, 2014), 1, 237, Kindle edition.

9. Donella H. Meadows, *Thinking in Systems: A Primer* (Chelsea, VT: Chelsea Green Publishing), 3, Kindle edition.

10. Joseph E. Stiglitz, *The Price of Inequality: How Today's Divided Society Endangers Our Future* (New York: W. W. Norton & Company, 2012), 121, Kindle edition.

11. Nick Hanauer, "The Pitchforks Are Coming . . . For Us Plutocrats," *Politico*, July/August 2014, http://www.politico.com/magazine/story/2014/06/the-pitchforks-are-coming-for-us-plutocrats-108014.html.

12. Julia La Roche, "Paul Tudor Jones: Income Inequality Will End in Revolution, Taxes, or War," *Business Insider*, March 19, 2015, http://www.businessinsider.com/paul-tudor-jones-on-inequality-2015-3.

13. Alec Hogg, "As Inequality Soars, the Nervous Super Rich Are Already Planning Their Escapes," *The Guardian*, January 23, 2015, http://www.theguardian.com/public-leaders-network/2015/jan/23/nervous-super-rich-planning-escapes-davos-2015.

CHAPTER 2

1. Michael T. Kaufman, *Soros: The Life and Times of a Messianic Billionaire* (New York: Vintage, 2010), Kindle Locations 1677–81, Kindle edition.

2. George Soros, *The New Paradigm for Financial Markets: The Credit Crisis of 2008 and What It Means* (New York: PublicAffairs, 2008), 102–105; George Soros, "Soros: General Theory of Reflexivity," *Financial Times*, October 27, 2009, http://www.ft.com/intl/cms/s/2/0ca06172-bfe9-11de-aed2-00144feab49a.html.

3. George Soros, *Soros on Soros: Staying Ahead of the Curve* (New York: Wiley, 1995), Kindle locations 1200–1204, Kindle edition.

4. For reference, see also: Taleb, *The Black Swan*, Kindle locations 4881–87.

5. Nicholas A. Christakis and James H. Fowler, *Connected: The Surprising Power of Our Social Networks and How They Shape Our Lives* (New York: Little, Brown and Company, 2009), 26, Kindle edition; Richard Koch and Greg Lockwood, *Superconnect: Harnessing the Power of Networks and the Strength of Weak Links* (New York: W. W. Norton, 2010), 13, Kindle edition; Duncan J. Watts, *Six Degrees: The Science of a Connected Age* (New York: W. W. Norton, 2004), Kindle location 599–670, Kindle edition.

6. Albert-Laszlo Barabasi and Jennifer Frangos, *Linked: The New Science of Networks* (New York: Basic Books, 2002), 106, Kindle edition.

7. Ibid., 221.

8. Koch and Lockwood, *Superconnect*, 184.

9. David Easley and Jon Kleinberg, *Networks, Crowds, and Markets: Reasoning about a Highly Connected World* (New York: Cambridge University Press, 2010), Kindle locations 11169–11252, Kindle edition; Barabasi and Frangos, *Linked*, 88; Koch and Lockwood, *Superconnect*, 184–185.

10. Barabasi and Frangos, *Linked*, 85.

11. Ibid., 87, 106; 85.

12. Meadows, *Thinking in Systems*, 17.

13. Watts, *Six Degrees*, Kindle location 318; Barabasi and Frangos, *Linked*, 110.

14. James Barron, "The Blackout of 2003: The Overview; Power Surge Blacks Out Northeast, Hitting Cities in 8 States and Canada; Midday Shutdown Disrupts Millions," *New York Times*, August 15, 2003.

15. Allen N. Berger, Thomas Kick, Michael Koetter, and Klaus Schaeck, "Does It Pay to Have Friends? Social Ties and Executive Appointments in Banking," *Journal of Banking & Finance* 37(6) (June 2013): 2087–2105, http://www.frankfurt-school.de/clicnetclm/fileDownload.do?goid=000000411442AB4.

16. Nikhil Swaminathan, "For the Brain, Cash Is Good, Status Is Better," *Scientific American*, April 24, 2008, http://www.scientificamerican.com/article.cfm?id=for-the-brain-status-is-better.

17. Sergey Gavrilets and Laura Fortunato, "The Altruistic Side of Aggressive Greed: Study Explains New Twist in Group Cooperation," National Institute for Mathematical and Biological Synthesis, press release, March 26, 2014, https://www.sciencedaily.com/releases/2014/03/140326092600.htm.

18. Phil Rosenzweig, *The Halo Effect: . . . And the Eight Other Business Delusions That Deceive Managers* (New York: Free Press, 2007), Kindle locations 1074–77, Kindle edition.

19. For reference: Jeffrey Pfeffer, *Power: Why Some People Have It—and Others Don't* (New York: HarperCollins, 2010), Kindle location 1782, Kindle edition.

20. Rob Cross, "The Most Valuable People in Your Network," *Harvard Business Review Blog Network*, March 8, 2011, https://hbr.org/2011/03/the-most-valuable-people-in-yo.

21. Robin Dunbar, *How Many Friends Does One Person Need? Dunbar's Number and Other Evolutionary Quirks* (Boston: Cambridge University Press, 2010), Kindle locations 40–42, Kindle edition; Drake Bennett, "The Dunbar Number: From the Guru of Social Networks," *Businessweek*, January 10, 2013, http://www.businessweek.com/articles/2013-01-10/the-dunbar-number-from-the-guru-of-social-networks.

22. Valdis Krebs, "Power in Networks," *Orgnet.com*, 2004, http://www.orgnet.com/PowerIn Networks.pdf.

23. John Field, *Social Capital* (London: Taylor and Francis, 2008), Kindle locations 1552–53, Kindle edition.

24. Elizabeth Bernstein, "The Friendship Bank: How and Why Even the Most Giving Friend Expects Payback," *Wall Street Journal*, Sept. 23, 2013, http://online.wsj.com/news/articles/SB10001424052702304713704579093141120660698.

25. Matthew D. Lieberman, *Social: Why Our Brains Are Wired to Connect* (New York: Crown, 2013), Kindle locations 3711–16, Kindle edition.

CHAPTER 3

1. Michael McLeay, Amar Radia and Ryland Thomas, "Money Creation in the Modern Economy," Quarterly Bulletin, Bank of England, 2014.

2. For reference, see also: Ralph Atkins, "Central Banks Shift into Shares as Low Rates Hit Revenues," *Financial Times*, June 15, 2014, https://next.ft.com/content/d9dfad02-f462-11e3-a143-00144feabdc0.

3. David Wessel, *In FED We Trust: Ben Bernanke's War on the Great Panic* (New York: Random House, 2009), 129, Kindle edition; Ben S. Bernanke, "Modern Risk Management and Banking Supervision," speech delivered at the Stonier Graduate School of Banking, Washington, D.C., June 12, 2006, http://www.federalreserve.gov/newsevents/speech/Bernanke20060612a.htm.

4. Pedro Nicolaci da Costa, "Fed Missed Crisis Due to Narrow Mindset, Says Study," *Wall Street Journal*, March 7, 2014, http://blogs.wsj.com/economics/2014/03/07/fed-missed-crisis-due-to-narrow-mindset-says-study.

5. Bob Ivry, Bradley Keoun and Phil Kuntz, "Secret Fed Loans Gave Banks $13 Billion Undisclosed to Congress," *Bloomberg*, Nov. 27, 2011, http://www.bloomberg.com/news/2011-11-28/secret-fed-loans-undisclosed-to-congress-gave-banks-13-billion-in-income.html.

6. Emma Coleman Jordan, "The Federal Reserve and a Cascade of Failures: Inequality, Cognitive Narrrowness and Financial Network Theory," Georgetown University Law Center, Faculty Research Workshop, April 17, 2014; Peter Coy, "Bernanke, the Reluctant Revolutionary," *Businessweek*, August 1, 2012, http://www.bloomberg.com/news/articles/2012-08-01/bernanke-the-reluctant-revolutionary.

7. Andrew Ross Sorkin, "What Timothy Geithner Really Thinks," *New York Times*, May 8, 2014, http://www.nytimes.com/2014/05/11/magazine/what-timothy-geithner-really-thinks.html.

8. Wessel, *In FED We Trust*, 209.

9. Adam LeBor, *Tower of Basel: The Shadowy History of the Secret Bank that Runs the World* (New York: PublicAffairs, 2013), Kindle edition.

10. For reference see: Liaquat Ahamed, *Lords of Finance: The Bankers Who Broke the World* (New York: Penguin, 2009), Kindle edition.

11. "About the IMF," The International Monetary Fund, http://www.imf.org/external/about.htm.

12. James Gleick, *The Information: A History, a Theory, a Flood* (New York: Random House, 2011), 9, Kindle edition.

13. Meadows, *Thinking in Systems*, 14.

14. Manuel Castells, *The Rise of the Network Society: The Information Age: Economy,*

Society, and Culture Volume I (Hoboken, NJ: Wiley-Blackwell, 2011), Kindle locations 569–71, Kindle edition.

15. Steven Kotler and Peter H. Diamandis, *Abundance: The Future Is Better Than You Think* (New York: Simon & Schuster, 2012), Kindle locations 3695–96, Kindle edition.

16. Erik Holm and Anupreeta Das, "Buffett Reminds His Top Managers: Reputation Is Everything," *Wall Street Journal*, December 19, 2014, http://blogs.wsj.com/moneybeat /2014/12/19/buffett-reminds-his-top-managers-reputation-is-everything.

17. Athena Vongalis-Macrow, "Assess the Value of Your Networks," *Harvard Business Review*, June 29, 2012, https://hbr.org/2012/06/assess-the-value-of-your-network.

18. Lauren H. Cohen and Christopher J. Malloy, "The Power of Alumni Networks," *Harvard Business Review*, October 2010, https://hbr.org/2010/10/the-power-of -alumni-networks.

19. Aruna Viswanatha, Kate Davidson, Brody Mullins and Christopher M. Matthews, "Questions About Leak at Federal Reserve Escalate to Insider-Trading Probe," *Wall Street Journal*, October 1, 2015, http://www.wsj.com/articles/questions-about-leak-at -federal-reserve-escalate-to-insider-trading-probe-1443650303.

20. Craig Torres, "Bernanke Raised Concern About Leaks Two Years Before 2012 Probe," *Bloomberg*, January 15, 2015, http://www.bloomberg.com/news/articles/2016-01-15 /bernanke-raised-concern-about-leaks-two-years-before-2012-probe.

21. Jo Becker and Gretchen Morgenson, "Geithner, Member and Overseer of Finance Club," *New York Times*, April 26, 2009, http://www.nytimes.com/2009/04/27/business /27geithner.html.

22. Daron Acemoğlu, Simon Johnson, Amir Kermani, James Kwak, Todd Mitton, "The Value of Connections in Turbulent Times: Evidence from the United States," MIT Department of Economics, Working Paper 13-22, November 27, 2013, http://ssrn .com/abstract=2363609.

23. Ibid.

24. Andrew Ross Sorkin, "Prophecies Made in Davos Do Not Always Come True," Dealbook, *New York Times*, January 21, 2013, http://dealbook.nytimes.com/2013/01/21 /prophesies-made-in-davos-dont-always-come-true.

25. Ambrose Evans-Pritchard, "Economic Bears Warn of Financial Crisis," *Daily Telegraph*, January 24, 2007, http://www.telegraph.co.uk/finance/4654397/Economic -bears-warn-of-financial-crisis.html.

26. Tim Harford, "An Astonishing Record—of Complete Failure," *Financial Times*, May 30, 2014, http://www.ft.com/intl/cms/s/2/14e323ee-e602-11e3-aeef-00144feabdc0 .html.

27. Ben S. Bernanke, "The Ten Suggestions," speech delivered at Princeton University, June 2, 2013, http://www.federalreserve.gov/newsevents/speech/bernanke20130602a .htm.

28. Steve Jobs' 2005 Stanford Commencement Address, "You've got to find what you love," *Stanford News*, June 14, 2005, http://news.stanford.edu/2005/06/14/jobs-061505/.

29. Carmen Marti, "EQ More Important than IQ When It Comes to Success," *Chicago-Booth News*, March 16, 2007, http://www.chicagobooth.edu/news/2007-03-16_dimon _fireside.aspx.

30. Andrew Ross Sorkin, *Too Big to Fail: The Inside Story of How Wall Street and Washington Fought to Save the Financial System—and Themselves* (New York: Penguin, 2010), 433, Kindle edition.

31. Watts, *Six Degrees*, Kindle locations 1663–71.

CHAPTER 4

1. Keith Dowding, *Encyclopedia of Power* (Thousand Oaks, CA: SAGE, 2011), 663.

2. Graydon Carter, "Dimon in the Rough," *Vanity Fair*, April 1, 2011, http://www.vanityfair .com/magazine/2011/04/graydon-201104.

3. Sheila Bair, *Bull by the Horns: Fighting to Save Main Street from Wall Street and Wall Street from Itself* (New York: Simon & Schuster, 2012), 2, Kindle edition.

4. Roger Lowenstein, "Jamie Dimon: America's Least-Hated Banker," *New York Times*, December 1, 2010, http://www.nytimes.com/2010/12/05/magazine/05Dimon-t.html.

5. Heidi N. Moore, "Scruffy Jamie Dimon Plays to Main Street," *Wall Street Journal*, January 29, 2009, http://blogs.wsj.com/deals/2009/01/29/jp-morgans-jamie-dimon -wears-scruff-supports-consumer.

6. Duff McDonald, *Last Man Standing: The Ascent of Jamie Dimon and JPMorgan Chase* (New York: Simon & Schuster, 2009), Kindle locations 2033–95, Kindle edition.

7. William Cohan, *House of Cards: A Tale of Hubris and Wretched Excess on Wall Street* (New York: Anchor, 2010), 142.

8. Marti, "EQ More Important than IQ When It Comes to Success."

9. Carl Benedikt Frey and Michael A. Osborne, "The Future of Employment: How Susceptible Are Jobs to Computerisation?" paper prepared for the Oxford Martin Programme on the Impacts of Future Technology, September 17, 2013, www .oxfordmartin.ox.ac.uk/downloads/academic/The_Future_of_Employment.pdf.

10. Roland Berger Strategy Consultants, "Perception Beats Performance," press release, July 29, 2014, http://www.rolandberger.de/pressemitteilungen/Perception_beats _Performance.html.

11. Andrew Goodmann, "Top 40 Buffett-isms: Inspiration to Become a Better Investor," *Forbes*, September 25, 2013, http://www.forbes.com/sites/agoodman/2013/09/25/the -top-40-buffettisms-inspiration-to-become-a-better-investor.

12. Stephen Foley, "Warren Buffett Rolls Out the Berkshire Hathaway Brand," *Financial*

Times, October 13, 2014, http://www.ft.com/intl/cms/s/0/9a685232-50a6-11e4-b73e
-00144feab7de.html.

13. Joseph S. Nye Jr., *The Future of Power* (New York: PublicAffairs, 2010), Kindle edition.

14. Kaufman, *Soros*, Kindle locations 2787–92.

15. Robert Rubin and Jacob Weisberg, *In an Uncertain World: Tough Choices from Wall Street to Washington* (New York: Random House, 2003), Kindle locations 171–73, Kindle edition.

16. "History," The World Economic Forum, http://www.weforum.org/history.

17. Ray Dalio, *Principles* (self-published, 2011), http://www.bwater.com/Uploads/File Manager/Principles/Principles-Bridgewater-Associates-Ray-Dalio-Principles.pdf.

18. Kathleen Morris, "The Reincarnation of Mike Milken," *Bloomberg*, May 10, 1999, http:// www.bloomberg.com/news/articles/1999-05-09/the-reincarnation-of-mike-milken.

19. Dionne Searcey, "Yellen Tells N.Y.U. Graduates to Expect Failure and Learn From It," *New York Times*, May 21, 2014, www.nytimes.com/2014/05/22/business/economy /at-nyu-yellen-praises-her-fed-predecessor.html.

20. Kaufman, *Soros*, Kindle locations 6284–87.

21. Rachel Feintzeig, "Are You Vain Enough to Get Ahead?" *Wall Street Journal*, January 13, 2014, http://blogs.wsj.com/atwork/2014/01/13/are-you-vain-enough-to-get-ahead.

22. Robert Hercz, "Psychopaths Among Us," *Saturday Night*, September 8, 2001, http:// www.hare.org/links/saturday.html.

23. Steven Davidoff Solomon, "A Mirror Can Be a Dangerous Tool for Some C.E.O.s," *New York Times*, March 6, 2012, http://dealbook.nytimes.com/2012/03/06/a-mirror -can-be-a-dangerous-tool-for-some-c-e-o-s.

24. John Darne and Jeffrey Gedmin, "Six Principles for Developing Humility as a Leader," *Harvard Business Review Blog Network*, September 9, 2013, http://blogs.hbr .org/2013/09/six-principles-for-developing.

25. Scott Patterson, "Something weird is going on with Bill Gross," June 19, 2014, 11:03 a.m., https://twitter.com/pattersonscott/status/479686007646728192.

26. Katherine Burton, "Gross on Gross: From Erotic Sneezes to His Dead Cat Bob," *Bloomberg*, September 26, 2014, http://www.bloomberg.com/news/articles/2014-09-26/gross -on-gross-from-erotic-sneezes-to-his-dead-cat-bob.

27. Kirsten Grind, "'Bond King' Bill Gross Loses Showdown at Firm," *Wall Street Journal*, September 26, 2014, http://www.wsj.com/articles/bond-king-bill-gross-loses -showdown-at-firm-1411773652.

28. Barbara Kiviat, "Even Bond Guru Bill Gross Can't Escape," *Time*, September 18, 2008, http://content.time.com/time/business/article/0,8599,1842501,00.html.

29. Robert Frank, "Elon Musk's Ex-Wife on Secret to Getting Rich: 'Be Obsessed,'" *CNBC*,

April 20, 2015, http://www.cnbc.com/2015/04/20/elon-musks-ex-wife-on-secret-to-getting-rich-be-obsessed.html.

30. Ray Dalio, *Principles*.

31. Michelle Celarier & Lawrence Delevingne, "Ray Dalio's Culture of Radical Truth," *Institutional Investor*, March 2, 2011, http://www.institutionalinvestor.com/Article/2775995/Ray-Dalios-radical-truth.html.

32. Kevin Roose, "Pursuing Self-Interest in Harmony with the Laws of the Universe and Contributing to Evolution Is Universally Rewarded," *New York*, April 10, 2011, http://nymag.com/news/business/wallstreet/ray-dalio-2011-4.

33. Bess Levin, "Bridgewater Associates: Be the Hyena. Attack the Wildebeest," *Dealbreaker*, May 10, 2010, http://dealbreaker.com/2010/05/bridgewater-associates-be-the-hyena-attack-the-wildebeest.

34. Lucy Kellaway, "Why Financiers Are Leaders in Drivel," *Financial Times*, August 2, 2010.

35. Lucy Kellaway, "Principles for Living We Could Do Without," *Financial Times*, May 23, 2010, http://www.ft.com/intl/cms/s/0/be8ce2ce-650d-11df-b648-00144feab49a.html.

36. Rob Copeland, "Schism Atop Bridgewater, the World's Largest Hedge Fund," *Wall Street Journal*, February 5, 2016, http://www.wsj.com/articles/schism-at-the-top-of-worlds-largest-hedge-fund-1454695374.

37. Ibid.

38. Mary Childs, "Bridgewater Succession Plan in Flux as Heir Greg Jensen Steps Back," *Financial Times*, February 7, 2016, http://www.ft.com/intl/cms/s/12ef2de6-cc72-11e5-be0b-b7ece4e953a0.

39. See Rob Copeland, note #36.

CHAPTER 5

1. Easley and Kleinberg, *Networks, Crowds, and Markets*, Kindle locations 1941–46.

2. Nicholas A. Christakis and James H. Fowler, *Connected: The Surprising Power of Our Social Networks and How They Shape Our Lives* (New York: Little, Brown and Company, 2009), 17, Kindle edition.

3. Koch and Lockwood, *Superconnect*, 184.

4. Berger, Kick, Koetter, and Schaeck, "Does It Pay to Have Friends?" 2087–2105.

5. Kristen Lamoreaux, "Hiring Managers: Personal Networks Hold Hiring Power for CIOs," *CIO.com*, January 27, 2010, http://www.cio.com/article/526363/Hiring_Managers_Personal_Networks_Hold_Hiring_Power_for_CIOs.

6. Miller McPherson, Lynn Smith-Lovin, and James M. Cook, "Birds of a Feather: Homophily in Social Networks," *Annual Review of Sociology* 27 (August 2001): 415–44, https://www.researchgate.net/publication/200110353_Birds_of_a _Feather_Homophily_in_Social_Networks.

7. Charles Kadushin, *Understanding Social Networks: Theories, Concepts, and Findings* (New York: Oxford University Press, 2011), Kindle locations 870–81, Kindle edition.

8. Niall Ferguson, *The Ascent of Money: A Financial History of the World* (New York: Penguin, 2008), Kindle locations 1098–1103, Kindle edition.

9. Andy Serwer and Melanie Shanley, "Wall Street's Hottest Hand Blackstone CEO Steve Schwarzman Has Built a Powerhouse Unlike Any Other," *Fortune*, June 9, 2003, http://archive.fortune.com/magazines/fortune/fortune_archive/2003/06/09/343947 /index.htm.

10. Tyler Cowen, "The Marriages of Power Couples Reinforce Income Inequality," *New York Times*, December 24, 2015, http://www.nytimes.com/2015/12/27/upshot /marriages-of-power-couples-reinforce-income-inequality.html.

11. Jordan Weissmann, "Ben Bernanke to Princeton Grads: The World Isn't Fair (and You All Got Lucky)," *The Atlantic*, June 3, 2013, http://www.theatlantic.com/business/ archive/2013/06/ben-bernanke-to-princeton-grads-the-world-isnt-fair-and-you-all -got-lucky/276471.

12. Sara Neville, "Top Firms' 'Poshness Test' Imposes Class Ceiling," *Financial Times*, June 15, 2015; Heather McGregor, "'Poshness Tests' Are About What You Know," *Financial Times*, June 19, 2015, http://www.ft.com/intl/cms/s/0/d647785e-1677-11e5-b07f -00144feabdc0.html; Lauren A. Rivera, "Guess Who Doesn't Fit In at Work," *New York Times*, May 30, 2015, http://www.nytimes.com/2015/05/31/opinion/sunday /guess-who-doesnt-fit-in-at-work.html.

13. Vicky Ward, "Lehman's Desperate Housewives," *Vanity Fair*, April 2010, http://www .vanityfair.com/news/2010/04/lehman-wives-201004.

14. Jonathan Wai, "Investigating America's Elite: Cognitive Ability, Education, and Sex Differences," *Intelligence* 41 (2013): 203–211, http://www.sciencedirect.com/science /article/pii/S0160289613000263.

15. Jonathan Rodkin, "Best Business Schools 2014: By the Numbers," *Businessweek*, November 11, 2014, http://www.bloomberg.com/bw/articles/2014-11-11/best -business-schools-2014-by-the-numbers.

16. Laura Newland, "How Elite Colleges Still Feed Wall St.'s Recruiting Machine," *New York Times*, April 30, 2012, http://dealbook.nytimes.com/2012/04/30/how -elite-colleges-still-feed-wall-streets-recruiting-machine/.

17. Matt Taibbi, *Griftopia: Bubble Machines, Vampire Squids, and the Long Con That Is Breaking America* (New York: Random House, 2010), 208.

18. Sherwin Rosen, "The Economics of Superstars," *The American Economic Review* (71)5 (December 1981): 845–58.

19. Xavier Gabaix and Augustin Landier, "Why Has CEO Pay Increased So Much?" The National Bureau of Economic Research, Working Paper 12365, July 2006, http://www.nber.org/papers/w12365.

20. Ulrike Malmendier and Geoffrey Tate, "Superstar CEOs," National Bureau of Economic Research, Working Paper 14140, June 2008, http://www.nber.org/papers/w14140.

21. Arch Patton, "What Is Executive Experience Worth? Rising Trainee Salaries Create Imbalance," *Business Horizons*, 11(5) (October 1968): 31–40.

22. Duff McDonald, "The Godfather of CEO Megapay: McKinsey Consultant Arch Patton Didn't Invent Wealth Inequality," *Observer*, August 13, 2013, http://observer.com/2013/08/the-godfather-of-ceo-megapay-mckinsey-consultant-arch-patton-didnt-invent-wealth-inequality.

23. David Mitchell, "Top Bankers Have One Special Skill: Convincing Us They Merit Millions," *The Guardian*, July 27, 2013, http://www.theguardian.com/commentisfree/2013/jul/28/bankers-special-skill-millions-david-mitchell.

24. Miles Johnson, "Top Hedge Fund Managers Made $21.5bn Last Year, Up 50% from 2012," *Financial Times*, May 6, 2014, http://www.ft.com/intl/cms/s/0/7b350ef8-d51a-11e3-9187-00144feabdc0.html; Alexandra Stevenson, "For Top 25 Hedge Fund Managers, a Difficult 2014 Still Paid Well," *New York Times*, May 5, 2015, http://www.nytimes.com/2015/05/05/business/dealbook/top-25-hedge-fund-managers-took-bad-14-all-the-way-to-the-bank.html; Stephen Taub, "The 2016 Rich List of the World's Top-Earning Hedge Fund Managers," *Institutional Investor's Alpha*, http://www.institutionalinvestorsalpha.com/Article/3552805/The-2016-Rich-List-of-the-Worlds-Top-Earning-Hedge-Fund-Managers.html.

25. Rupert Neate, "Top 25 Hedge Fund Managers Earned $13bn in 2015—More Than Some Nations," *The Guardian*, May 10, 2016, https://www.theguardian.com/business/2016/may/10/hedge-fund-managers-salaries-billions-kenneth-griffin-james-simon.

26. Tracy Alloway and Tom Braithwaite, "M Stanley Chief Warns on Wall St Pay," *Financial Times*, October 4, 2012, https://next.ft.com/content/96e3261c-0654-11e2-bd29-00144feabdc0.

CHAPTER 6

1. World Economic Forum, "History," http://www.weforum.org/history.

2. Neil Parmar, "Klaus Schwab: Inside the World Economic Forum," *Wall Street Journal*, September 4, 2014, http://www.wsj.com/articles/klaus-schwab-inside-the-world-economic-forum-1409843416.

3. Derek Thompson, "How Your Face Shapes Your Economic Chances," *The Atlantic*, August 1, 2014, http://www.theatlantic.com/business/archive/2014/08/the-economics-of-your-face/375450.

4. Gillian Tett, "Klaus Schwab Opens Door for His Davos Successor," *Financial Times*, May 19, 2015, https://next.ft.com/content/0fcb6966-fdfd-11e4-9f10-00144feabdc0.

5. Jaron Lanier, *You Are Not a Gadget: A Manifesto* (New York: Random House, 2009), Kindle locations 121–26, Kindle edition.

6. Mark Bauerlein, *The Digital Divide: Arguments for and Against Facebook, Google, Texting, and the Age of Social Networking* (New York: Penguin, 2011), Kindle location 60, Kindle edition; Sherry Turkle, *Alone Together: Why We Expect More from Technology and Less from Each Other* (New York: Perseus Books Group, 2011), Kindle edition.

7. Keith Hampton, Lauren Sessions Goulet, Eun Ja Her, and Lee Rainie, "Social Isolation and New Technology," The Pew Internet & American Life Project, November 4, 2009, http://www.pewinternet.org/2009/11/04/social-isolation-and-new-technology.

8. Hans-Georg Wolff and Klaus Moser, "Effects of Networking on Career Success: A Longitudinal Study," *Journal of Applied Psychology* 94 (2009): 196–97, http://psycnet.apa.org/journals/apl/94/1/196.

9. Malcolm Gladwell, *The Tipping Point: How Little Things Can Make a Big Difference* (New York: Hachette, 2006), 41.

10. Barabasi and Frangos, *Linked*, 55–56.

11. Carmine Gallo, "The Maya Angelou Quote That Will Radically Improve Your Business," *Forbes*, May 31, 2014, http://www.forbes.com/sites/carminegallo/2014/05/31/the-maya-angelou-quote-that-will-radically-improve-your-business.

12. Ben Knight, "Axel Weber Snubs Deutsche Bank for Swiss Financial Giant," *Deutsche Welle*, July 1, 2011, http://www.dw.de/axel-weber-snubs-deutsche-bank-for-swiss-financial-giant/a-15204477.

13. Christakis and Fowler, *Connected*, 8.

14. Rosabeth Moss Kanter, "Why You Need Charisma," *Harvard Business Review*, September 11, 2012, http://blogs.hbr.org/2012/09/why-you-need-charisma.

15. Alessandra Stanleyjan, "Schwarzman Scholars Announces Inaugural Class to Study in China," *New York Times*, January 10, 2016, http://www.nytimes.com/2016/01/11/business/dealbook/schwarzman-scholars-announces-inaugural-class-to-study-in-china.html.

16. "Networking Can Make Some Feel Dirty Says New Study," Rotman School of Management, press release, September 10, 2014, http://www.eurekalert.org/pub_releases/2014-09/uotr-ncm091014.php.

17. Adam M. Grant, *Give and Take: Why Helping Others Drives Our Success* (New York: Penguin Group, 2013), Kindle edition.

18. "Current Members," Group of Thirty, http://group30.org/members.

19. "About the Bretton Woods Committee," The Bretton Woods Committee, http://www.brettonwoods.org/page/about-the-bretton-woods-committee.

CHAPTER 7

1. Adam Smith, *The Money Game: Lunch at Scarsdale Fats'* (New York: Open Road Media, 2015), Kindle location 2874, Kindle edition.

2. Susan Pulliam, Kate Kelley, and Carrick Mollenkamp "Hedge Funds Try 'Career Trade' Against Euro," *Wall Street Journal*, February 26, 2010, http://www.wsj.com /articles/SB10001424052748703795004575087741848807439.

3. Susan Pulliam, Kate Kelly, and Carrick Mollenkamp "Hedge Funds Try 'Career Trade' Against Euro," *Wall Street Journal*, February 26, 2010, http://www.wsj.com /articles/SB10001424052748703795004575087741848074392; Katherine Burton and David Scheer, "U.S. Said to Tell Hedge Funds to Save Euro Records," *Bloomberg*, March 3, 2010, http://www.bloomberg.com/news/articles/2010-03-03/u-s -said-to-tell-hedge-funds-to-save-euro-records; Matthew Goldstein and Svea Herbst-Bayliss, "Hedge Fund Dinner Party Sparks U.S. Euro Probe," Reuters, March 3, 2010, http://www.reuters.com/article/2010/03/03/markets-euro-investigation -dinnertalk-idUSN0311646820100303.

4. Dorie Clark, "Networking When You Hate Talking to Strangers," *Harvard Business Review*, May 5, 2015, https://hbr.org/2015/05/networking-when-you-hate -talking-to-strangers.

5. "About: Chatham House Rule," Chatham House, http://www.chathamhouse.org /about/chatham-house-rule.

6. Kerry A. Dolan and Luisa Kroll, "Forbes 2016 World's Billionaires: Meet the Richest People on the Planet," *Forbes*, March 1, 2016, http://www.forbes.com /sites/luisakroll/2016/03/01/forbes-2016-worlds-billionaires-meet-the-richest -people-on-the-planet.

7. James C. McKinley Jr., "Julian Niccolini, Co-Owner of Four Seasons Restaurant, Pleads Guilty to Misdemeanor Assault," *New York Times*, March 24, 2016, http:// www.nytimes.com/2016/03/25/nyregion/julian-niccolini-co-owner-of-four-seasons -restaurant-pleads-guilty-to-misdemeanor-assault.html.

8. Janey Morrissey, "Sitaras Fitness, Where Business Titans Work Out," *New York Times*, March 3, 2012, http://www.nytimes.com/2012/03/04/business/sitaras-fitness-where -business-titans-work-out.html.

9. Roland Lindner, "Sitaras Fitness in New York: Wo George Soros ins Schwitzen kommt," *Frankfurter Allgemeine*, April 2012, http://www.faz.net/aktuell/wirtschaft /menschen-wirtschaft/sitaras-fitness-in-new-york-wo-george-soros-ins-schwitzen -kommt-11709768-p2.html.

10. Matthew Bishop and Michael Green, *Philanthrocapitalism: How the Rich Can Save the World* (London: Bloomsbury, 2010), Kindle locations 174–75, Kindle edition.

11. "Virtuous in New York," *Economist*, September 23, 2008, http://www.economist .com/node/12285516.

CHAPTER 8

1. David Tweed and Aaron Kirchfeld, "Momentum Is Building on Greek Debt Swap, IIF's Dallara Says," *Bloomberg*, March 2, 2012, http://www.bloomberg.com/news/2012-03-02 /momentum-is-building-on-greek-debt-swap-iif-s-dallara-says.html.

2. Paul Anastasi and Garry White, "Greek Debt Deal Hits Setback as Talks Suspended," *The Telegraph*, January 21, 2012, http://www.telegraph.co.uk/finance/financialcrisis /9030163/Greek-debt-deal-hits-setback-as-talks-suspended.html.

3. Dawn Kopecki, "Young Bankers Fed Up With 90-Hour Weeks Move to Startups," *Bloomberg*, May 9, 2014 http://www.bloomberg.com/news/articles/2014-05-09 /young-bankers-fed-up-with-90-hour-weeks-move-to-startups.

4. David F. Larcker, Allan L. McCall, and Brian Tayan, "Separation Anxiety: The Impact of CEO Divorce on Shareholders," Rock Center for Corporate Governance at Stanford University Closer Look Series: Topics, Issues and Controversies in Corporate Governance and Leadership No. CGRP-36, September 28, 2013, http://corpgov.law .harvard.edu/2013/12/03/the-impact-of-ceo-divorce-on-shareholders.

5. Lorenz Wagner, "Endlich gut genug," *Süddeutsche Zeitung*, Heft 37, 2014 http://sz -magazin.sueddeutsche.de/texte/anzeigen/42184/2/1

6. Stefan Niggemeier, "When Tabloids Turn: Powerful Media Ally Abandons German President," *Spiegel*, January 3, 2012, http://www.spiegel.de/international/germany /when-tabloids-turn-powerful-media-ally-abandons-german-president-a-806982 .html.

7. "Goldman Sachs Wives Hate to Wait," *Page Six*, August 5, 2009, http://pagesix.com /2009/08/05/goldman-sachs-wives-hate-to-wait.

8. Matt Phillips, "Goldman Sachs' Blankfein on Banking: 'Doing God's Work,'" *Wall Street Journal*, November 9, 2009, http://blogs.wsj.com/marketbeat/2009/11/09 /goldman-sachs-blankfein-on-banking-doing-gods-work.

9. Matthew Holehouse, "Bob Diamond's Daughter Attacks George Osborne," *The Telegraph*, July 3, 2012,http://www.telegraph.co.uk/finance/newsbysector /banksandfinance/9373342/Bob-Diamonds-daughter-attacks-George-Osborne .html.

10. Laura Dimon, "The Last Office Taboo for Women: Doing Your Business at Work," *Daily Beast*, April 27, 2013, http://www.thedailybeast.com/witw/articles/2013/04 /27/the-last-office-taboo-for-women-doing-your-business-at-work.html.

11. Jen Wieczner, "Is There a Suicide Contagion on Wall Street?" *Fortune*, February 27, 2014, http://fortune.com/2014/02/27/is-there-a-suicide-contagion-on-wall-street.

12. Jessica Silver Greenberg and Susanne Craig, "Citi Chairman Is Said to Have Planned Chief's Exit Over Months," *New York Times*, October 25, 2012, http://www.nytimes .com/2012/10/26/business/citi-chairman-is-said-to-have-planned-pandits-exit-for -months.html; Kevin Roose and Joe Coscarelli, "The Tuesday Massacre: The Details

Behind Vikram Pandit's Ouster at Citigroup," *New York*, October 16, 2012, http://nymag.com/daily/intelligencer/2012/10/vikram-pandit-out-as-citigroup-ceo.html; Joe Weisenthal, "Stunning NYT Report Explains How Vikram Pandit Was Really Fired From Citi," *Business Insider*, October 26, 2012, http://www.businessinsider.com/how-vikram-pandit-was-ousted-from-citi-2012-10; Joe Hagan, "Most Powerless Powerful Man on Wall Street," *New York Magazine*, March 1, 2009, http://nymag.com/news/businessfinance/55035.

13. "Einigung in Rechtsstreit: Deutsche Bank zahlt Kirch-Erben mehr als 775 Millionen Euro," *Spiegel Online*, February 20, 2014, http://www.spiegel.de/wirtschaft/unternehmen/deutsche-bank-zahlt-kirch-erben-fast-eine-milliarde-euro-a-954613.html; Gisela Friedrichsen, "Deutsche-Bank-Prozess: 'Ein Freispruch, wie er sich gehört,'" *Spiegel Online*, April 25, 2016, http://www.spiegel.de/wirtschaft/unternehmen/deutsche-bank-juergen-fitschen-erleichtert-josef-ackermann-kopfschuettelnd-a-1089192.html.

14. "Mannesmann Defendants Not Guilty," *BBC News*, July 22, 2004, http://news.bbc.co.uk/2/hi/business/3915717.stm.

15. Maria Petrakis, "Davos-Man Ackermann Lured to Cyprus Bank by Billionaires," *Bloomberg*, November 10, 2014, http://www.bloomberg.com/news/articles/2014-11-11/davos-man-ackermann-lured-to-cyprus-bank-by-billionaires.

16. Ibid.

CHAPTER 9

1. Fabio Benedetti-Valentini, "Women Rare at Top of European Banks as ECB's Nouy Ascends," *Bloomberg*, February 19, 2014, http://www.bloomberg.com/news/2014-02-19/women-rare-at-top-of-european-banks-as-ecb-s-nouy-ascends.html; For reference, see also: Gillian Tett, "Central Banking: Still a Man's World," *Financial Times*, August 9, 2013, http://www.ft.com/intl/cms/s/2/2d8c1ac4-ffba-11e2-b990-00144feab7de.html.

2. Patrick McGeehan, "Discrimination on Wall St.? The Numbers Tell the Story," *New York Times*, July 14, 2004, http://www.nytimes.com/2004/07/14/business/14place.html.

3. Fabio Benedetti-Valentini, "Women Rare at Top of European Banks as ECB's Nouy Ascends," *Bloomberg*, February 19, 2014, http://www.bloomberg.com/news/articles/2014-02-19/women-rare-at-top-of-european-banks-as-ecb-s-nouy-ascends; Anna Brown, "Perceptions about Women Bosses Improve, but Gap Remains," *FactTank*, blog of the Pew Research Center, August 7, 2014, http://www.pewresearch.org/fact-tank/2014/08/07/perceptions-about-women-leaders-improve-but-gap-remains.

4. Tim Smedley, "The Evidence Is Growing—There Really Is a Business Case for Diversity," *Financial Times*, March 15, 2014, http://www.ft.com/intl/cms/s/0/4f4b3c8e-d521-11e3-9187-00144feabdc0.html.

5. Debora L. Spar, *Wonder Women: Sex, Power, and the Quest for Perfection* (New York: Farrar, Straus and Giroux, 2013), Kindle locations 3463–65, Kindle edition.

6. Cathy Benko and Bill Pelster, "How Women Decide," *Harvard Business Review*, September 2013, https://hbr.org/2013/09/how-women-decide.

7. Olimpia Zagnoli, "Why Some Teams Are Smarter Than Others," *New York Times*, January 16, 2015, http://www.nytimes.com/2015/01/18/opinion/sunday/why-some-teams-are-smarter-than-others.html.

8. Stephen Foley, "Is Gender a Factor in Fund Performance?" *Financial Times*, February 9, 2015, http://www.ft.com/intl/cms/s/0/92007f04-b035-11e4-92b6-00144feab7de.html.

9. Chris Newlands, "The Fall of the Female Fund Manager," *Financial Times*, February 22, 2015.

10. Carolin Ströbele, "Mit 50plus ist für Karrierefrauen Feierabend," *Karriere.de*, July 7, 2015, http://www.karriere.de/karriere/mit-50plus-ist-fuer-karrierefrauen-feierabend-167863.

11. Tracey Lien, "Why Are Women Leaving the Tech Industry in Droves?" *Los Angeles Times*, February 22, 2015, http://www.latimes.com/business/la-fi-women-tech-20150222-story.html.

12. Nina Burleigh, "What Silicon Valley Thinks of Women," *Newsweek*, January 28, 2015, http://www.newsweek.com/2015/02/06/what-silicon-valley-thinks-women-302821.html.

13. Bair, *Bull by the Horns*, 98.

14. Pamela Ryckman, *Stiletto Network: Inside the Women's Power Circles That Are Changing the Face of Business* (New York: AMACOM, 2013), Kindle edition; Sara Murray, "Ex-Banker Heads Up 'Broad' Effort at Boosting Women in Business," *Wall Street Journal*, January 31, 2014, http://online.wsj.com/news/articles/SB10001424052702304856504579340971127508490; Diane Brady, "Sallie Krawcheck and the Value of Women's Networks," *Bloomberg Businessweek*, May 16, 2013, http://www.businessweek.com/articles/2013-05-16/sallie-krawcheck-and-the-value-of-womens-networks.

15. For reference, see also: Brady, "Sallie Krawcheck and the Value of Women's Networks."

16. Richard L. Zweigenhaft and G. William Domhoff, *Diversity in the Power Elite: How It Happened, Why It Matters* (Lanham, MD: Rowman & Littlefield, 2006), 58, Kindle edition.

17. Benedetti-Valentini, "Women Rare at Top of European Banks."

18. Joanna Barsh and Lareina Yee, "Unlocking the Full Potential of Women in the US Economy," McKinsey & Company, April 2011, http://www.mckinsey.com/client_service/organization/latest_thinking/unlocking_the_full_potential.

19. John Darne and Jeffrey Gedmin, "Six Principles for Developing Humility as a

Leader," *Harvard Business Review Blog Network*, September 9, 2013, http://blogs.hbr
.org/2013/09/six-principles-for-developing.

20. Sheryl Sandberg, *Lean In: Women, Work, and the Will to Lead* (New York: Knopf
Doubleday, 2013), 17, Kindle edition.

21. Adam Grant and Sheryl Sandberg, "Madam C.E.O., Get Me a Coffee: Sheryl Sandberg
and Adam Grant on Women Doing 'Office Housework,'" *New York Times*, February 6, 2015, http://www.nytimes.com/2015/02/08/opinion/sunday/sheryl-sandberg
-and-adam-grant-on-women-doing-office-housework.html.

22. Victoria L. Brescoll, "Who Takes the Floor and Why: Gender, Power, and Volubil-
ity in Organizations," Harvard Kennedy School, Women and Public Policy Program, 2011, http://gap.hks.harvard.edu/who-takes-floor-and-why-gender-power
-and-volubility-organizations.

23. Amanda Terkel, "Jamie Dimon Wants to Mansplain Banking to Elizabeth Warren,"
June 10, 2015, http://www.huffingtonpost.com/2015/06/10/jamie-dimon-elizabeth
-warren_n_7555204.html.

24. "Microsoft CEO Satya Nadella: Women, Don't Ask for a Raise," *The Guardian*,
October 9, 2014, https://www.theguardian.com/technology/2014/oct/10/microsoft
-ceo-satya-nadella-women-dont-ask-for-a-raise.

25. Katty Kay and Claire Shipman, "The Confidence Gap, Evidence Shows That Women
Are Less Self-Assured than Men—and That to Succeed, Confidence Matters as Much
as Competence," *The Atlantic*, April 14, 2014, http://www.theatlantic.com/features
/archive/2014/04/the-confidence-gap/359815.

26. Margo Epprecht, "The Real Reason Women Are Leaving Wall Street," *The Atlantic*,
September 5, 2013, http://www.theatlantic.com/business/archive/2013/09/the-real
-reason-why-women-are-leaving-wall-street/279379; Carrick Mollenkamp, "Sallie
Krawcheck on Taking the Fall—Again," *Marie Claire*, April 17, 2012, http://www
.marieclaire.com/career-money/jobs/sallie-krawcheck-interview.

27. Andrew Clark, "Lehman Brothers' Golden Girl, Erin Callan: Through the Glass Ceiling—and Off the Glass Cliff," *Guardian*, March 19, 2010, http://www.theguardian
.com/business/2010/mar/19/lehmans-erin-callan-glass-cliff.

28. Gillian Tett, "Lunch with the FT: Christine Lagarde," *Financial Times*, September 12,
2014, http://www.ft.com/intl/cms/s/0/4c506aec-3938-11e4-9526-00144feabdc0.html.

29. Andrew Ross Sorkin, "Do Activist Investors Target Female C.E.O.s?" *New York
Times*, February 9, 2015, http://dealbook.nytimes.com/2015/02/09/the-women
-of-the-s-p-500-and-investor-activism.

30. Debora L. Spar, *Wonder Women: Sex, Power, and the Quest for Perfection* (New York:
Farrar, Straus and Giroux, 2013), Kindle locations 3222–25, Kindle edition.

31. Sandberg, *Lean In*, 71.

32. Ibid., 72.

33. Madison Marriage, "FTfm Survey: Fund Market Rocked by Sexism Claims," *Financial Times*, September 8, 2013, http://www.ft.com/intl/cms/s/0/4e57770e-1639-11e3-a57d-00144feabdc0.html.

34. Chris Newlands and Madison Marriage, "Chauvinistic Boys' Club Still Rules Asset Management," *Financial Times*, November 24, 2013, http://www.ft.com/intl/cms/s/0/3ee96d7c-52a2-11e3-8586-00144feabdc0.html; Zweigenhaft and Domhoff, *Diversity in the Power Elite*, 62–63.

35. Karen Gullo, "Goldman Must Turn Over Female Employee Complaints in Suit," *Bloomberg*, October 16, 2013, http://www.bloomberg.com/news/2013-10-15/goldman-must-turn-over-female-employee-complaints-in-suit.html.

36. Zweigenhaft and Domhoff, *Diversity in the Power Elite*, 62–63; Gullo, "Goldman Must Turn Over Female Employee Complaints in Suit."

37. Tett, "The Female Face of the Crisis Quits the Spotlight."

38. Jenna Johnson, "Paul Tudor Jones: In Macro Trading, Babies Are a 'Killer' to a Woman's Focus," *Washington Post*, May 23, 2013, http://www.washingtonpost.com/local/education/paul-tudor-jones-in-macro-trading-babies-are-a-killer-to-a-womans-focus/2013/05/23/1c0c6d4e-c3a6-11e2-9fe2-6ee52d0eb7c1_story.html.

39. Kelly Bit, "Tudor Jones Says to Sell U.K. Gilts During Late Summer," *Bloomberg*, May 5, 2014, http://www.bloomberg.com/news/articles/2014-05-05/-tudor-s-jones-said-macro-funds-need-central-bank-viagra.

40. Gillian B. White, "Women Are Owning More and More Small Businesses," *The Atlantic*, April 17, 2015, http://www.theatlantic.com/business/archive/2015/04/women-are-owning-more-and-more-small-businesses/390642/.

41. Ann-Marie Slaughter, "Why Women Still Can't Have It All," *The Atlantic*, July/August 2012, http://www.theatlantic.com/magazine/archive/2012/07/why-women-still-cant-have-it-all/309020; Indra Nooyi, "Why PepsiCo CEO Indra K. Nooyi Can't Have It All," *The Atlantic*, July 2014, http://www.theatlantic.com/business/archive/2014/07/why-pepsico-ceo-indra-k-nooyi-cant-have-it-all/373750.

42. Danielle Paquette, "Why Women Are Judged Far More Harshly Than Men for Leaving Work Early," *The Washington Post*, June 10, 2015, http://www.washingtonpost.com/blogs/wonkblog/wp/2015/06/10/why-women-are-judged-far-more-harshly-than-men-for-leaving-work-early.

43. Abby W. Schachter, "A More Dire Assessment of Work-Life Balance: Erin Callan vs. Sheryl Sandberg," *Acculturated*, March 15, 2014, http://acculturated.com/a-more-dire-assessment-of-work-life-balance-erin-callan-vs-sheryl-sandberg.

44. Erin Callan, "Is There Life after Work?" *New York Times*, March 9, 2013, http://www.nytimes.com/2013/03/10/opinion/sunday/is-there-life-after-work.html.

45. Erin Callan Montella, *Full Circle: A Memoir of Leaning In Too Far and the Journey Back* (Triple M Press, 2016), Kindle locations 2216–20, Kindle edition.

46. Susanne Craig, "Lehman's Straight Shooter, Finance Chief Callan Brings Cool Jolt

of Confidence to Credit-Rattled Street," *Wall Street Journal*, May 17, 2008, http://online.wsj.com/news/articles/SB121098034130400069.

47. Christine Lagarde, "Dare the Difference, Finance & Development," *IMF* 50(2) (June 2013), https://www.imf.org/external/pubs/ft/fandd/2013/06/straight.htm; Renee Montagne and Christine Lagarde, "IMF's Lagarde: Women in Workforce Key to Healthy Economies," *NPR*, March 28, 2014, http://www.npr.org/2014/03/28/294715846/imfs-lagarde-women-in-workforce-key-to-healthy-economies; Christine Lagarde, "Women and the World Economy," *Project Syndicate*, September 24, 2013, http://www.project-syndicate.org/commentary/how-to-increase-women-s-participation-in-the-workforce-by-christine-lagarde.

48. "The 2011 International Best-Dressed List," *Vanity Fair*, August 3, 2011, http://www.vanityfair.com/news/2011/08/revealed-vfs-2011-international-best-dressed-list; Diane Johnson, Christine Lagarde, *Vogue*, August 22, 2011, http://www.vogue.com/865416/christine-lagarde-changing-of-the-guard; Gillian Tett, "Lunch with the FT: Christine Lagarde," *The Financial Times*, September 12, 2014, http://www.ft.com/cms/s/0/4c506aec-3938-11e4-9526-00144feabdc0.html; Molly Guinness, "Is This the World's Sexiest Woman (and the Most Powerful)?" *The Guardian*, July 16, 2011, https://www.theguardian.com/world/2011/jul/17/christine-lagarde-worlds-sexiest-woman; Raquel Laneri, "Christine Lagarde's Power Dressing," *Forbes*, August 25, 2011, http://www.forbes.com/sites/raquellaneri/2011/08/25/christine-lagardes-power-dressing; Liaquat Ahamed, "Money and Tough Love: On Tour with the IMF," *Visual Editions*, August 2014.

49. Liz Alderman, "Mme. Lagarde Goes to Washington," *New York Times*, September 24, 2011, http://www.nytimes.com/2011/09/25/business/economy/christine-lagarde-new-imf-chief-rocks-the-boat.html.

50. Ibid.

51. Spar, *Wonder Women*, Kindle locations 3453–60.

52. Gillian Tett, "Lunch with the FT: Christine Lagarde," *Financial Times*, September 12, 2014, http://www.ft.com/intl/cms/s/0/4c506aec-3938-11e4-9526-00144feabdc0.html.

CHAPTER 10

1. Jake Bernstein, "Secret Tapes Hint at Turmoil in New York Fed Team Monitoring JPMorgan," *ProPublica*, November 17, 2014, http://www.propublica.org/article/secret-tapes-hint-at-turmoil-in-new-york-fed-team-monitoring-jpmorgan; Jake Bernstein, "Inside the New York Fed: Secret Recordings and a Culture Clash," *ProPublica*, September 26, 2014, http://www.propublica.org/article/carmen-segarras-secret-recordings-from-inside-new-york-fed; Jake Bernstein, "High-Level Fed Committee Overruled Carmen Segarra's Finding on Goldman," *ProPublica*, December 29, 2014, http://www.propublica.org/article/high-level-fed-committee-overruled-carmen-segarras-finding-on-goldman.

2. David Rothkopf, *Power, Inc.: The Epic Rivalry between Big Business and Government—and the Reckoning That Lies Ahead* (New York: Macmillan, 2012), 16, Kindle edition.

3. Bill Moyers, "The Washington–Wall Street Revolving Door Keeps Spinning," January 23, 2012, http://billmoyers.com/2012/01/23/the-washington-wall -street-revolving-door-keeps-spinning.

4. Max Nisen, "Ben Bernanke Has Earned More from One Speech than He Did Last Year at the Fed," *Quartz*, March 6, 2014, http://qz.com/184431/ben -bernankes-250000-speech-shows-why-people-leave-the-public-sector.

5. Patrick Jenkins and Arash Massoudi, "King takes on Citigroup role despite past criticism of bankers," *Financial Times*, July 29, 2016 http://www.ft.com/cms /s/0/3b770d76-55a5-11e6-9664-e0bdc13c3bef.html#axzz4GfYx3xyl.

6. Bair, *Bull by the Horns*, 142.

7. Joseph Kahn and Alessandra Stanley, "Enron's Many Strands: Dual Role; Rubin Relishes Role of Banker as Public Man," *New York Times*, February 11, 2002, http:// www.nytimes.com/2002/02/11/business/enron-s-many-strands-dual-role-rubin -relishes-role-of-banker-as-public-man.html.

8. William D. Cohan, "Rethinking Robert Rubin," *Business Week*, September 30, 2012, http://www.businessweek.com/articles/2012-09-19/rethinking-robert-rubin.

9. Carol J. Loomis and Research Associate Patricia Neering, "The Larger-Than-Life Life of Robert Rubin," *Fortune*, December 8, 2003, http://archive.fortune.com/magazines /fortune/fortune_archive/2003/12/08/355123/index.htm.

10. Aaron Bartley, "How Robert Rubin's Bright-Eyed Proteges Came to Dominate Wall Street," alternet.org, March 15, 2009, http://www.alternet.org/story/131568 /how_robert_rubin%27s_bright-eyed_proteges_came_to_dominate_wall_street.

11. Sarah Ellison, "The Which Blair Project," *Vanity Fair*, December 18, 2014, http:// www.vanityfair.com/news/2015/01/tony-blair-profile.

12. Philip Stephens, "The manic mission that is Blair's dismal last act," *Financial Times*, May 1, 2014, http://www.ft.com/cms/s/0/15f6aa2c-cf90-11e3-bec6-00144feabdc0 .html#axzz4HGsINdXm.

13. Robert Mendick, and Edward Malnick, "Tony Blair widens his web via the stock markets," January 13, 2014, http://www.telegraph.co.uk/news/politics/tony -blair/9797837/Tony-Blair-widens-his-web-via-the-stock-markets.html.

14. Daniel W. Drezner, *The System Worked: How the World Stopped Another Great Depression* (New York: Oxford University Press, 2014), Kindle edition.

15. Andrew Ross Sorkin, *Too Big to Fail: The Inside Story of How Wall Street and Washington Fought to Save the Financial System—and Themselves* (New York: Penguin, 2010), 52, 237, Kindle edition.

16. Henry M. Paulson, *On the Brink: Inside the Race to Stop the Collapse of the Global Financial System* (New York: Grand Central, 2013), 50, Kindle edition.

17. Ibid.

18. Jane Mayer, "Schmooze or Lose," *New Yorker*, August 27, 2012, http://www
.newyorker.com/magazine/2012/08/27/schmooze-or-lose.

19. Nomi Prins, *All the Presidents' Bankers: The Hidden Alliances That Drive American
Power* (New York: Nation Books, 2014), 413, Kindle edition.

20. Martin Reyher, "Goldman Sachs, JP Morgan, Josef Ackermann: Mit diesen Lob-
byisten traf sich die Bundesregierung," *Abgeordnetenwatch*, February 21, 2013,
https://www.abgeordnetenwatch.de/2013/02/21/goldman-sachs-jp-morgan-josef
-ackermann-mit-diesen-lobbyisten-traf-sich-die-bundesregierung.

21. Lawrence Lessig, *Republic, Lost: How Money Corrupts Congress—and a Plan to Stop
It* (New York: Grand Central, 2011), 109, Kindle edition.

22. Jeff Connaughton, *The Payoff: Why Wall Street Always Wins* (Westport, CT: Easton
Studio Press, 2012), Kindle locations 438–45, Kindle edition.

23. Marianne Bertrand, Matilde Bombardini, Francesco Trebbi, "Is It Whom You Know
or What You Know? An Empirical Assessment of the Lobbying Process," NBER
Working Paper No. 16765, February 2011, http://www.nber.org/papers/w16765.

24. University Warwick, "Economists Calculate True Value of 'Who' You Know, Rather
than 'What' in US Politics," press release, December 12, 2012, http://www.eurekalert
.org/pub_releases/2012-12/uow-ect121212.php.

25. Eric Lipton and Ben Protess, "Banks' Lobbyists Help in Drafting Financial Bills,"
New York Times, May 23, 2013, http://dealbook.nytimes.com/2013/05/23/banks
-lobbyists-help-in-drafting-financial-bills.

26. Maria M. Correia, "Political Connections and SEC Enforcement," paper for the London Business School, April 14, 2014, http://papers.ssrn.com/sol3/papers.cfm?abstract
_id=1458478.

27. Bair, *Bull by the Horns*, 8.

28. Ibid., 130.

29. Ben Protess and Peter Lattman, "A Legal Bane of Wall Street Switches Sides,"
New York Times, July 22, 2013, http://dealbook.nytimes.com/2013/07/22/a-legal
-bane-of-wall-street-switches-sides.

30. Tony Barber, "Saving the Euro: Dinner on the Edge of the Abyss," *Financial Times*,
October 10, 2010, http://www.ft.com/intl/cms/s/0/190b32ae-d49a-11df-b230-
00144feabdc0.html; Neil Irwin, "Three Days That Saved the World Financial System," *The Washington Post*, April 1, 2013, http://www.washingtonpost.com/business
/three-days-that-saved-the-world-financial-system/2013/03/28/d5b9a38c-94ef-11e2
-b6f0-a5150a247b6a_story.html; Neil Irwin, *The Alchemists: Three Central Bankers
and a World on Fire* (New York: Penguin, 2013), Kindle edition.

31. Barabasi and Frangos, *Linked*, 208–209.

32. Vitali, Glattfelder, and Battiston, "The Network of Global Corporate Control;"

"State of Power 2014: A Corporate Planet" Transnational Institute, January 21, 2014, http://www.tni.org/stateofpower2014;

Guido Caldarelli and Michele Catanzaro, *Networks: A Very Short Introduction* (Oxford, UK: Oxford University Press), Kindle locations 709–12, Kindle edition.

CHAPTER 11

1. James B. Stewart and Peter Eavis, Revisiting the Lehman Brothers Bailout That Never Was," *New York Times*, September 29, 2014, http://www.nytimes.com/2014/09/30/business/revisiting-the-lehman-brothers-bailout-that-never-was.html.

2. John Gittelsohn and Hui-Yong Yu, "Ex-Lehman CEO Sells Sun Valley Estate in Record for Auction," *Bloomberg*, September 17, 2015, http://www.bloomberg.com/news/articles/2015-09-18/dick-fuld-s-sun-valley-estate-sets-u-s-record-at-home-auction.

3. "Let Them Eat Pollution," *The Economist* February 8, 1992, http://isites.harvard.edu/fs/docs/icb.topic1188138.files/Week_11/Summers_1991.pdf

4. "Seeing Crimson," *The Economist*, January 3, 2002, http://www.economist.com/node/923104; Jenny Lawhorn, "Cornel West Outlines, 'Pull toward Princeton' and 'Push from Harvard' in Exclusive Interview with NPR's Tavis Smiley," press release, NPR, April 15, 2002, http://www.npr.org/about/press/020415.cwest.html.

5. Lawrence H. Summers, "Remarks at NBER Conference on Diversifying the Science & Engineering Workforce," Cambridge, Massachusetts, January 14, 2005, http://www.harvard.edu/president/speeches/summers_2005/nber.php.

6. Sam Dillonjan, "Harvard Chief Defends His Talk on Women," *New York Times*, January 18, 2005, http://www.nytimes.com/2005/01/18/us/harvard-chief-defends-his-talk-on-women.html; Lawrence H. Summers, "Letter from President Summers on Women and Science," January 19, 2005, http://www.harvard.edu/president/speeches/summers_2005/womensci.php.

7. Maureen Dowd, "Summers of Our Discontent," *New York Times*, August 13, 2013, http://www.nytimes.com/2013/08/14/opinion/dowd-summers-of-our-discontent.html.

8. Connie Bruck, *The Predators' Ball: The Inside Story of Drexel Burnham and the Rise of the Junk Bond Raiders* (New York: Penguin, 1989).

9. "Strauss-Kahn Hired by Ukraine Billionaire Viktor Pinchuk," *BBC*, February 3, 2016, http://www.bbc.com/news/business-35488200.

10. Christine Haughney and Peter Lattman, "The Man at the Center of a Dispute at the Dakota," New York Times, February 25, 2011, http://www.nytimes.com/2011/02/26/nyregion/26dakota.html.

11. Suzanna Andrews, "Sex, Lies, and Lawsuits," *Vanity Fair*, March 1, 2013, http://www.vanityfair.com/style/scandal/2013/03/buddy-fletcher-ellen-pao.

12. Leah Mennies, "Buddy Fletcher: Financial Genius—or a Fake?" Boston Magazine, March 27, 2012, http://www.bostonmagazine.com/2012/02/is-harvard -graduate-buddy-fletcher-financial-genius-or-fake.

13. Steve Eder, "Risky Business: Fund Backs Filmmaker," Wall Street Journal, August 27, 2012, http://www.wsj.com/articles/SB100008723963904449003045775817322 24646356.

14. Rachel Abrams, "Pension Funds Sue on a Deal Gone Cold," New York Times, February 24, 2014 http://dealbook.nytimes.com/2014/02/24/pension-funds-sue -on-a-deal-gone-cold/?_r=0

15. Suzanna Andrews, "Sex, Lies, and Lawsuits," Vanity Fair, March 1, 2013, http://www .vanityfair.com/style/scandal/2013/03/buddy-fletcher-ellen-pao
Adam Lashinsky and Katie Benner, "A tale of money, sex and power: The Ellen Pao and Buddy Fletcher affair," Fortune, October 25, 2012, http://fortune.com/2012/10/25 /ellen-pao-buddy-fletcher/.
Rachel Abrams, "Skadden to Pay $4.25 Million in Fletcher Bankruptcy Case," New York Times, March 21, 2014, http://dealbook.nytimes.com/2014/03/21 /skadden-to-pay-4-25-million-in-fletcher-bankruptcy-case/.

16. Dan Primack, "How a hedge fund bust 'may' relate to Kleiner Perkins suit," Fortune, July 5, 2012, http://fortune.com/2012/07/05/how-a-hedge-fund-bust-may -relate-to-kleiner-perkins-suit/.
David Streitfeld, "Lawsuit Shakes Foundation of a Man's World of Tech," New York Times, June 2, 2012, http://www.nytimes.com/2012/06/03/technology/lawsuit -against-kleiner-perkins-is-shaking-silicon-valley.html.
Adam Lashinsky and Katie Benner, "A tale of money, sex and power: The Ellen Pao and Buddy Fletcher affair," Fortune, October 25, 2012, http://fortune.com/2012/10/25 /ellen-pao-buddy-fletcher/.

17. Maya Kosoff, "Ellen Pao Is Writing a Tell-All About Silicon Valley's 'Toxic Culture,'" Vanity Fair, June 8, 2016, http://www.vanityfair.com/news/2016/06/ellen-pao -memoir-silicon-valley-toxic-culture.

CHAPTER 12

1. Roger Lowenstein, When Genius Failed: The Rise and Fall of Long-Term Capital Management (New York: Random House, 2001), Kindle locations 575–6, Kindle edition.

2. Mitchell, Complexity, Kindle locations 4250–55.

3. Richard Dobbs, Susan Lund, Jonathan Woetzel, and Mina Mutafchieva, "Debt and (Not Much) Deleveraging," McKinsey Global Institute, February 2015, http:// www.mckinsey.com/global-themes/employment-and-growth/debt-and-not -much-deleveraging.

4. Stephen G. Cecchetti and Enisse Kharroubi, "Reassessing the Impact of Finance on

Growth," Bank for International Settlements, Working Papers No. 381, July 2012, http://www.bis.org/publ/work381.htm.

5. Özgür Orhangazi, "Financialization and Capital Accumulation in the Non-Financial Corporate Sector," Political Economy Research Institute, University of Massachusetts Amherst, Working Paper Series Number 149, October 2007, http://scholarworks .umass.edu/cgi/viewcontent.cgi?article=1120&context=peri_workingpapers.

6. Satyajit Das, *The Age of Stagnation: Why Perpetual Growth Is Unattainable and the Global Economy Is in Peril* (New York: Prometheus Books, 2016) 598, Kindle edition.

7. "The American Middle Class Is Losing Ground," Pew Research Center, December 9, 2015, http://www.pewsocialtrends.org/2015/12/09/the-american-middle-class -is-losing-ground.

8. Lawrence Mishel, Elise Gould, and Josh Bivens, "Wage Stagnation in Nine Charts," Economic Policy Institute, January 6, 2015, http://www.epi.org/publication/charting -wage-stagnation.

9. Peter Georgescu, "Capitalists, Arise: We Need to Deal With Income Inequality," *New York Times*, August 7, 2015, http://www.nytimes.com/2015/08/09/opinion/sunday /capitalists-arise-we-need-to-deal-with-income-inequality.html.

10. Lawrence Mishel, Elise Gould, and Josh Bivens, "Wage Stagnation in Nine Charts."

11. "The American Middle Class Is Losing Ground," Pew Research Center.

12. Tim Montgomerie, "The World Lost Faith in Capitalism?" *Wall Street Journal*, November 6, 2015, http://www.wsj.com/articles/has-the-world-lost-faith-in -capitalism-1446833869.

13. Edward Luce, "The End of American Meritocracy," *Financial Times*, May 8, 2016; Sabrina Tavernise, "U.S. Suicide Rate Surges to a 30-Year High," *New York Times*, April 22, 2016, http://www.nytimes.com/2016/04/22/health/us-suicide-rate-surges-to -a-30-year-high.html; James Gallagher, "Recession 'led to 10,000 suicides,'" *BBC*, June 12, 2014, http://www.bbc.com/news/health-27796628.

14. "The Gini Index," World Bank, 2015, http://data.worldbank.org/indicator/SI .POV.GINI.

15. Joseph E. Stiglitz, *The Great Divide: Unequal Societies and What We Can Do About Them* (New York: W. W. Norton & Company, 2015), 15, Kindle edition.

16. Libby Nelson, "A Top Expert on Tax Havens Explains Why the Panama Papers Barely Scratch the Surface," *Vox*, April 16, 2016, http://www.vox.com/2016/4/8/11371712 /panama-papers-tax-haven-zucman.

17. Das, *The Age of Stagnation*, 208.

18. Kali Holloway, "Gordon Gekko for Bernie: Inspiration for "Wall Street" Villain Endorses Sanders for President," *Salon*, March 12, 2016, http://www.salon.com /2016/03/12/gordon_gecko_for_bernie_master_of_the_universe_endorses_sanders _for_president_partner.

19. "The Global Risk Report 2016," World Economic Forum, 44, http://www3.weforum.org/docs/Media/TheGlobalRisksReport2016.pdf.

20. Zbigniew Brzezinski, "Major Foreign Policy Challenges for the Next US President," *International Affairs* 85(1) (2009): 53–60, http://onlinelibrary.wiley.com/doi/10.1111/j.1468-2346.2009.00780.x/pdf.

21. "2016 Edelman Trust Barometer," 2016 Annual Global Study, http://www.edelman.com/insights/intellectual-property/2016-edelman-trust-barometer.

22. "Poverty in the UK," Oxfam Policy & Practice, http://policy-practice.oxfam.org.uk/our-work/poverty-in-the-uk.

23. Andrew Mayeda, "Next Financial Crisis Could Overwhelm World's Defenses, IMF Says," *Bloomberg*, March 17, 2016, http://www.bloomberg.com/news/articles/2016-03-17/next-financial-crisis-could-overwhelm-world-s-defenses-imf-says.

24. "BIS Quarterly Review March 2016" remarks by Claudio Borio and Hyun Song Shin, March 4, 2016, http://www.bis.org/publ/qtrpdf/r_qt1603_ontherecord.pdf.

25. Andrew Haldane, "How Low Can You Go?" speech given for the Bank of England, September 18, 2015, http://www.bankofengland.co.uk/publications/Pages/speeches/2015/840.aspx.

26. Mervyn King, *The End of Alchemy: Money, Banking, and the Future of the Global Economy* (New York: W. W. Norton & Company, 2016), Kindle locations 4822–23, Kindle edition.

27. Sheila Bair, "Sheila Bair: Why I Recommend Tim Geithner's Book," *Fortune*, May 20, 2014, http://fortune.com/2014/05/20/sheila-bair-why-i-recommend-tim-geithners-book.

28. Bair, *Bull by the Horns*, 8.

29. "Lord Mayor's Banquet for Bankers and Merchants of the City of London," speech given by Mervyn King at the Mansion House, London, June 17, 2009, http://www.bankofengland.co.uk/archive/Documents/historicpubs/speeches/2009/speech394.pdf.

30. Mervyn King, *The End of Alchemy*, Kindle locations 60–65.

31. Adair Turner, *Between Debt and the Devil: Money, Credit, and Fixing Global Finance* (Princeton, NJ: Princeton University Press, 2015), 163, Kindle edition.

32. Peter Eavis, "New York Fed Chief Calls for Improved Wall Street Culture," *New York Times*, November 5, 2015, http://www.nytimes.com/2015/11/06/business/dealbook/new-york-fed-chief-calls-for-improved-wall-street-culture.html.

33. Barabasi and Frangos, *Linked*, 131; Easley and Kleinberg, *Networks, Crowds, and Markets*, Kindle locations 730–37.

34. Andrew G. Haldane, "Rethinking the Financial Network," speech at the Financial Student Association, Amsterdam, 28 April 2009, http://www.bis.org/review/r090505e.pdf; Ross A. Hammond, "Systemic Risk in the Financial System: Insights from Network

Science," Pew Charitable Trust, Financial Reform Project, Briefing Paper No. 12, 2009, http://www.brookings.edu/research/papers/2009/10/23-network-science-hammond.

35. Haldane, "Rethinking the Financial Network."

36. Meadows, *Thinking in Systems*, 155.

37. Neel Kashkari, "Lessons from the Crisis: Ending Too Big to Fail," speech at the Brookings Institution, Washington, D.C., February 16, 2016, https://www.minne-apolisfed.org/news-and-events/presidents-speeches/lessons-from-the-crisis-ending-too-big-to-fail.

38. Kelly Shue, "Executive Networks and Firm Policies: Evidence from the Random Assignment of MBA Peers," University of Chicago, Booth School of Business, January 12, 2013, http://rfs.oxfordjournals.org/content/26/6/1401.abstract.

39. Stephen Haines, *Systems Thinking: The New Frontier—Discovering Simplicity in an Age of Complexity* (Self-published, 2011), Kindle locations 106–29; Meadows, *Thinking in Systems*, 7.

40. Haines, *Systems Thinking*, Kindle location 16, 69.

41. Immanuel Wallerstein, *World-Systems Analysis: An Introduction* (Durham, NC: Duke University Press, 2004), Kindle location 136, Kindle edition.

42. James Gleick, *Chaos: Making a New Science* (Open Road Media, 2011), 8, 23, Kindle edition; Mitchell, *Complexity*, Kindle locations 419–21.

43. Wallerstein, *World-Systems Analysis*, 77.

44. Adam Taylor, "Is Vladimir Putin Hiding a $200 Billion Fortune?" *Washington Post*, February 20, 2015, http://www.washingtonpost.com/blogs/worldviews/wp/2015/02/20/is-vladimir-putin-hiding-a-200-billion-fortune-and-if-so-does-it-matter.

45. Douglas Rushkoff, *Throwing Rocks at the Google Bus: How Growth Became the Enemy of Prosperity* (New York: Penguin Publishing Group, 2016), 4, 15, 22, Kindle edition.

46. Meadows, *Thinking in Systems*, Kindle location 42–46; xi; Donella Meadows, Jorgen Randers, and Dennis Meadows, *Limits to Growth: The 30-Year Update* (Chelsea, Vermont, Chelsea Green Publishing, 2004), Kindle location 119, Kindle edition.

47. Robert J. Gordon, *The Rise and Fall of American Growth: The U.S. Standard of Living since the Civil War* (Princeton, NJ: Princeton University Press, 2016), Kindle locations 82, 176, 178, 180, 222, Kindle edition.

48. Alan Greenspan, "Federal Reserve Board's Semiannual Monetary Policy Report to the Congress," testimony before the Committee on Banking, Housing, and Urban Affairs, U.S. Senate, July 16, 2002, http://www.federalreserve.gov/boarddocs/hh/2002/july/testimony.htm.

49. "Pope Francis: Humanity's Future Is in the Hands of the Poor," press release, Catholic News Agency, July 9, 2015, http://www.catholicnewsagency.com/news/pope-francis-humanitys-future-is-in-the-hands-of-the-poor-66764.

50. The White House Office of the Press Secretary, "Remarks by the President to GM Lordstown Assembly Plant Employees in Ohio," September 15, 2009, https:// www.whitehouse.gov/the-press-office/remarks-president-gm-lordstown-assembly -plant-employees-ohio-9152009.

51. Wang Long, Deepak Malhotra, and J. Keith Murnighan. "Economics Education and Greed," *Academy of Management Learning & Education* 10(4) (December 2011): 643–60, http://www.hbs.edu/faculty/Pages/item.aspx?num=44223.

52. Caroline Binham and Martin Arnold, "Bank of England Governor Mark Carney to Extend Market Abuse Rules," *Financial Times*, June 11, 2015, http://www.ft.com/intl/cms /s/0/d24ce466-0f8b-11e5-b968-00144feabdc0.html.

53. John Kay, *Other People's Money: The Real Business of Finance* (New York: PublicAffairs, 2015), Kindle locations 4924–25, Kindle edition.

54. Steve Denning, "Can Complexity Thinking Fix Capitalism?" *Forbes*, February 27, 2013, http://www.forbes.com/sites/stevedenning/2013/02/27/can-complexity -thinking-advance-management-and-fix-capitalism.

55. "Banking Conduct and Culture, A Call for Sustained and Comprehensive Reform" (S. 12), Group of Thirty, July 2015, http://group30.org/images/uploads/publications/G30 _BankingConductandCulture.pdf.

56. Ibid.

57. Alain Cohn, Ernst Fehr, and M. A. Maréchal, "Business Culture and Dishonesty in the Banking Industry," Maréchal, Department of Economics, University of Zurich, December 4, 2014; 516(7529): 86–89. doi: 10.1038/nature13977, http://www.ncbi.nlm .nih.gov/pubmed/25409154.

58. Shannon Hall, "Investment Bankers Severely Dissociate Their Sense of Self from Their Work," *Scientific American*, January 1, 2016, http://www.scientificamerican.com/article /investment-bankers-severely-dissociate-their-sense-of-self-from-their-work.

59. Zachary Grossman and J. van der Weele, "Self-Image and Willful Ignorance in Social Decisions," *Journal of the European Economic Association*, March 21, 2013, http://papers .ssrn.com/sol3/papers.cfm?abstract_id=2237496.

60. Margaret Heffernan, *Willful Blindness* (London: Bloomsbury Publishing, 2011), Kindle locations 25, 3017, 4561, Kindle edition.

61. "Banking Conduct and Culture," Group of Thirty.

62. Ibid.

63. Fred Kiel, "Return on Character: The Real Reason Leaders and Their Companies Win," *Harvard Business Review*, April 7, 2015, https://hbr.org/product/return-on -character-the-real-reason-leaders-and-their-companies-win/16899-HBK-ENG.

64. Peter Eavis, "New York Fed Chief Calls for Improved Wall Street Culture," *New York Times*, November 5, 2015, http://www.nytimes.com/2015/11/06/business/dealbook /new-york-fed-chief-calls-for-improved-wall-street-culture.html.

65. Das, *The Age of Stagnation*, 210–11.

66. Matt Turner, "Warren Buffett Nailed the Problem with Wall Street Pay—and Offered a Draconian Solution," *Business Insider*, March 13, 2016, http://www.businessinsider .com/warren-buffett-on-wall-street-pay-2016-3.

67. Rana Foroohar, *Makers and Takers: The Rise of Finance and the Fall of American Business* (New York: Crown Business, 2016), Kindle locations 5373–75, Kindle edition.

68. Klaus Schwab, "The Profitability of Trust," *Economia*, December 9, 2014, http://economia.icaew.com/opinion/december-2014/the-profitability-of-trust.

69. The Archbishop of Westminster, "Character and Virtue Key to Business Success Says Archbishop of Westminster in Address to City," speech given at St Paul's Cathedral, April 17, 2013, http://cvcomment.org/2013/04/17/character-and-virtue-key-to -business-success-says-archbishop-of-westminster-in-address-to-city.

70. Eavis, "New York Fed Chief Calls for Improved Wall Street Culture."

71. Stefanie K. Johnson and David R. Hekman, "Women and Minorities Are Penalized for Promoting Diversity," *Harvard Business Review*, March 23, 2016, https://hbr .org/2016/03/women-and-minorities-are-penalized-for-promoting-diversity.

72. Warren, *A Fighting Chance*, Kindle locations 1874–77.

73. Gerald Weinberg, *An Introduction to General Systems Thinking* (Weinberg & Weinberg, 2011), Kindle locations 815–17, Kindle edition.

74. Stiglitz, *The Price of Inequality*, 28.

For a complete bibliography visit www.beyond-global.com.

Index

A

Abdullah, King of Jordan, 114
Abu Dhabi, 171
Abu Dhabi Investment Authority,
    203
Academic achievements, 62, 81
Access
    description of, 23–25
    to information, 42–44
    to network platforms, 112
    shows of support as method of,
        174
    social capital and, 26
    to superhubs, 23–26, 174
Access gap, 148–151
"Accommodative monetary
    policies," 211
Achleitner, Paul, 121
Ackermann, Josef
    Angela Merkel and, 143–144
    Deutsche Bank leadership by,
        141–142. *See also* Deutsche
        Bank
    at EQT Partners, 144
    family of, 136
    general references to, 101, 118, 120
    International Institute of Finance
        and, 131
    legal charges against, 142–143

Mannesmann AG and, 142–143
Pierre Wauthier suicide and, 138,
    144
    public relations mistakes by, 143
    at Zürich Insurance, 144
"Age of irresponsibility," 222
Ahamed, Liaquat, 160
AIG, 31, 48, 183–184, 217
Air France, 193
"Airport test," 80
Albania, 27
Alibada Group, 103
Allen & Company Sun Valley
    Conference, 112
Alpha personality, 55–58
Alps, 38, 93, 122
Altman, Roger, 121
Alumni networks, 81
Al-Waleed, Prince of Saudi Arabia,
    205
Amazon, 199
Amygdala, 98
"Analysis paralysis," 51
Analytical thinking, 218
Anarchy, 213
Andreessen Horowitz, 189
Anger, 57
Annan, Kofi, 27
Ant colonies, 6
"Anthropocene," xxvii

Apollo Global Management, 88
Appaloosa Management, 88
Arab Spring, 226
Arabella Sheraton Hotel Seehof, 115
Arbitrage traders, 166, 208
Arcadia Conference, 34
Archbishop of Westminster, 226
Aristotle, 79
Arrow, Kenneth, 185
"Ask gap," 153
Aspen Institute, 112, 200
Assess the Value of Your Networks,
    41
Assessment gap, 152–153
"Assortative mating," 80
Athleticism, 126
Atlantic Council, 158
Avenue Capital Group, 90
AXA, 179
Axel Springer, 136
Azerbaijan, 171

B

Babacan, Ali, 120
Bacall, Lauren, 199
Bacon, Louis, 109
Bailouts, 10–11, 216
Bair, Sheila, 56, 150, 168, 172–173,
    176, 214
Baker & McKenzie, 154, 159
Banamex Bank, 167
Banco Santander, 121, 148
Bank(s)
    bailouts of, 10–11, 216
    central, xxv, 6, 10, 32–33, 37
    CEOs of, 38, 87–88, 174
    commercial, 37

description of, xxv
investment, 38
postcrisis regulation of, 218
private, 37
private equity firms and, 61
regular, 37
savings, 37
shadow, 38
"too big to fail," 216
Bank Credit-Dnepr, 195
Bank for International Settlements,
    37, 78, 214
Bank of America, 115, 151, 183
Bank of Cyprus, 144–145
Bank of England, xxv, 32, 43, 57, 84,
    106, 165, 214–215, 222
Bank of Israel, 36, 84
Bank of New York, 196
Bank One, 65
Banking Conduct and Culture, 223
Banque de France, 39
Barabasi, Albert-László, 19
Barak, Ehud, 9
Barclays, 43, 137, 179, 183, 205
Basel Committee on Banking
    Supervision, 37
BASF, 115
Bass, Kyle, 154
Baur au Lac Hotel, 38
Bear Stearns, 41, 56–57, 198
Beaux-Arts style, 34
Behavior of networks, 20
Beijing, 103, 194
"Believability index," 72
"Believability matrices," 71
Belvédère Hotel, 3, 9, 29
Berkeley Hotel, 43
Berkshire Hathaway, 60
Berlusconi, Silvio, 177–178

Bernanke, Ben
  annual salary of, 165
  as Federal Reserve chairman,
      34–37, 188
  background on, 36
  at Bilderberg conference, 121
  in Euro crisis, 177–178
  in financial crisis of 2007–2008
      management, 11, 36–37, 84,
      172
  Medley Global Advisors leak and,
      43
  power of, 35
  Princeton University graduation
      speech by, 50, 80
  successor to, 188
Bernstein, Leonard, 199
Beverly Hills Hotel, 192
Bieber, Justin, 67
"Big data analysis" programs, 72
Bild, 136
Bilderberg conference, 120–122
Bilderberg Group, 96, 112
Bilderberg Steering Committee,
      142
Billionaires, 123
BIS. *See* Bank for International
      Settlements
Bishop, Matthew, 128
Black, Leon, 190
  at Milken Institute conference,
      192
  net worth of, 88, 123
  parties attended by, 92, 129
  residence of, 91
Black, Steve, 140
Blackouts, 20
BlackRock, xxv, 29–31, 43–44, 53,
      64, 106, 121

Blackstone Group, xxvii, 27, 30, 53,
      60–61, 79, 88, 109, 203
Blair, Tony, 9, 170–172, 192, 205
Blankfein, Lloyd
  AIG and, 183
  Barack Obama and, 174
  Ben Bernanke and, 36
  at Bilderberg conference, 121
  media scrutiny of, 136
  net worth of, 88
  parties attended by, 92
  residence of, 91
  Robin Hood Foundation and, 76
Blige, Mary J., 115
Bloomberg, Michael, 75
Bloomberg Tower, 125
Bodmer mansion, 122
Bolten, Joshua, 85
Bolton, Tamiko, 27
Bonino, Emma, 27
Bono, 27
Borio, Claudio, 214
Botin, Ana, 121, 148
Boulud, Daniel, 205
Brain, 6
Branson, Richard, 115
Bretton Woods Committee, 106
Bretton Woods Conference, 38, 106
Breuer, Rolf, 143
Brevan Howard, 43
Brexit, 213–214, 218
Bridgewater Associates, xxvii, 63,
      70–71, 88
Brin, Sergey, 114
Brookings Institution, 105, 168–169
Brosens, Frank, 170
Brown, Gordon, 107, 205
Brzezinski, Zbigniew, 212
Budapest Festival Orchestra, 27

Buffett, Warren, 225
  Barack Obama and, 174
  Berkshire reputation and, 40,
    59–60
  family and, 135, 137
  "Giving Pledge" participation by,
    70, 128
Buiter, Willem, 45
Bull by the Horns, 56, 176
Bundesbank, 32, 37, 42, 120, 223
Burda DLA Nightcap, 115
Burnout, 137
Bush, George H. W., 16
Bush, George W., 24, 61, 84–85, 173,
  183
Business schools, 81
"Butterfly effect," 219
Buying of influence, 176

C

Calello, Paul, 138
Calgene, 201
Callan, Erin, 157–158
Camdessus, Michel, 39
Cantor Fitzgerald, 76
Capital
  human, 26, 80
  network, 189
  political, 169
  relational, 97
  social. *See* Social capital
  transactional, 168
Capitalism, 209–213, 219, 221
Caramoor Estate, 27
"Carlton affair," 194–195
Carlyle Bank, 105
Carney, Mark, 39, 43, 57, 222

Cass, Stephen, 201
Catalonia, 212
"Catch me if you can" culture, 223
Cayman Islands, 211
Cayne, James, 56
Central bank(s), xxv, 6, 10, 32–33, 37
Central Bank of Canada, 57
Central Bank of Italy, 177
Central bankers
  conflicts of interest, 42
  description of, 33
  financiers and, 43
  proximity to, 42
Central Park, 90, 199
Centre for Economic Policy
    Research, 43
Centre for Financial Analysis, 43
CEOs. *See also* Executives; *specific
    CEO*
  as brand masters, 59
  as role models, 224
  of banks, 38, 87–88, 174
  compensation of, 85–87
  coups d'état of, 139–141
  divorce effects on, 135
  egos of, 65–69
  of financial institutions, 86, 174
  innovation by, 51
  ousting of, 139
  pay packages for, 87–88
  private equity, 88
  renumeration of, 87–88
  risk taking by, 66
  salaries of, 87–88, 211
  social responsibility by, 226
  succession of, 141
  women as, 148, 154, 157
CERN. *See* European Organization
    for Nuclear Research

Change, 227
Chaos, 213
Character, 22, 224
Charisma, 102
Charity events, 128–129
Charm, 102
Chatham House Rule, 39, 121
Children, 135–137
China, 103, 171–172
Chopra, Deepak, 71
Chu, Victor, 115
Churchill, Winston, 34, 219
CIA, 226
Çirağan Cad, 141
Çirağan Palace, 119
CIT Group, 90
Citadel, 42, 76, 87, 121
Citi Wealth Management, 150
Citigroup, 23, 45, 56–57, 65, 84,
       88, 131, 139–140, 150, 165,
       167–169, 204
Clarida, Richard, 44
"Class traitors," 212
Cleary Gottlieb, 166
Clinton, Bill, 24, 84, 164, 166
Clinton, Hillary, 164, 174
Clinton administration, 165, 186
Clinton Global Initiative, 27, 129,
       164
Club of Rome, 220
CNBC, 29, 115
Coeuré, Benoît, 43–44
Cognitive ability, 62, 81
Cognitive biases in human
       thinking, 50
Cognitive capture, 163–164, 217–218
Cohen, Steven, 24, 59, 86, 88, 123,
       192
Cohn, Gary, 52

Collective thought, 50
Cologny, 93
Columbia University, 107
Commercial banks, 37
Commerzbank, 120
Committee on Payment and
       Settlement Systems, 37
Committee on the Global Financial
       System, 37
Common good, 225
Communication
   executives' skills in, 59
   face-to-face, 100
   network power through, 41
   nonverbal, 99–100
Communism, 219
Compensation
   of CEOs, 85–87
   of financial sector employees, 225
   of hedge fund managers, 87–88
   on Wall Street, 221
   performance-based, 86
Competitive advantage, 59
"Conference curve," 120
Conflict resolution, 71
Conflicts of interest, 42, 44, 164
Congress, 35, 173
Congress Centre, 3–4, 9, 114
Congressional Budget Office, 168
Connections
   networking to create, 100–101
   personal. See Personal
       connections
Conspiracy theories, 111
Consultancy firms, 43
Consulting, 49
Consumer Financial Protection
       Bureau, 153
Contagion effect, 217

Contextual intelligence, 62, 97
"Convening power," 25
Cooperatives, 90
Corbat, Michael, 88, 174
Corporate culture, 223–224
Corporations, global, 178–179
Corzine, Jon, 85
Council of Economic Advisers,
    47–48, 84, 188
Council on Foreign Relations, 105,
    166, 168, 170
Council on Systemic Financial Risk,
    1
Coups d'état, 139–141
Credibility, 25
Credit Suisse, 2–3, 138
Crisis of Global Capitalism, The, 65
Crony capitalism, 212
Cult of failure, 64–65
Cultural capture, 46
"Cultural fit," 80
Culture, 220–221, 223–224
Currency
    information as, 39–41
    misinformation as, 41

D

D. E. Shaw, 188
Dakota building, 199–200
Daley, William, 165
Dalio, Ray, xxvii
    Anthony Scaramucci and, 24
    background on, 69–72
    meditation by, 62, 70
    net worth of, 88
    Principles, 63, 71
    Robin Hood Foundation and, 76

    spouse of, 135
Dallara, Charles, 27, 107, 131–133
Dallara, Peixin, 131–133
D'Andrea Tyson, Laura, 185
Das, Satyajit, 210
Davos
    access to, 113
    attendees of, 2, 4, 113–114
    central bankers at, 33
    critics of, 95
    description of, 1–4, 96, 112–116
    drawbacks of, 113
    environment of, 2–3
    hierarchy at, 114
    hotels in, 2–3
    networking at, 113–114
    parties at, 114–116
    peer-to-peer networking at, 5, 9
    purpose of, 4
    status markers at, 114
    superhubs at, 8–12
Dealbreaker, 71
Debt, 210
Decision makers, proximity to, 42
Dell, Michael, 115
Democratic Party, 168
Den of Thieves, 190
Depression, 137
Deripaska, Oleg, 9, 69
Deutsche Bank, 27, 42, 101, 105, 118,
    120–121, 131, 136, 141, 143,
    176
Diamond, Bob, 43, 137, 205
Dijsselbloem, Jeroen, 121
DiMartino, Joseph, 199
Dimon, Jamie
    alma mater of, 174
    as superhub, 11, 56
    as type A personality, 56–57

background on, 55–58
charity by, 76
Elizabeth Warren and, 225
financial losses by, 23, 51
firings by, 140–141
general references to, xxv, 79
at JPMorgan, 9. *See also*
    JPMorgan
"mansplaining" by, 153
media scrutiny of, 137
net worth of, 88
personal life of, 135
profiles of, 56
reputation of, 23
Weill's firing of, 65
"Diplomatic Quartet," 171
Discrimination
gender, 201
of minorities, 148
racial, 198, 200–201, 203
sexual, 155–156
Dispute Resolver, 71
Divorce, 135
Doerr, John, 199
Dombret, Andreas, 223
Domino effect, 216
Döpfner, Matthias, 136
Dormant ties, 41
Dot Collector, 71
Dougan, Brady, 2
Dow Chemical, 205
Dowd, Maureen, 189
Draghi, Mario, 44, 48, 84, 121,
    177–178
Drew, Ina, 154
Dreyfus Family of Funds, 199
Druckenmiller, Stan, 27, 52, 59, 87,
    123
Dubin, Glenn, 90

Dudley, William, 215
Dukakis, Michael, 185–186
"Dunbar's Number," 24

E

East Timor, 171
ECB. *See* European Central Bank
Eccentricity, 66
Eccles Building, 34
ECFR. *See* European Council on
    Foreign Relations
École nationale d'administration, 159
Economic growth, 219–220
Economic power, 164
Economics, 50
"Economics of superstars," 85
Economist, 65, 129, 187
Economists, as thought leaders, 49
Edelman, Asher, 210
Ego, 65–69
85 Broads, 151
Einhorn, David, 110
Einstein, Albert, 218
El Mirador, 126–127
Electrical blackouts, 20
El-Erian, Mohamed, 44, 68
Elite academic affiliations, 81–82
Elite schools, 81–83
Ellevate, 151
Élysée Palace, 132
Emotional intelligence, 49, 58–59,
    97, 189
Empathy, 58
End of Alchemy, The, 214
Englander, Israel "Izzy," 90
Epstein, Edward Jay, 194
EQT Partners, 144

Erdogan, Recep Tayyip, 119
Esma Sultan Palace, 120
Estonia, 27
Ethical behavior, 223–224
Ethical standards, 223
Ethics, 222–223
Ethics code, 223
Eton Park Capital Management,
        109, 170
Euro crisis, 109–110, 176–178
European Banking Congress, 33
European Central Bank, xxv, 32, 37,
        44, 48, 84, 106, 177
European Commission, 32, 110
European Council on Foreign
        Relations, 17
European Organization for Nuclear
        Research, 93
European Union, 110, 213
Evercore, 121
"Evidence-based meritocracy," 71
"Executive contagion," 216–218
Executive networking, 108
Executives. *See also* CEOs
    collective behavior by, 217
    communication skills of, 59
    emotional intelligence of, 58
    friendships among, 78
    homogeneity among, 78–79
    microcommunity of, 77
    personal backgrounds of, 80–81
    private-sector, 165
    sales skills of, 59
    shared backgrounds of, 77–79
    similarities among, 217
    spouses of, 79–81
    traits commonly shared by, 77–78
    wealth of, 85
Exhaustion, 137–138

F

Fabius, Laurent, 160
Face, 98
"Face time," 134
Facebook, 198
Face-to-face communication, 100
Failure
    cult of, 64–65
    of financial systems, 215
Failure gap, 154
Family
    children, 135–137
    of superhub, 133
    work-family life imbalance,
        135–136, 157
Family office gatherings, 122–124
Family offices, 122–123
Favors, 25–26, 104
FDIC. *See* Federal Deposit
        Insurance Corporation
Fear, 52
Federal Cross of Merit, 84
Federal Deposit Insurance
        Corporation, 150, 173
Federal Open Market Committee,
        48
Federal Reserve
    Bernanke as chairman of, 34–37
    checks and balances by, 217
    description of, 20, 30, 32–33, 84
    Eccles Building of, 34
Federal Reserve Bank, 215
Feedback loops, xxvii
Ferguson, Niall, 103
Feriye Lokantasi restaurant, 141
Fidelity Investments, 148
Finance
    as gross domestic product, 12

information as currency in, 39
politics and, 163
wealth gap caused by, 12
Financial crises
in future, 214
networks and, xxvii
risk of, 214
Financial crisis (of 2007–2008)
bailouts of, 10–11
Bernanke's intervention in, 35–37
financial leaders in, 10
health effects on superhubs,
137–138
personal relationships used in
problem solving during,
172–173
policy makers' and politicians'
cooperation in addressing,
176–178
printing money for, 178
recovery from, 219–220
residential mortgages and, 12
Rubin's presence during, 167
Troubled Asset Relief Program
for, 35, 153, 173
Financial decision making, 79
Financial industry
information in, 39–41
male-dominant nature of,
148–150
misinformation in, 41
regulatory errors in, 176
reputation in, 23
salaries in, 22
Financial institutions
bailout of, 11
CEOs of, 86, 174
intermediation by, 10
leaders of. See Financial leaders

lobbyists of, 176
payment systems provided by, 10
Financial leaders
corporate sector leaders and,
178–179
description of, 10–11
educational degrees of, 81
interconnections of, 83–84
Financial Services Authority
license, 171
Financial services industry, 210
Financial Stability Board, 37, 57
Financial system
as network, 18
as self-organizing system, 6
behavior of, 218
boards of, 226
central network position in, 21
collapse of, 218–219
complexity of, xxvi
conspiracy theories in, 111
culture and, 9–10
dependence on, xxv
failure of, 215
feedback loops in, xxvii, 216, 227
fragility of, xxvii, 12–13, 216, 218
global, 177
hubs in, 19
hyperconnectivity in, 214
interconnectedness of, xxvii, 215
language used in, 10
network science application to,
6–7
nodes in, 19–20
oblique actions in, 222
personal connections in, 7–8
purpose of, 225
recalibration of, 221–227
rules that govern, 6–7

Financial system *(Cont.)*
   self-correction of, xxvii, 215–216
   self-reinforcing dynamics of, 12
   societal importance of, 9–10
   stability of, 214
   superhubs in, 19, 26
Financial Times, 43, 65, 71, 89, 115,
      125, 149, 155, 160
Financialization, xxvi, 8, 12, 77, 210
Financiers
   central bankers and, 43
   compensation of, 86
   residences of, 89–90
   super-elite as, 12
Fink, Larry, xxv, xxvii
   background on, 29–31
   BlackRock, xxv, 29–31, 43–44, 53,
      64, 106, 121
   Council on Foreign Relations
      participation by, 105–106
   power lunches by, 124
   risk analysis systems created by,
      53, 64
   Robin Hood Foundation and, 76
First Boston, 30
Fischer, Stanley, 36, 84, 224
Fitness clubs, 125–126
Fletcher, Buddy, 196–203
Fletcher, Geoffrey, 196, 201
Fletcher, Todd, 196
Fletcher Asset Management, 199
"Flocking effect," 89
Focus, 69
Forbes, 115
"Force field" of similarity, 79
Fortress Investments, 109
Four Seasons restaurant, 124–125
France, 178, 194
Freakonomics, 140

Frenkel, Jacob, 48
Freud, Matthew, 115
Friends, making, 100–102
Friendster, 100
FSB. *See* Financial Stability Board
Fuld, Dick, 56, 158, 181–184

G

Ganek, David, 90–91
Gap(s)
   access, 148–151
   "ask gap," 153
   assessment, 152–153
   failure, 154
   gender, 147, 158–161
   mentoring, 154–155
   networking, 151, 161–162
   resilience, 156–158
   sexism, 155–156
   wage, 153–154
   wealth. *See* Wealth gaps
Gates, Bill, 4, 70, 128
Geithner, Timothy
   AIG and, 183
   appointment as U.S. treasury
      secretary, 188
   background on, 45–46
   at Bilderberg conference, 121
   CEO relationships with, 174
   Jamie Dimon and, 57
   Larry Fink and, 30–31
   in Lehman Brothers collapse,
      172–173
   Nouriel Roubini and, 47
   personal relationships and, 11,
      172
   in public and private sectors, 165

relationship with Bernanke and
    Paulson, 11
Robert Rubin and, 168
Gekko, Gordon, 191, 210
Gender discrimination, 201
Gender gap, 147, 158–161
Genentech, 199
Generosity, 105
Geneva, Switzerland, 93
Gergiev, Valery, 116
Germany, 37, 39, 84, 116, 141–142,
    174, 178, 190
Gini coefficient, 211
Give and Take, 104
"Givers," 104–105
"Giving Pledge," 70, 126
"Glass cliff," 154
Glass-Steagall Act, 167, 188
Glencore, 171, 205
Global Competitiveness Report, 96
"Global corporate citizenship," 63,
    95
Global corporations, 178–179
Global Risk Report, 212
Globalization, xxvi, 8, 95, 97, 211,
    213, 220
Goethe, 76
Goethe University Frankfurt, 142
Goldman Sachs, 23, 36, 44, 52, 76,
    84, 88, 91, 121, 136, 151, 156,
    165–166, 168, 184, 189, 217
Goodbye Gordon Gekko, 24
Google, 40, 114, 199
Gorbachev, Mikhail, 16
Gordon, Robert, 220
Gorman, James, 89
Grant, Adam M., 104
Great Britain, 9
Great Depression, 34, 36, 186, 219

Greece, 27, 110, 132, 177, 194
Greed, 220–221
Green, Michael, 128
Greenspan, Alan, 35–36, 42, 44, 220
Gregory, Joe, 182
Griffin, Kenneth, 76, 82, 87, 121
Grill Room, 124
Grímsson, Olafur Ragnar, 9
Gross, Bill, 53, 65–69
Gross domestic product
    debt versus, 210
    finance as, 12
Group of Thirty, 106, 118, 222–224
Groupthink, 51
Guanxi, 103
Guardian, 87, 160
Guare, John, 18

H

Haakon, Prince of Norway, 114
Haines, Stephen, 218
Haldane, Andrew, 214
"Halo effect," 23
Hamilton, Alexander, 167
Hamilton Project, 168–169
Hamptons, 91
Hanauer, Nick, 13, 212
"Hard power," 225
Harvard Business Review, 87, 152
Harvard Business School, 41, 57, 61,
    199
Harvard Club, 195
Harvard Corporation, 168
Harvard Gay & Lesbian Caucus,
    200
Harvard Kennedy School of
    Government, 96

Harvard Law School, 23, 199
Harvard University, 36, 47, 81–82,
        153, 166, 174, 185, 187, 198
Hawking, Stephen, xxvi
Hedge fund(s), 23–24, 27, 63, 70–71,
        75, 82, 86–87, 111, 188
Hedge fund managers
    earnings by, 87–88
    residences of, 90
    women as, 149
Heffernan, Margret, 224
Henry Crown Fellowship Program,
    200
Herrhausen, Alfred, 136
Heterophily, 147
Hierarchy
    creditworthiness and, 51
    opposition to change by, 227
    purposes of, 225
    social, 22
    status and, 22
    at World Economic Forum,
        114
Highbridge Capital Management,
    90
"High-Level Conference on the
    International Monetary
    System," 38
Hildebrand, Philipp, 30, 39, 43,
    121
Homogeneity
    description of, 78–79
    familiarity and, 102
    hegemony of, 79–92
Homophily, 75–92
    description of, 41
    mentoring based on, 155
    shared background and, 79
    in spouse selection, 79–80

Hotel De Bilderberg, 120
Hubs
    definition of, 19
    in financial system, 19
    links to, 19
    network efficiency affected by,
        20
    system failures caused by failure
        of, 20
Human capital, 26, 80
Human networks
    formation of, 98
    homophily influences on, 76
    position of individuals in, 21
    social capital in, 25
Human relationships
    description of, 7–8, 105
    links in, 19
Human thinking, 50, 218
Humor, 102
Hyperconnectivity, 214

I

Iceland, 27
Ideologies, 63–64
IGWEL. See Informal Gatherings of
        World Economic Leaders
Illness, 138
IMF. See International Monetary
        Fund
Implosion
    of Buddy Fletcher, 196–203
    of Dick Fuld, 181–184
    of Dominique Strauss-Kahn,
        193–196
    of Ellen Pao, 196–203
    of Larry Summers, 187–188

of Lehman Brothers, 182–183
of Michael Klein, 203–205
of Mike Milken, 190–193
In an Uncertain World: Tough Choices from Wall Street, 63, 168
Incentives, 224–225
Income inequality, 13, 210–212
Inequality, 13, 210–212, 221
INET. *See* Institute for New Economic Thinking
Informal Gatherings of World Economic Leaders, 113
Information
  access to, 42–44
  asymmetrical access to, 44
  leaks of, 43
  in networks, 39–41
  personal contacts as conduits of, 41–42
  unequal access to, 44
  verifiable, 40
Information currency, 31
Inside Job, 47
Institute for New Economic Thinking, 13, 17, 106–108
Institutional Investor, 65
Integrity, reputation from, 59
Intellectual construct, 63, 168
Intellectual discipline, 64
Intelligence
  contextual, 62, 97
  emotional, 49, 58–59, 97, 189
Interconnectedness, xxvii, 8
Intercontinental Hotel, 114
Intermediation, 10
International Crisis Group, 17
International Institute of Finance, 27, 118–119, 131

International Monetary Fund
  Christine Lagarde at, 159–161
  description of, xxiv–xxv, 4, 6, 11, 16, 27, 38–39, 78, 106, 112, 226
  Dominique Strauss-Kahn at, xxv, 39, 84, 116, 118, 154, 159, 177, 193
  history of, 117
  Istanbul meeting of, 118–120
  meetings of, 117–120
  in Washington, D.C., 117–118
Internet, 40
Interpersonal skills, 66, 81
Intrinsic aptitude, 188
Introspection, 62
Introverts, 104
Intuition, 62, 64
Investment banks, 38
IQ, 81
Isolationism, 212
Israel, 9
"Issue logs," 71
Istanbul, 118–120
Italy, 27, 84
It's a Wonderful Life, 217
Ives Hendrik, Toomas, 27

J

Jackson Hole, 33
Janus Capital, 53, 68
Jensen, Greg, 72
Jim Young Kim, 27
John, Elton, 75, 91
John Bates Clark medal, 185
Johnson, Abigail, 148
Johnson, Rob, 13, 107
Johnson, Simon, 45

Jones, Paul Tudor III
   Barack Obama fund-raising by,
      174, 196, 199
   income inequality and, 13, 212
   meditation by, 62
   Robin Hood Foundation of,
      75–76, 103
   at Soros's wedding, 27
   women and, 157
JPMorgan, xxv, 9, 11, 23, 56–57, 65,
      141, 154, 156, 165, 170, 179,
      225
JPMorgan Advisory Council, 170
Junk bonds, 190–191

K

Kagame, Paul, 171, 192
Kashkari, Neel, 216
Kay, John, 222
Kazakhstan, 171
Kempe, Fred, 158
Khuzami, Robert, 176
Kidder, Peabody & Co., 198, 201
Kindness, 105
King, Mervyn, 43, 84, 165, 215
Kirch, Leo, 143
Kirchner Museum, 9
Kirkland & Ellis, 176
Kissinger, Henry, 45, 124
Kissinger Associates, 45
Klein, Michael, 203–205
Kleiner Perkins Caufield & Byers,
      199, 201–203
Koch-Weser, Caio, 27, 120
Kohlberg Kravis Roberts (KKR) &
      Co., 76, 88, 121
Kravis, Henry, 76, 88, 91–92, 121

Krawcheck, Sallie, 150–151
Krugman, Paul, 36, 49
Kuchma, Leonid, 195
Kuwait, 171

L

Lady Gaga, 75
Lagarde, Christine, 226
   as superhub, 11, 158–162
   background on, 158–162
   at Baker & McKenzie, 154
   compensation of, 85
   education of, 159
   general references to, 4
   at International Monetary Fund
      conference, 39
   male criticism of, 160
   at Soros's wedding, 27
   worldwide network of, 161
Lake Geneva, 93–94
Lake Zürich, 38, 122
Las Vegas, 193
Lasry, Marc, 90
Laws, 222–223
Lazard, 165
Le Tricorne, 124
Leaders
   of financial institutions. See
      Financial leaders
   thought, 47–51
LeFrak, Richard, 129, 192
Legal norms, 222
"Legalized corruption," 175–176
Lehman Brothers, 8, 20, 41, 56, 61,
      157, 172, 177, 181–183, 205
Lending Club, 189
Lennon, John, 199

Levitt, Steven, 140
Leyne, Strauss-Kahn & Advisors, 195
Leyne, Thierry, 195
Liar's Poker, 221
Liberia, 27, 171
Limits to Growth, The, 220
Links
  definition of, xxvi
  to hubs, 19
  in human relationships, 19
  system stability through, 215
Lipton, David, 165
Liversis, Andrew, 205
Lloyds, 137
Lobbying, 122
Lobbyists, 175
Loeb, Daniel, 91, 109
London, 43
London Business School, 48, 166, 175
London School of Economics, 16, 63, 142
"London Whale," 57
Long Term Capital Management, 207–209
Loungani, Prakash, 50
Louvre, 132
Lowenstein, Roger, 208
Loyalty, 23
LTCM. *See* Long Term Capital Management
"Lucky Sperm Club," 137
Lutnick, Howard, 76

M

Ma, Jack, 103
Macroeconomic trends, 70

Magic Mountain, The, 2
"Magic roundabout," 134
Malloch-Brown, Lord Mark, 27
Manchurian Candidate, The, 67
Mankiw, Greg, 84
Mann, Thomas, 2
Mannesmann AG, 142–143
"Mansplaining," 152–153
Marks, Howard, 90
Marrakech, 194
Marron, Donald, 209
Marx, Karl, 219
Massachusetts Institute of Technology, 36, 81, 84, 149, 185
Masters, Blythe, 156
"Matchers," 104
Matrix Advisors, 184
"Matthew Effect," 52
McDonough, William J., 209
McKinsey, 87, 115, 152
Meade, Michael, 201
Media scrutiny, 136–137
Meditation, 62, 70
Medley, Richard, 43
Mentoring gap, 154–155
Meritocracy, 71, 80, 83, 213
Meriwether, John, 207–209
Merkel, Chancellor Angela
  banker interactions with, 174
  at Davos, 114
  in Euro crisis, 177
  general references to, 39, 61, 193
  Josef Ackermann and, 142–144
Merrill Lynch, 56, 179, 183
Merton, Robert, 52, 208
Metropolitan Museum of Art's Costume Institute Benefit, 76
Metzler, Jakob von, 136

Microsoft, 153
Middle East, 171
Milgram, Stanley, 18
Miliband, Ed, 137
Milken, Lowell, 191
Milken, Mike, 63–64, 129, 190–193
Milken Institute, 190, 192
Min Zhu, 27
Mindich, Eric, 109, 170
"Mind-reading," 149
Minimum wage, 211
Minorities
    discrimination against, 148
    integration of, 226
    old boys' network exclusion of, 82
Misinformation, 41
MIT. See Massachusetts Institute of
    Technology
Mitchell, David, 87
Mittelstand, 123
Money. See also Wealth
    creation of, 32
    network power of, 31
    status associated with, 22
Mongolia, 171
Monness Crespi Hardt & Co.,
    110
Monoculture, 227
"Monopoly power," 224
Monti, Mario, 84
Moore Capital, 109
Morgan Stanley, 89, 139
Moyers, Bill, 164
Moynihan, Brian, 115
Mozambique, 171
Murdoch, Elizabeth, 115
Musk, Elon, 69
Musk, Justine, 69
Myspace, 100

N

Nadella, Satya, 153
National Bureau of Economic
    Research, 86
National Economic Council, 39,
    165–166, 168, 184, 186
Nazarbayev, Nursultan, 171
Nazre, Ajit, 201
Negotiation, 153
Netherlands, 120
Netscape, 199
Network(s). See also Human
    networks
    in academia, 48
    access in, 23–25
    alumni, 81
    architecture of, 18–19
    behavior of, 20
    building of, 24, 103
    collapse of, 193–196
    competition in, 97
    connectivity in, 20
    creation of, 173
    detrimental effects of, xxvii
    efficiency of, 20
    exclusive, 101–102
    expansion of, 19
    financial crises and, xxvii
    financial system as, 18
    gravitational force of, 4–14
    growth of, 77
    hub effects on, 20
    human activity affected by, 18
    information as currency in, 39–41
    intelligence of, 97
    links in, xxvi
    location of, 89
    money's power in, 31

negative notions on, 104–105
nodes in. *See* Nodes
opportunity gap caused by, 13
plutocracy of, 82–85
of policy makers, 48
psychological support from, 102
strength of, 97–98
Network capital, 189
Network platforms
access to, 112
Davos as. *See* Davos
need for, 112
Network power
communication used to form, 41
description of, xxv
of Klaus Schwab, 95
network strength and, 97
Network science
description of, xxvi
financial system viewed through, 6–7
human relationships viewed through, 7
patterns in, 7
Networkers, 100–101
Networking
at charity events, 128–129
at Davos, 5, 9
family office platform for, 123–124
at fitness clubs, 125–126
mind-set of, 100–101
power lunches for, 124–125
at Private parties, 126–128
purpose of, 100, 104, 108
resistance to, 104
by Superhubs, 100
by women, 151
Networking gap, 151, 161–162

New York
charity events in, 128
Four Seasons restaurant in, 124
real estate in, 90–91
New York Fed, 45–46, 183, 208–209, 215
New York Times, 17, 56, 71, 125, 148, 158, 189
New York University, 36, 47, 64
New Zealand, 13
Newsweek, 80
Niccolini, Julian, 124
Niederauer, Duncan, 85
Nodes
definition of, xxvi
description of, 18–19
failure of, 216
in financial system, 19–20
hierarchy of, 19
with limited connections, 20
links to, 19
preferential attachment of, xxvi
senior, 77
superhub connections to, 19–20
Nonverbal communication, 99–100, 149
Nooyi, Indra, 157
Norms, 222
Northwestern University, 220
Norway, 114
Novogratz, Michael, 109
Noyer, Christian, 160

O

Oaktree Capital Management, 90
Obama, Barack, 58, 165, 168, 173–174, 188–189, 196
Observer, 87

Obsessiveness, 69
Och, Dan, 170
Och-Ziff, 170
"Office housework," 152
Office of the Chief Economist, 164
Old boys' network, 82–85, 150
Old Lane Partners, 139
On the Brink, 172
On Tour with the IMF, 160
O'Neal, Stanley, 56
O'Neill, Michael, 140
Open-mindedness, 62
Opportunities, 52–53
Opportunity gap, 13
Orszag, Peter, 168
Osborne, George, 121, 137
Osório, Horta, 137
Oxfam, 213

P

Pain, 71
Paine Webber, 209
Palantir Technologies, 72
Panama Papers, 211
Pandit, Vikram, 23, 53, 57, 139–140, 203
Pao, Ellen, 196–203
Papandreou, George, 27
Paranoia, 71
Paris, 131–132
Parties
  private, 126–128
  at World Economic Forum, 114–116
Patton, Arch, 87
Paulson & Co., 42, 88
Paulson, Hank
  AIG and, 183
  Alan Greenspan and, 36
  as U.S. treasury secretary, 36, 167
  background on, 172
  at Bilderberg conference, 121
  networking by, 172–173, 182
  personal relationships, 11
  in public and private sectors, 165
  revolving door phenomenon and, 165
  Robert Rubin and, 167
Paulson, John, xxvii, 7, 82, 88, 129
Pax Ellevate Global Women's Index Fund, 151
Peer-to-peer networking
  at Davos, 5, 9
  by women, 151
P=EFT formula, 63–64, 192
Pelosi, Nancy, 27, 173
Peltz, Nelson, 154
People's Bank of China, 209
Pepsi, 157
Perfectionism, 137
Performance-based assessments, 152
Performance-based compensation, 86
"Perma-bears," 48
Perry, Richard, 170
Perry Capital, 170
Personal connections
  access and, 52
  benefits of, 45–46
  description of, 7–8, 10–12
  in financial crisis of 2007–2008 resolution, 172–173
  influence of, 41–42
  information from, 41–42
  leveraging of, 175
  need for, 98

networking to create, 100–101
technology's role in, 99–100
value of, 175
Peterson, Pete, 27, 30, 53, 61, 79, 124
Peterson Institute, 107
Petraeus, General David, 121
Petro Saudi, 170
"Philanthrocapitalism," 128
Philanthropy, 17, 70, 75–76, 128–
129, 169, 171, 192, 199
Philippe, King of Belgium, 114
Picasso, Pablo, 124–125
Piketty, Thomas, 49
PIMCO, 42, 44, 53, 66–67, 69
Pinchuk, Victor, 195
Place Vendôme, 132
Plato, 79
Plaza Hotel, 158
Point72 Asset Management, 88
Policy makers, 85
Political capital, 169
Political protection, 175–176
Politics, finance and, 163
Ponzi schemes, 196, 201–202
Pool Room, 124
Pope, 220
Portugal, 177
"Positive linking," 100
Potential versus performance,
152–153
Poverty, 213
Power
network. See Network power
undue concentration of, 164
Power lunches, 124–125
Power of Alumni Networks, The, 42
"Power-law distribution," 20
"Predators' Ball," 192
Predictions, 50

Preferential attachment, xxvi
"Pricelings," 103
Prince, Chuck, 56, 139–140, 203
Princeton University, 36, 50, 157,
199
Principles, 63, 71
Printing money, 178, 211
Private banks, 37
Private equity firms, 61, 144
Private parties, 126–128
Private sector, 164–165
Prostitution, 194
Protectionism, 212
Psychological detachment, 223–224
Psychopaths, 66
Public sector, 164–165, 168
Purcell, Philip, 139
Putin, Vladimir, 114–116, 219

Q

Qatari ruling family, 171

R

Racial discrimination, 198, 200–
201, 203
"Radical truth," 71
Rainbow Room, 109–110
Rama, Edi, 27
Rand, Ayn, 71
Rania, Queen, 114
Reddit, 203
Reflexivity theory, 63
Regular banks, 37
Regulatory capture, 164, 217–218
Reinhart, Carmen, 107

Relational capital, 97
Relational capture, 163, 217
Renaissance Technologies, 87–88
Renova Group, 144
"Rent-seeking," 12, 22
Renumeration, 87
Reputation
  integrity as source of, 59
  methods of bolstering, 40
  status and, 22–23
Research firms, 43
Reset, 203
Residences, 89–92
Residential mortgages, 12
Resilience gap, 156–158
"Revolving door" phenomenon
  description of, 10–11, 163, 218
  Robert Rubin as example of,
    163–170
  Tony Blair as example of, 170–172
Rhodes, Bill, 131
Rice, Condoleezza, 172
"Rich-get-richer phenomenon,"
    xxvii, 19, 77, 92
Rikers Island, 39, 193
"Rise of the Overclass, The," 80
Risk, 30
Risk management systems, 30, 64
Risk taking, 66, 225
Ritz Hotel, 132
Robbins, Tony, 23
Robertson, Julian, 27
Robin Hood charity gala, 75–76
Robin Hood Foundation, 75–76, 103
Robinson, James D. III, 125
Rockefeller, John D., 90, 123
Rockefeller Plaza, 109
Rogoff, Kenneth, 36, 107
Romney, Mitt, 193

Roosevelt, Franklin, 34
Rosen, Aby, 124
Rosen, Sherwin, 85–86
Ross, Wilbur, 92, 144, 199
Rothschilds, 79
Roubini, Nouriel, 229
  as superhub, 11
  as thought leader, 47–49
  charm of, 103
  Dominique Strauss-Kahn and,
    193–194
  general references to, 34, 39, 109
  Jamie Dimon and, 56
  Larry Summers and, 184
  networks as viewed by, 48
  at Soros' eightieth birthday party,
    27
Roubini Global Economics, 109
Royal Dutch Shell, 142
Rubin, Robert, 182
  as superhub, 169
  as U.S. treasury secretary, 84, 168
  at Bildersberg conference, 121
  capital network of, 170
  at Citigroup, 167
  Council on Foreign Relations
    participation by, 105, 168, 170
  education of, 166
  at Goldman Sachs, 170
  Hamilton Project, 169
  Larry Summers and, 168, 186, 189
  on National Economic Council,
    166
  personality of, 169, 186
  power of, 166
  in private sector, 167
  revolving door phenomenon and,
    165–170
  thought constructs by, 63

Vikram Pandit and, 139, 204
"Rubinomics," 167
Rules, 221–222, 225
Rumors, 41
Rüschlikon, 122
Rushkoff, Douglas, 8, 220
Russia, 144, 208, 219
Russian Direct Investment Fund, 194
Russian Federation, 115
Rwanda, 171, 192
Ryan, Michelle, 154

S

SAC Capital, 88
Sachs, Jeffrey, 107
Sadikoğlu, Kahraman, 120
Sales skills, 59, 62
Salomon Brothers, 208
SALT. See SkyBridge Alternatives Conference
Samuelson, Paul, 185
Sandberg, Sheryl, 153, 155, 157
Sanford C. Bernstein, 150
Sarkozy, Nicolas, 24, 159, 177–178
Saudi Arabia, 205
Savarona, 120
Savings banks, 37
Scaramucci, Anthony, 23, 53
Scarsdale Equities, 109
Schatzalp Hotel, 115
Schmidt, Eric, 40, 114
Scholes, Myron, 208
Schumer, Chuck, 27
Schwab, Klaus
    background on, 93–96
    Christine Lagarde and, 158

common good and, 225
    at Davos, 116
    digital technology and, 99
    education of, 96
    network power of, 95, 101
    stakeholder principle of, 63
    World Economic Forum and, 25, 93–96, 101. See also World Economic Forum
Schwarzman, Steve
    background on, 59–62
    Blackstone Group, xxvii, 27, 30, 53, 60–61, 79, 88, 109, 204
    at charity events, 129
    earnings by, 88
    education of, 61
    general references to, xxvii, 4, 9, 76, 109, 192
    at Milken Institute conference, 192
    net worth of, 88, 123
    partnerships by, 79
    philanthropy by, 82
    power lunches by, 124
    residences of, 89–92
    in think tanks, 106
Schwarzman Scholars program, 103
Scotland, 212
Scowcroft, Brent, 45
Seagram Building, 124–125
SEC. See Securities and Exchange Commission
Securities and Exchange Commission, 87, 175–176, 217
Self-confidence, 102
Sense of self, 66
Seoul, 194
Sex scandals, 196

Sexism gap, 155–156

Sexual discrimination, 155–156

Sexual harassment, 156, 201

Shadow banking system, 10

Shadow banks, 38

Shadow government, 121

Shaming, 225

Shiller, Robert, 4

Sickness, 138

Siemens AG, 142, 144

Sierra Leone, 171

Silicon Valley, 201

Simons, James, 87–88

Sirleaf, Ellen Johnson, 27

Sitaras, John, 126

Sitaras Fitness, 125–126

Six degrees of separation theory, 18

Skadden, Arps, 201

Skepticism, 64

SkyBridge Alternatives Conference, 24

SkyBridge Capital, 23–24, 53

Slaughter, Anne-Marie, 157

Sleep deprivation, 134

Sleeping pills, 134

Social capital
   accumulation of, 51
   description of, 23, 25–27, 78, 202
   exchange of, 52
   opportunities associated with, 52–53

Social connections, 45–46

"Social connections meets the crisis," 46

Social corrosion, 221

Social hierarchies, 22

Social Isolation and New Technology, 100

Social networks, 100

Social responsibility, 226

Social skills, 58

Social standing, 22, 225

Socialism, 219

Society
   financial system's importance in, 9–10
   rules of, 221
   social standing and status in, 21–22
   stereotype of women by, 153
   value for, 225–226

"Soft power," 225

Sorkin, Andrew Ross, 172

Soros, George
   access to other superhubs by, 26–27
   annual earnings by, 88
   as superhub, 15–18, 21, 26–27
   background on, 15–16, 62
   in Barack Obama presidency, 173–174
   Bedford estate of, 127
   convening power of, 25
   eightieth birthday party of, 27
   El Mirador estate of, 126–127
   failures by, 65
   general references to, xxv, 2, 7, 11, 13, 15–18, 21, 53, 59, 76, 86, 106, 109–110, 194, 196, 199, 209, 229
   humor by, 103
   income inequality warnings by, 212
   Institute for New Economic Thinking creation by, 106–108
   net worth of, 88, 123
   network creation by, 103

philanthropy by, 17
private parties given by, 126–127
reflexivity theory, 63
reputation of, 16
residences of, 90, 126–128
at Sitaras Fitness, 125
wedding to Tamiko Bolton, 27
at World Economic Forum in
    Davos, 15, 21
*Soros: The Life and Times of a
    Messianic Billionaire*, 62
Soros Fund Management, 107
South Sudan, 194
Soviet Union, 226
Spain, 177, 212
Sperling, Gene, 168, 185
Spouses, 79–81, 135, 225
Square, 189
Sri Lanka, 194–195
Stakeholder principle, 63, 95–96
Stanford Business School, 36
Stanford University, 81
"State secrets," 49
State Street, 179
Status
    convening power effects on, 25
    description of, 21–22
    favors and, 25–26
    hierarchy and, 22
    reputation and, 22–23
    wealth effects on, 22
Steinbrück, Peer, 142
Stephanopoulos, George, 185
Stern School of Business, 47
Stewart, Jimmy, 217
Stockholm Syndrome, 163
Stone, Oliver, 24, 47
Strauss-Kahn, Dominique, xxv
    arrest of, 39, 193–194

downfall of, 193–194
in Euro crisis, 177–178
at International Monetary Fund,
    117–118, 193
Leyne, Strauss-Kahn & Advisors,
    195
in money management, 195
resignation of, 84, 154
Stress, 138
Subprime crisis, 140, 183, 223
Success
    criteria for achieving, 18
    wealth and, 85
Suicide, 138, 195, 211
Summers, Larry, 227
    as U.S. treasury secretary, 186
    background on, 184–190
    at Bildersberg conference, 121
    Cornel West and, 187
    Council of Economic Advisers
        leadership by, 188
    education of, 36
    Federal Reserve chairman
        campaign by, 188–189
    general references to, 4
    implosion of, 187–188
    at INET conference, 107
    interconnections of, 84
    International Monetary Fund
        and, 39
    on Bretton Woods Committee,
        106
    personality of, 186–187, 190
    in private sector, 165
    professional rise of, 185–186
    Robert Rubin and, 168, 186, 189
    Schwarzman Scholars program
        participation by, 103
    "toxic memo gate," 187

Superhubs. *See also specific*
          superhub
    access to, 23–26, 53, 174
    characteristics of, 11, 30, 55–56,
          64, 80
    children of, 135–136
    competitiveness of, 55
    "convening power" of, 25
    at Davos, 8–12
    definition of, xxiv, xxvi, xxviii, 11
    degrees of separation for, 19
    divorce rates among, 135
    in financial system, 19, 26
    financial systems affected by,
          215
    habitat of, 89–92
    homogeneity among, 78–79
    implosion of. *See* Implosion
    influence of, 20
    lifestyle of, 133–135
    media scrutiny of, 136–137
    net worth of, 88
    networking by, 100
    node connections by, 19–20
    open-mindedness of, 62
    personal relationships among,
          10–12
    power of, 14, 25–26
    "power-law distribution" of, 20
    pressure on, 227
    prioritization by, 24
    quest for power by, 55–56
    recognizing of, 21
    residences of, 89–92
    self-reinforcing feedback loops
          for, 13
    wealth of, 85–89
"Superhuman paradox," 157
Swiss Federal Council, 94

Swiss Federal Institute of
          Technology, xxv, 179
Swiss National Bank, 30, 38–39, 43
Swiss Re Centre, 122
Switzerland, 122, 144
Systems thinking, xxvi–xxvii, 218

T

Taconic Capital, 170, 189
"Takers," 104
Taleb, Nassim, 49
TARP. *See* Troubled Asset Relief
          Program
Technologization, xxvi, 8
Technology, 99
"Teflonic identity maneuvering,"
          224
Telecommunications, 99
Tepper, David, 88
Tepper, Ray, 24
Tett, Gillian, 160
TGG, 140
Thain, John, 56, 85, 90, 182
Thatcher, Margaret, 16
Theron, Charlize, 115
Thiel, Peter, 121
Thiel Capital, 121
Think tanks, 105–106
Third Point, 109
Thought construct, 63
Thought leaders, 47–51
Thought leadership, 96
*Throwing Rocks at the Google Bus:
          How Growth Became the
          Enemy of Prosperity*, 220
Time, 65
Times of London, 136

Timken, William, 196
Tony Blair Associates, 170
Too Big to Fail, 172
"Toxic memo gate," 187
Transactional capital, 168
Transactional relationships, 104
Transcendental meditation, 70
Transnational financial elite, 77–78
Transparency International, 17
"Transparency library," 71
Travelholics, 134
Trichet, Jean-Claude, 118, 177–178
Trilateral Committee, 142
Troubled Asset Relief Program, 35, 153, 173
Trust, 13, 78–79, 98–99, 222–223
Tsinghua University, 103
Tucker, Paul, 43
Turner, Lord Adair, 27, 107, 215
Type A personality, 56
Tyson, Laura, 48

U

U2, 27
UBS, 42, 106, 179
UCLA, 30
U.K. Financial Services Authority, 107
Ukraine, 116
Unethical behavior, 224
United Nations, 27, 129
United Nations World Food Programme, 205
United States
  billionaires in, 123
  electrical blackout in, 20
  income inequality in, 13, 210–211
  life expectancy in, 211
  treasury secretary of, 167, 186, 188
  wealth accumulation in, 13
  wealth gap in, 210–211
University of Chicago, 85
University of Toronto, 104
University of Warwick, 175
University of Zürich, 223
U.S. Federal Reserve, xxv, 84
U.S. Senate Banking Committee, 107
U.S. Treasury Department, 20, 30, 35, 45, 47

V

Value of Connections in Turbulent Times, The, 45
Vanguard, 179
Vanity Fair, 56, 160
Vekselberg, Viktor, 144
Venture capitalist industry, 149–150
Venture philanthropy, 76
Verifiable information, 40
Video conferences, 99
Violet & Daisy, 201
Vodafone Group, 142
Vogue, 160
Volcker, Paul, 107, 125–126
Volkswagen, 224

W

Wachovia, 140
Wage gap, 153–154
Wall Street
  description of, 46, 165

Wall Street *(Cont.)*
  excessive compensation on, 221
  male-dominant nature of, 148
  Washington and, relationship
      between, 176
Wall Street, 212, 221
Wall Street II, 24, 47
Wall Street Journal, 17, 67, 72, 158,
  200
Wallerstein, Immanuel, 218–219
Warburg Pincus, 165
Warren, Elizabeth, 153, 225, 227
Warsh, Kevin, 36
Washington Post, 2, 91
Wauthier, Pierre, 138, 144
Wealth. *See also* Money
  displays of, 60
  exclusivity associated with, 77
  family accumulation of, 123
  global, 211
  status affected by, 22
  in tax havens, 211
Wealth gap
  finance as reason for, 12
  globalization effects on, 213
  Institute for New Economic
      Thinking discussions about,
      107
  unethical behavior and, 222
  in United States, 210–211
Weber, Axel, 42, 120
Weill, Sandy, 57, 65, 91, 140, 167,
  203
Welch, Jack, 125, 135
Wellington, 44
Wells Fargo, 140
West, Cornel, 187
Weymouth, Lally, 2, 91
When the Genius Failed, 208

WHO. *See* World Health
    Organization
Wien, Byron, 27
Willful blindness, 223–224
Willful Blindness, 224
Wilson, Kendrik, 30
Winters, Bill, 140–141
Women
  access gap for, 148–151
  as "buffer zones," 151
  as CEOs, 148, 154, 157
  as hedge fund managers, 149
  assessment gap for, 152–153
  childbearing by, 157
  failure gap in, 154
  gender gap for, 147, 158–161
  integration of, 226
  mentoring gap for, 154–155
  "mind-reading" by, 149
  negotiation by, 153
  networking gap for, 151, 161–162
  "office housework" by, 152
  old boys' network exclusion of,
      82, 150
  on Wall Street, 148
  performance-based assessments
      of, 152
  promotion of, 154
  reasons for inclusion of, 148–149
  resilience gap for, 156–158
  sexism gap for, 155–156
  sexual discrimination against,
      155–156
  sexual harassment against, 156
  at Sitaras Fitness, 126
  societal stereotype of, 153
  "superhuman paradox" for, 157
  in venture capitalist industry,
      149–150

  wage gap for, 153–154
Work hours, 134
Workalcoholics, 132, 134
Work-family life imbalance,
        135–136, 157
Workouts, 125–126
World Bank, 27, 106, 185, 187
World Economic Forum
  attendees of, 113–114
  at Davos. *See* Davos
  description of, xxiv, 1, 3, 25, 94,
        112
  dinners at, 115
  Geneva headquarters of, 93–94
  Global Risk Report, 212
  hierarchy at, 114
  Informal Gatherings of World
        Economic Leaders, 113
  Klaus Schwab of, 94–96, 158
  membership fees for, 113
  mission of, 95
  networking at, 113–114
  parties of, 114–116
  stakeholder principle application
        to, 95–96
  status markers at, 114
  succession plan at, 96
  transparency of, 113
World Health Organization, 93

World War I, 37
World War II, 34

X

Xstrata, 171, 205

Y

Yale Club, 196
Yale Law School, 166
Yale University, 61, 82, 185
Yalta, 194
Yellen, Janet, 48, 64, 85, 188
Yilmaz, Durmuş, 119

Z

Zoellick, Robert, 84, 121
Zuckerberg, Mark, 198
Zuckerman, Mort, 192
Zunfthaus zur Meisen, 39
Zürich, 38–39
Zürich Insurance Group, 138, 144,
        170